JAC LES

THE NEW ADVENT OF JACK AND JACK

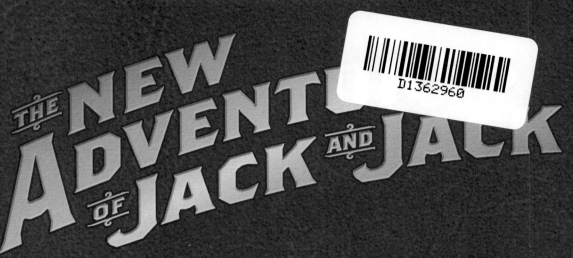

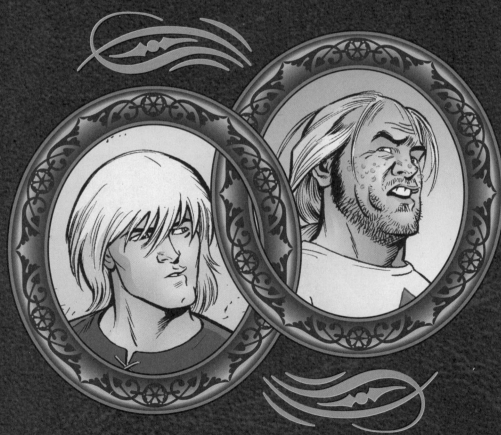

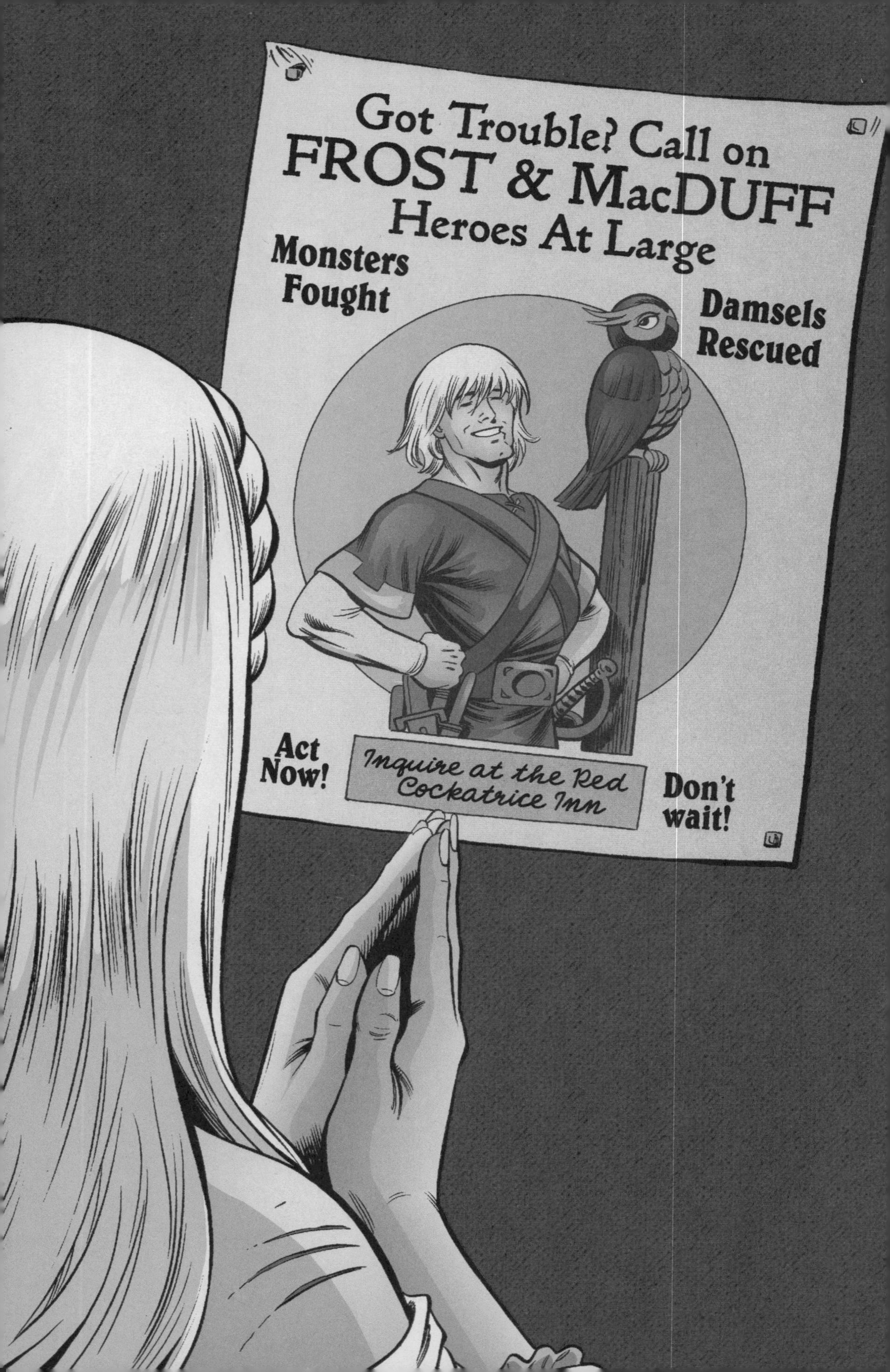
Got Trouble? Call on
FROST & MacDUFF
Heroes At Large
Monsters Fought
Damsels Rescued
Act Now!
Inquire at the Red Cockatrice Inn
Don't wait!

JACK of FABLES

THE NEW ADVENTURES of JACK and JACK

BILL WILLINGHAM
MATTHEW STURGES
CHRIS ROBERSON
WRITERS

RUSS BRAUN ✳ **TONY AKINS**
PENCILLERS

JOSÉ MARZÁN, JR. ✳ **ANDREW PEPOY**
TONY AKINS ✳ **RUSS BRAUN**
INKERS

DANIEL VOZZO
COLORIST

TODD KLEIN
LETTERER

BRIAN BOLLAND
ORIGINAL SERIES COVERS

Jack of Fables created by **BILL WILLINGHAM**

Cover illustration by BRIAN BOLLAND
Logo design by JAMES JEAN

JACK OF FABLES: THE NEW ADVENTURES OF JACK AND JACK

Published by DC Comics. Cover and compilation Copyright © 2010 DC Comics.
All Rights Reserved. Originally published in single magazine form as JACK OF FABLES 36-40.
Copyright © 2009, 2010 Bill Willingham and DC Comics. All Rights Reserved. All characters,
their distinctive likenesses and related elements featured in this publication are trademarks of
Bill Willingham. VERTIGO is a trademark of DC Comics. The stories, characters and incidents
featured in this publication are entirely fictional. DC Comics does not read or accept unsolicited
submissions of ideas, stories or artwork.

DC Comics, 1700 Broadway, New York, NY 10019
A Warner Bros. Entertainment Company.
Printed in the USA. First Printing.
ISBN: 978-1-4012-2712-8

SUSTAINABLE
FORESTRY
INITIATIVE

Certified Fiber Sourcing
www.sfiprogram.org

Fiber used in this product line meets the
sourcing requirements of the SFI program.
www.sfiprogram.org PWC-SFICOC-260

TABLE OF CONTENTS

Dramatis Personae

Jack

Also known as Little Jack Horner, Jack B. Nimble, Jack the Giant Killer and countless other aliases, our hero Jack of the Tales embodies the archetype of the lovable rogue (minus, according to many, the lovability).

Gary, the Pathetic Fallacy

A timid, impressionable and warm-hearted fellow who used to be one of the most powerful beings on the planet.

Jack Frost

The son of Jack Horner and Lumi, the Snow Queen, now grown up and looking for a direction in life.

Robin Page

One of the three Page Sisters, former chief librarians and enforcers for the now-defunct Fable prison known as the Golden Boughs Retirement Village.

Babe

A blue ox given to flights of fancy.

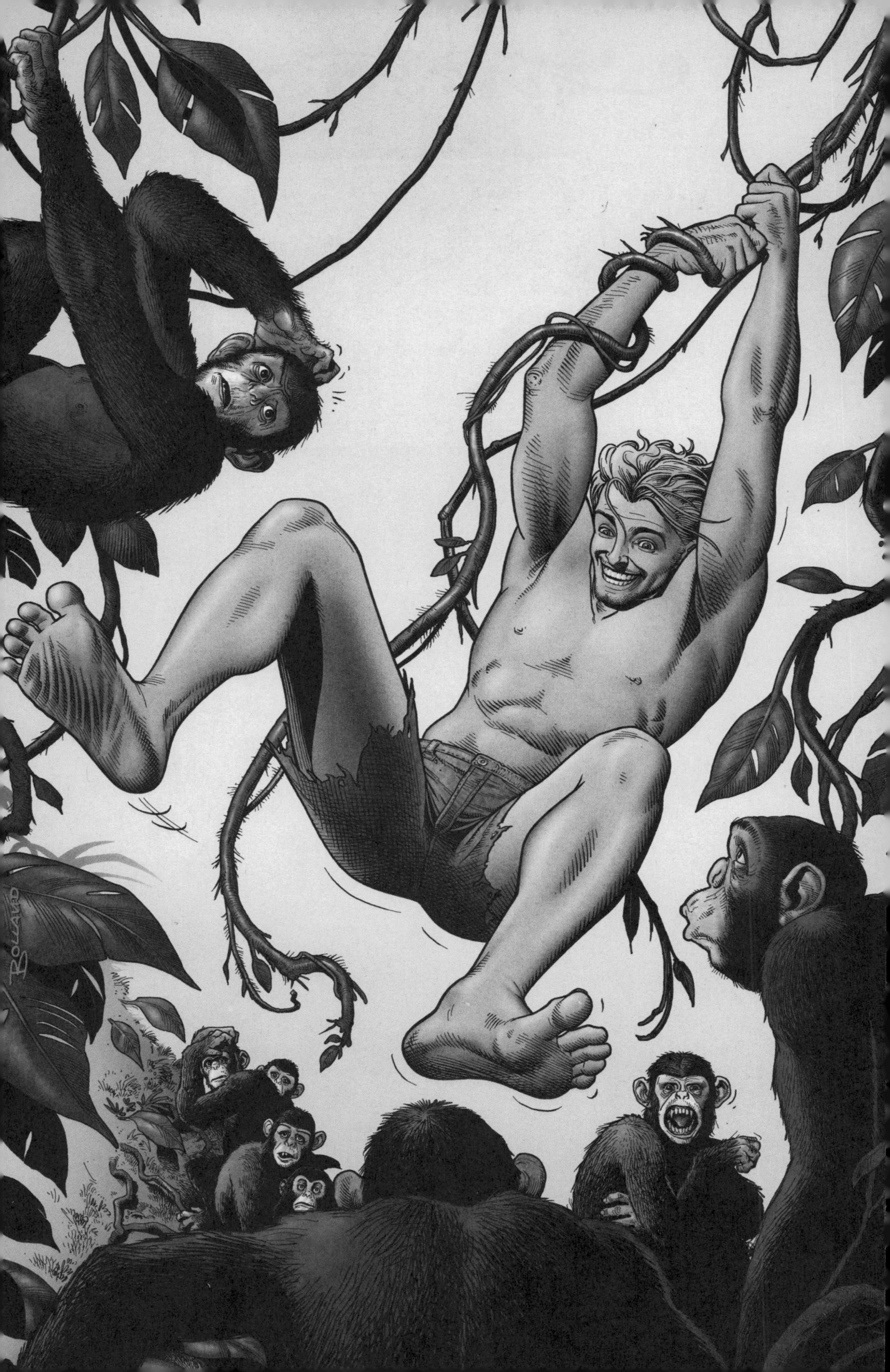

"WHO KNEW THAT MUSLIMS WOULD TAKE OFFENSE TO A COMBINATION BROTHEL AND GAMBLING HOUSE?"

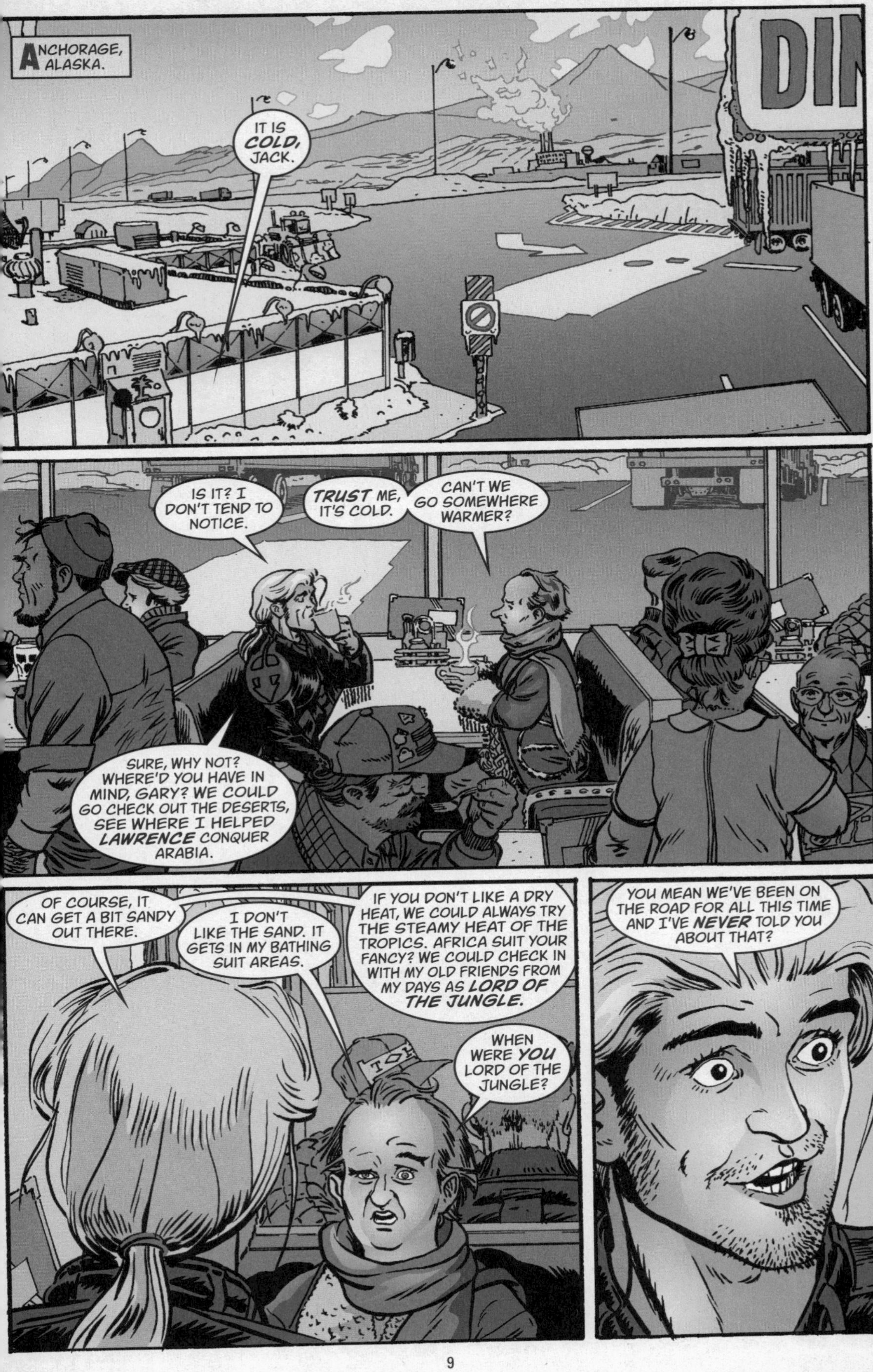
ANCHORAGE, ALASKA.
IT IS COLD, JACK.
IS IT? I DON'T TEND TO NOTICE.
TRUST ME, IT'S COLD.
CAN'T WE GO SOMEWHERE WARMER?
SURE, WHY NOT? WHERE'D YOU HAVE IN MIND, GARY? WE COULD GO CHECK OUT THE DESERTS, SEE WHERE I HELPED LAWRENCE CONQUER ARABIA.
OF COURSE, IT CAN GET A BIT SANDY OUT THERE.
I DON'T LIKE THE SAND. IT GETS IN MY BATHING SUIT AREAS.
IF YOU DON'T LIKE A DRY HEAT, WE COULD ALWAYS TRY THE STEAMY HEAT OF THE TROPICS. AFRICA SUIT YOUR FANCY? WE COULD CHECK IN WITH MY OLD FRIENDS FROM MY DAYS AS LORD OF THE JUNGLE.
WHEN WERE YOU LORD OF THE JUNGLE?
YOU MEAN WE'VE BEEN ON THE ROAD FOR ALL THIS TIME AND I'VE NEVER TOLD YOU ABOUT THAT?

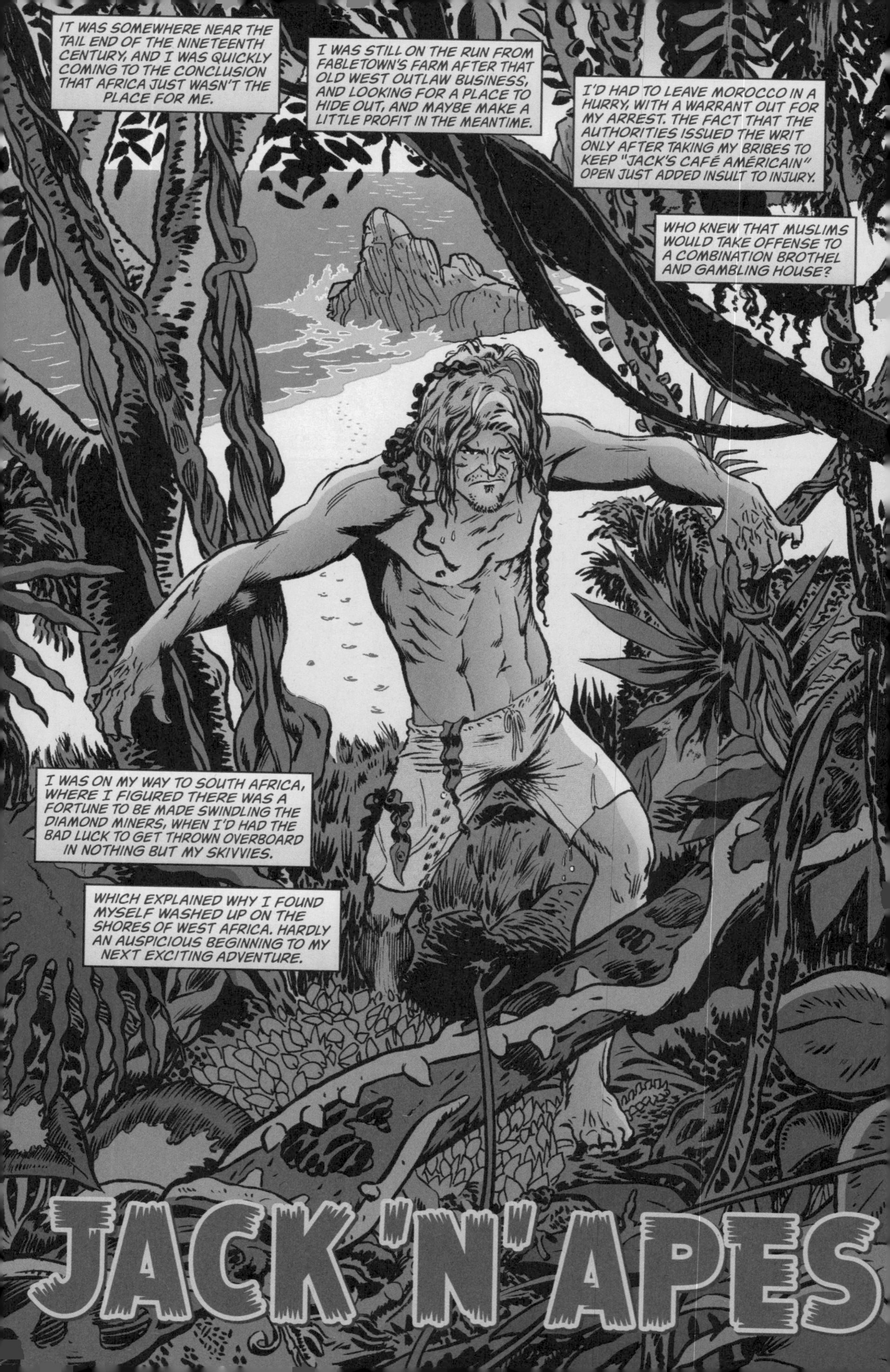
IT WAS SOMEWHERE NEAR THE TAIL END OF THE NINETEENTH CENTURY, AND I WAS QUICKLY COMING TO THE CONCLUSION THAT AFRICA JUST WASN'T THE PLACE FOR ME.
I WAS STILL ON THE RUN FROM FABLETOWN'S FARM AFTER THAT OLD WEST OUTLAW BUSINESS, AND LOOKING FOR A PLACE TO HIDE OUT, AND MAYBE MAKE A LITTLE PROFIT IN THE MEANTIME.
I'D HAD TO LEAVE MOROCCO IN A HURRY, WITH A WARRANT OUT FOR MY ARREST. THE FACT THAT THE AUTHORITIES ISSUED THE WRIT ONLY AFTER TAKING MY BRIBES TO KEEP "JACK'S CAFÉ AMÉRICAIN" OPEN JUST ADDED INSULT TO INJURY.
WHO KNEW THAT MUSLIMS WOULD TAKE OFFENSE TO A COMBINATION BROTHEL AND GAMBLING HOUSE?
I WAS ON MY WAY TO SOUTH AFRICA, WHERE I FIGURED THERE WAS A FORTUNE TO BE MADE SWINDLING THE DIAMOND MINERS, WHEN I'D HAD THE BAD LUCK TO GET THROWN OVERBOARD IN NOTHING BUT MY SKIVVIES.
WHICH EXPLAINED WHY I FOUND MYSELF WASHED UP ON THE SHORES OF WEST AFRICA. HARDLY AN AUSPICIOUS BEGINNING TO MY NEXT EXCITING ADVENTURE.
JACK'N'APES

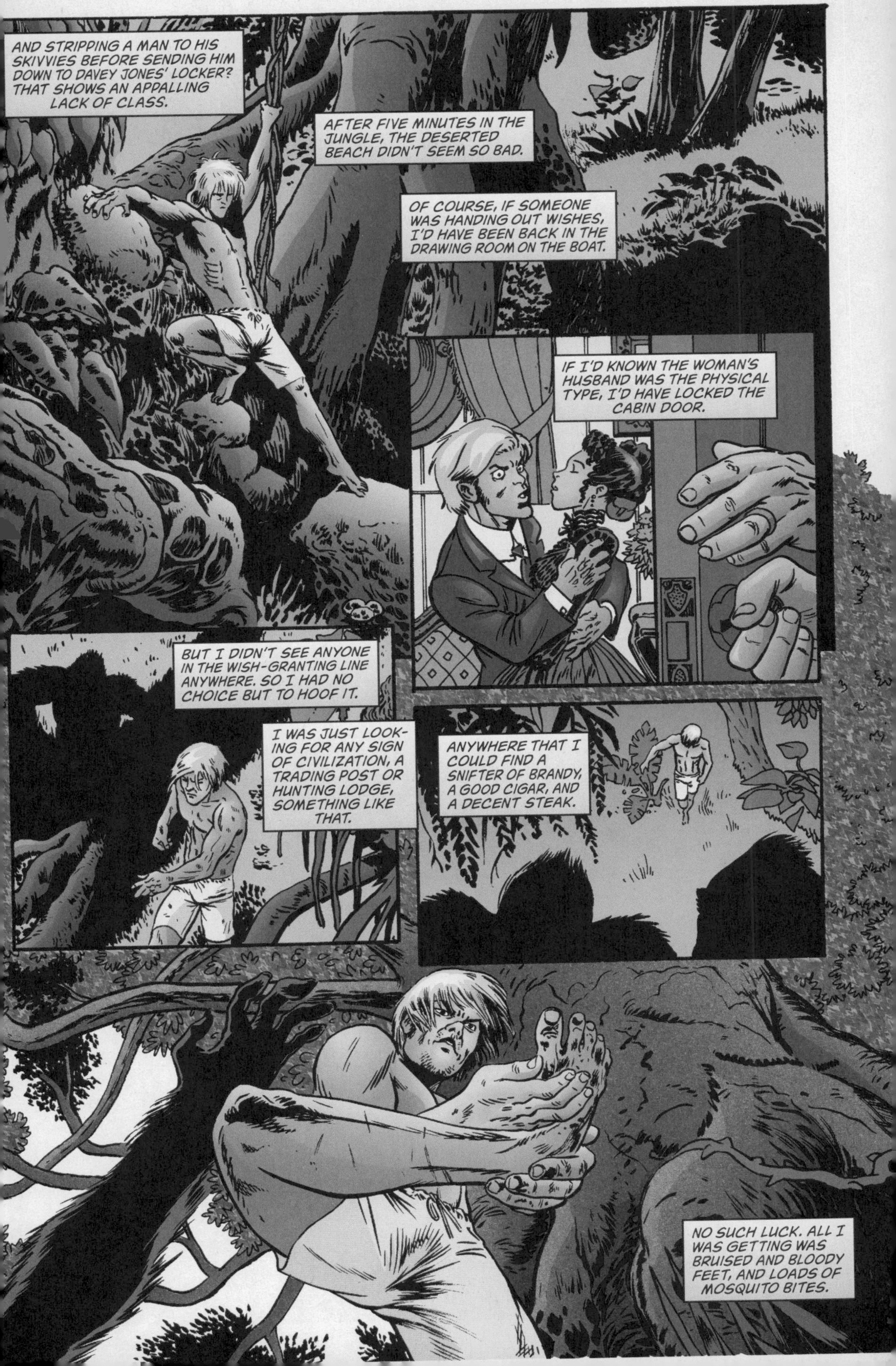
AND STRIPPING A MAN TO HIS SKIVVIES BEFORE SENDING HIM DOWN TO DAVEY JONES' LOCKER? THAT SHOWS AN APPALLING LACK OF CLASS.
AFTER FIVE MINUTES IN THE JUNGLE, THE DESERTED BEACH DIDN'T SEEM SO BAD.
OF COURSE, IF SOMEONE WAS HANDING OUT WISHES, I'D HAVE BEEN BACK IN THE DRAWING ROOM ON THE BOAT.
IF I'D KNOWN THE WOMAN'S HUSBAND WAS THE PHYSICAL TYPE, I'D HAVE LOCKED THE CABIN DOOR.
BUT I DIDN'T SEE ANYONE IN THE WISH-GRANTING LINE ANYWHERE. SO I HAD NO CHOICE BUT TO HOOF IT.
I WAS JUST LOOKING FOR ANY SIGN OF CIVILIZATION, A TRADING POST OR HUNTING LODGE, SOMETHING LIKE THAT.
ANYWHERE THAT I COULD FIND A SNIFTER OF BRANDY, A GOOD CIGAR, AND A DECENT STEAK.
NO SUCH LUCK. ALL I WAS GETTING WAS BRUISED AND BLOODY FEET, AND LOADS OF MOSQUITO BITES.

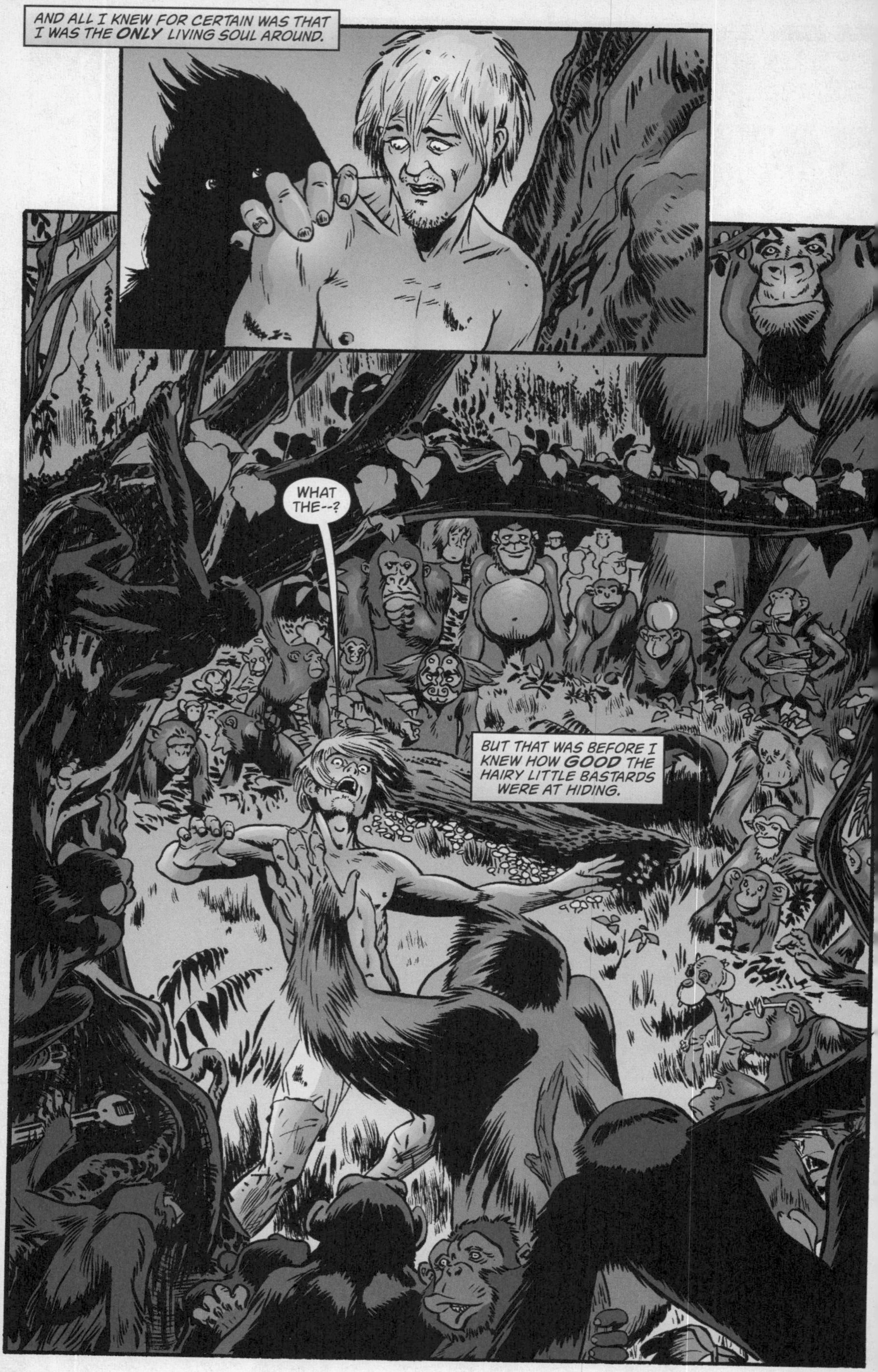
AND ALL I KNEW FOR CERTAIN WAS THAT I WAS THE ONLY LIVING SOUL AROUND.
WHAT THE--?
BUT THAT WAS BEFORE I KNEW HOW GOOD THE HAIRY LITTLE BASTARDS WERE AT HIDING.

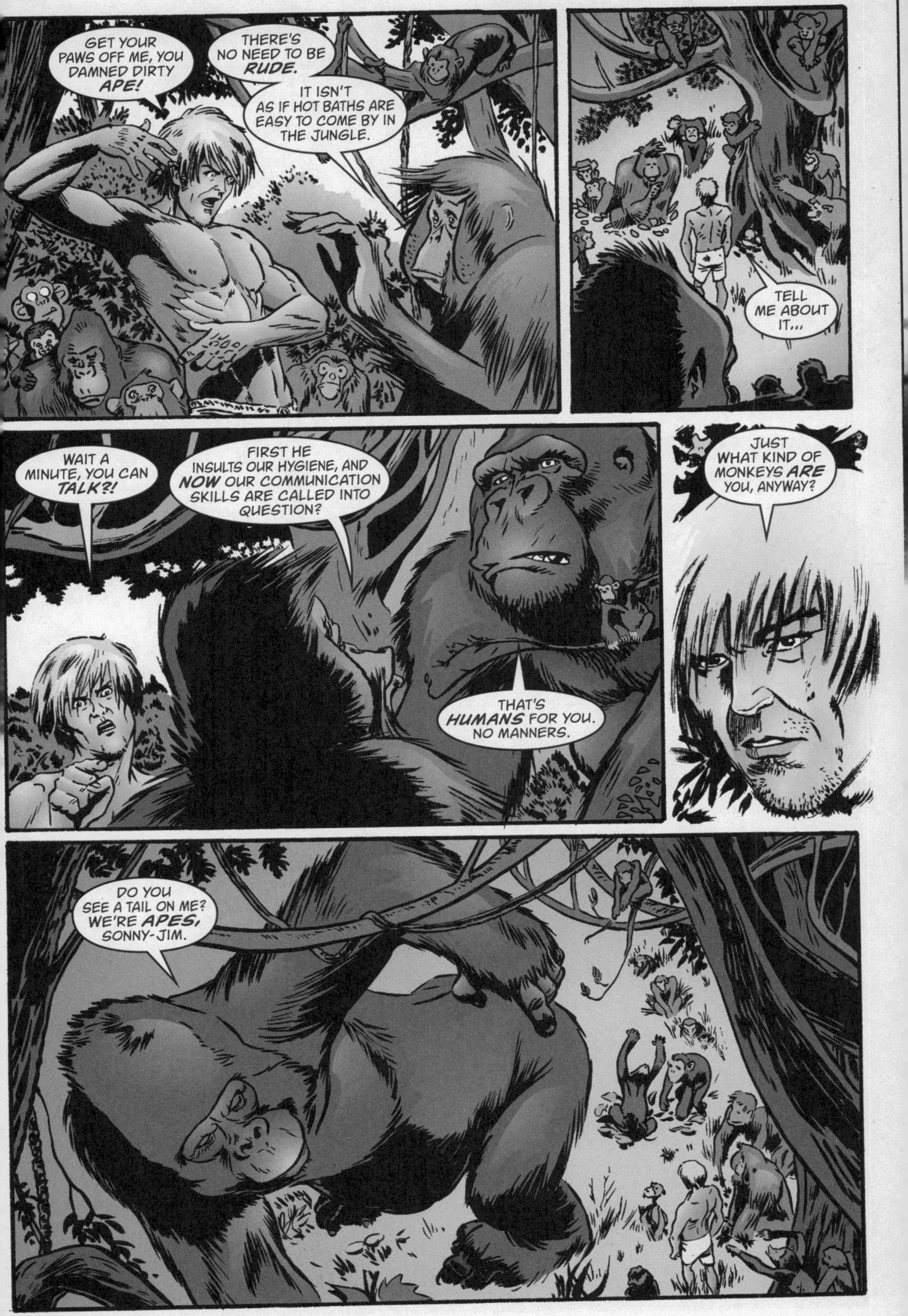
GET YOUR PAWS OFF ME, YOU DAMNED DIRTY APE!
THERE'S NO NEED TO BE RUDE.
IT ISN'T AS IF HOT BATHS ARE EASY TO COME BY IN THE JUNGLE.
TELL ME ABOUT IT...
WAIT A MINUTE, YOU CAN TALK?!
FIRST HE INSULTS OUR HYGIENE, AND NOW OUR COMMUNICATION SKILLS ARE CALLED INTO QUESTION?
THAT'S HUMANS FOR YOU. NO MANNERS.
JUST WHAT KIND OF MONKEYS ARE YOU, ANYWAY?
DO YOU SEE A TAIL ON ME? WE'RE APES, SONNY-JIM.

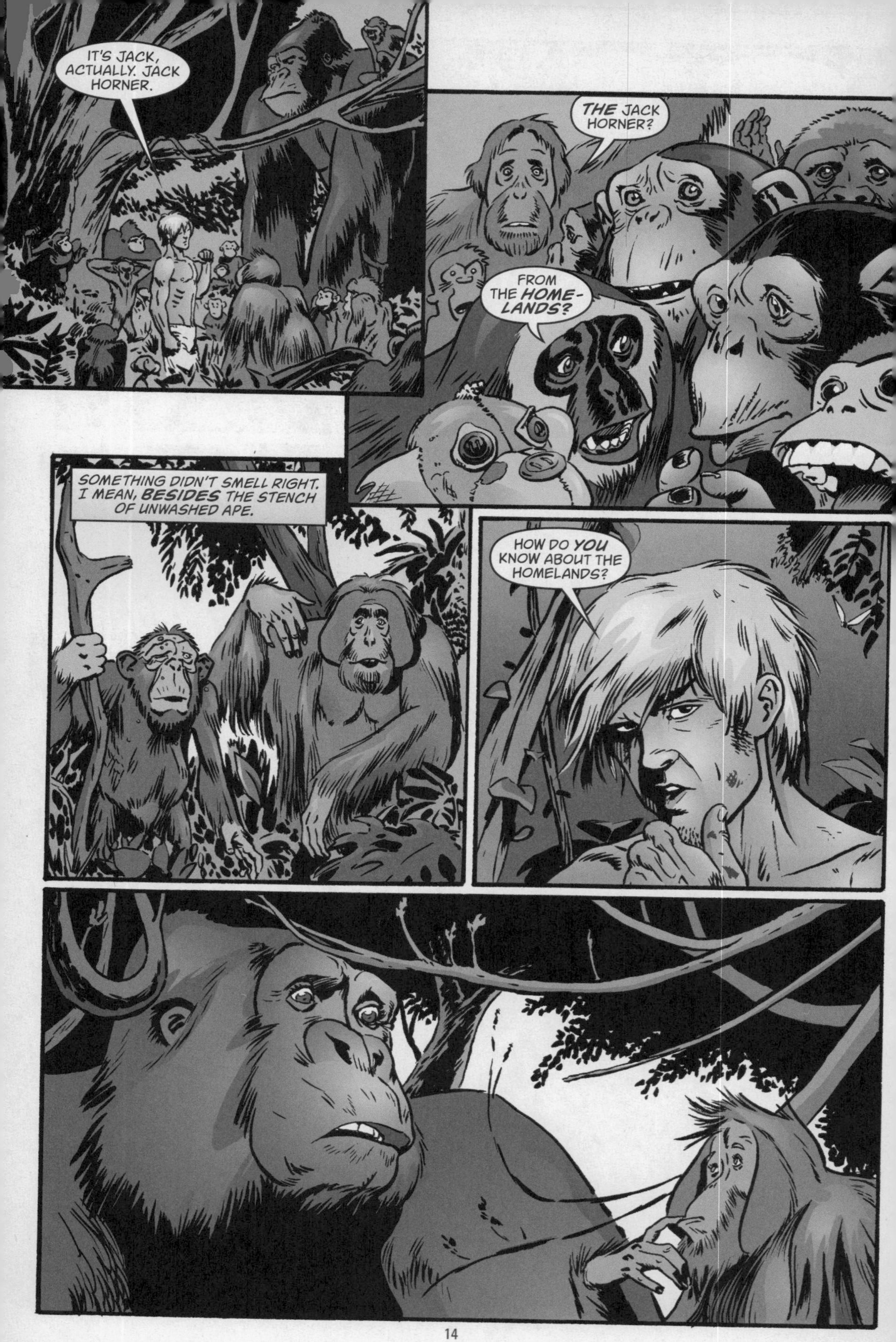
IT'S JACK, ACTUALLY. JACK HORNER.
THE JACK HORNER?
FROM THE HOME-LANDS?
SOMETHING DIDN'T SMELL RIGHT. I MEAN, BESIDES THE STENCH OF UNWASHED APE.
HOW DO YOU KNOW ABOUT THE HOMELANDS?

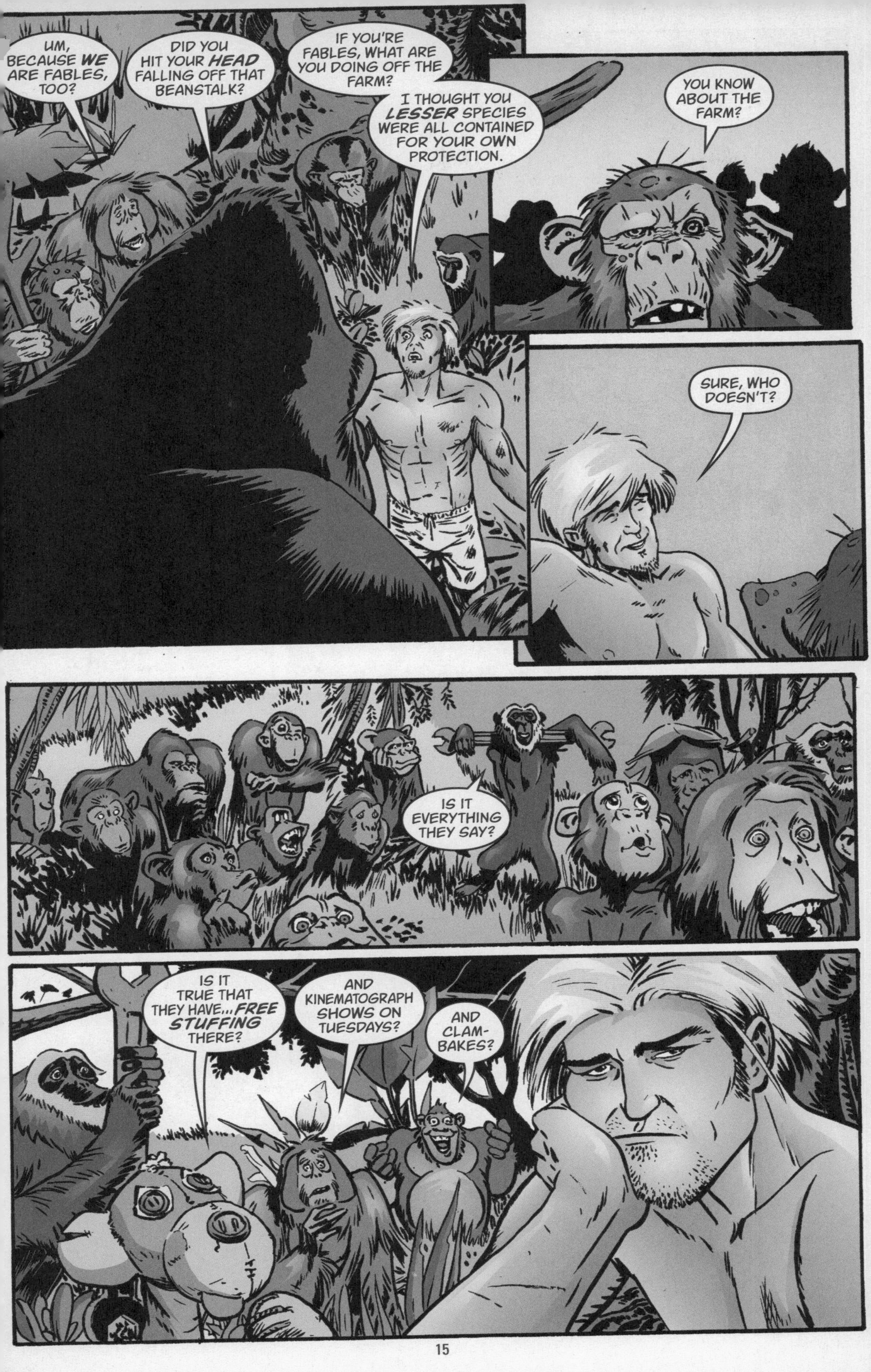
UM, BECAUSE WE ARE FABLES, TOO?
DID YOU HIT YOUR HEAD FALLING OFF THAT BEANSTALK?
IF YOU'RE FABLES, WHAT ARE YOU DOING OFF THE FARM?
I THOUGHT YOU LESSER SPECIES WERE ALL CONTAINED FOR YOUR OWN PROTECTION.
YOU KNOW ABOUT THE FARM?
SURE, WHO DOESN'T?
IS IT EVERYTHING THEY SAY?
IS IT TRUE THAT THEY HAVE... FREE STUFFING THERE?
AND KINEMATOGRAPH SHOWS ON TUESDAYS?
AND CLAM-BAKES?

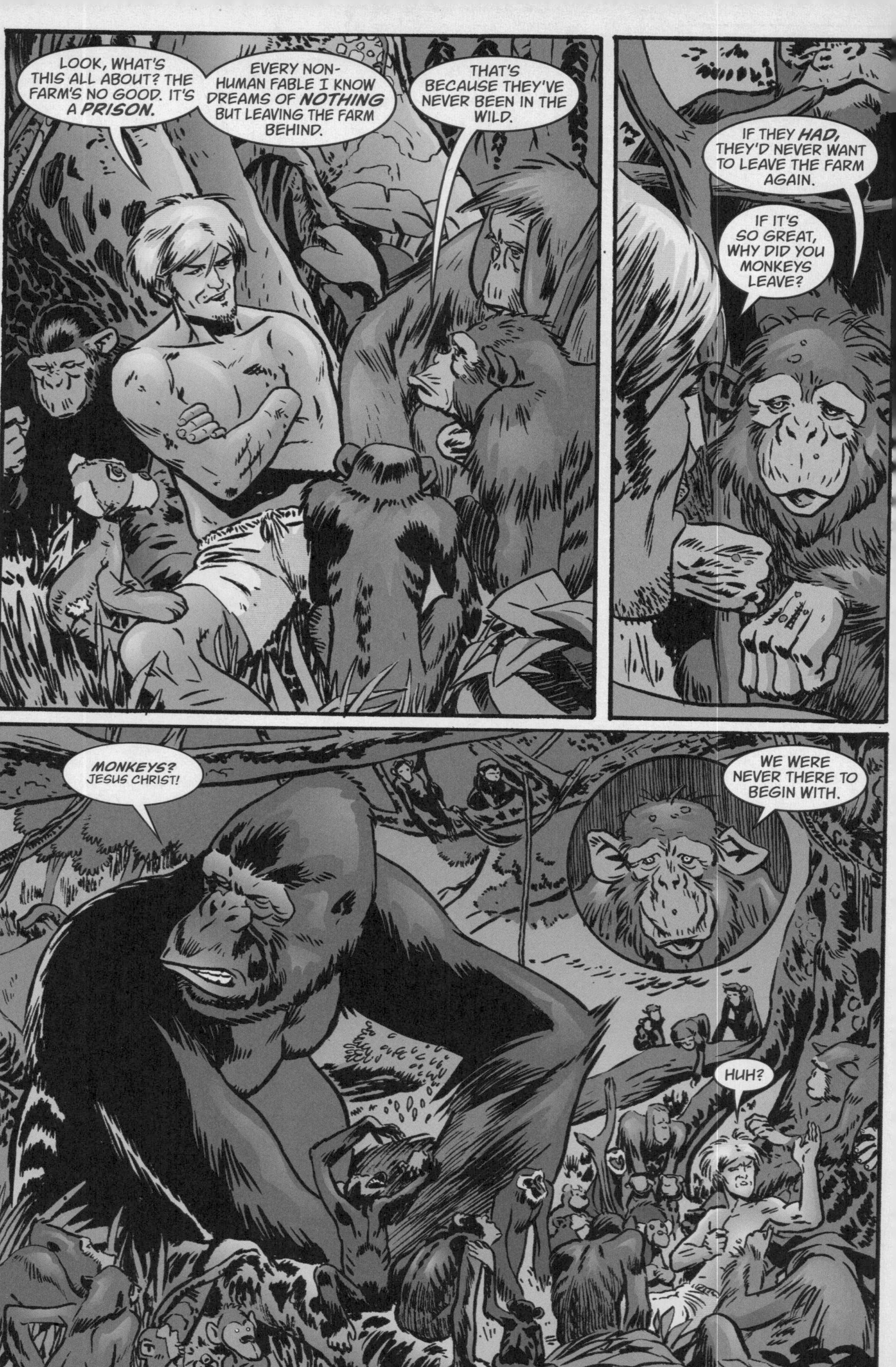

LOOK, WHAT'S THIS ALL ABOUT? THE FARM'S NO GOOD. IT'S A *PRISON.*
EVERY NON-HUMAN FABLE I KNOW DREAMS OF *NOTHING* BUT LEAVING THE FARM BEHIND.
THAT'S BECAUSE THEY'VE NEVER BEEN IN THE WILD.
IF THEY *HAD,* THEY'D NEVER WANT TO LEAVE THE FARM AGAIN.
IF IT'S SO GREAT, WHY DID YOU MONKEYS LEAVE?
MONKEYS? JESUS CHRIST!
WE WERE NEVER THERE TO BEGIN WITH.
HUH?

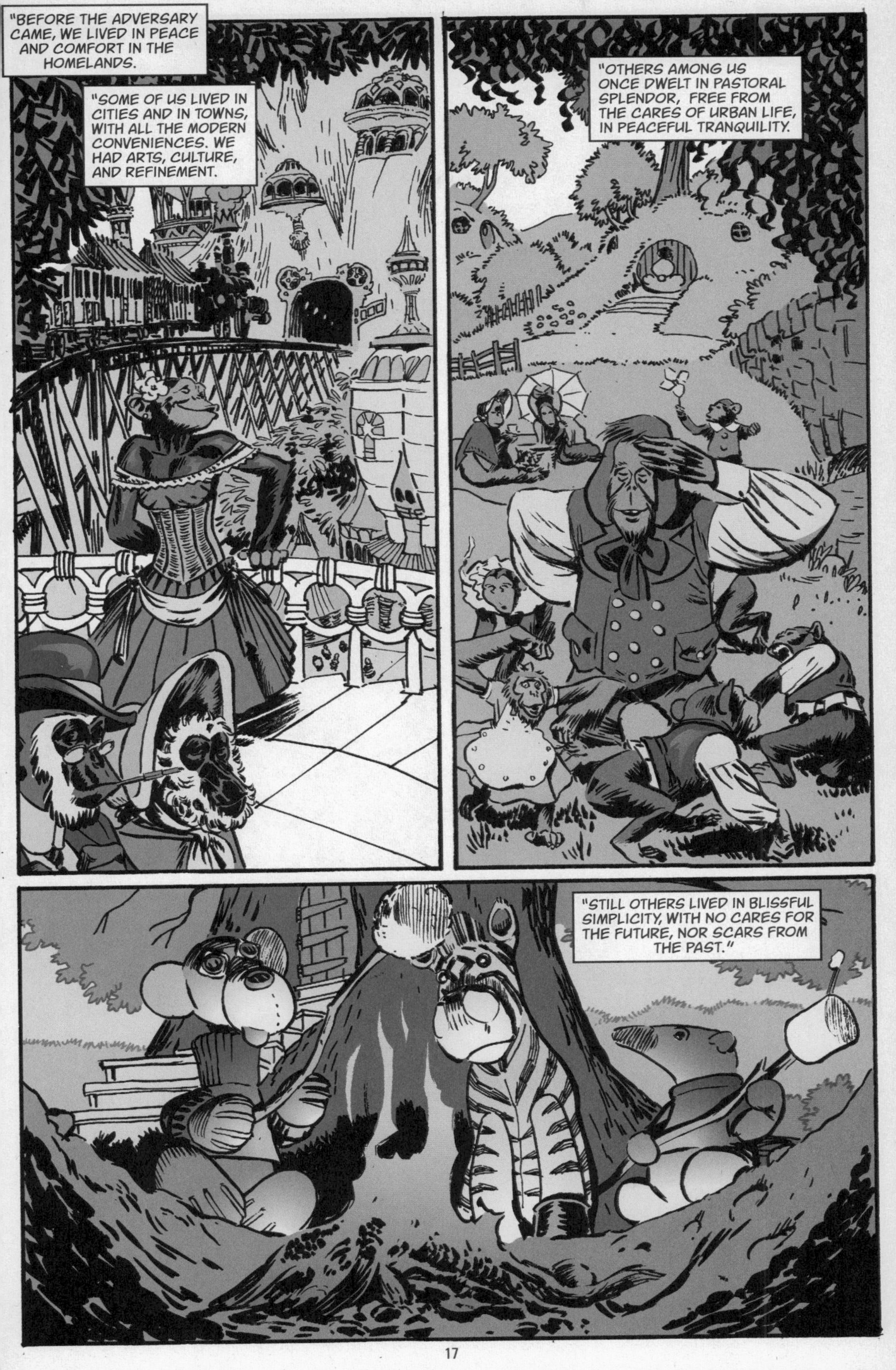
"BEFORE THE ADVERSARY CAME, WE LIVED IN PEACE AND COMFORT IN THE HOMELANDS.
"SOME OF US LIVED IN CITIES AND IN TOWNS, WITH ALL THE MODERN CONVENIENCES. WE HAD ARTS, CULTURE, AND REFINEMENT.
"OTHERS AMONG US ONCE DWELT IN PASTORAL SPLENDOR, FREE FROM THE CARES OF URBAN LIFE, IN PEACEFUL TRANQUILITY.
"STILL OTHERS LIVED IN BLISSFUL SIMPLICITY, WITH NO CARES FOR THE FUTURE, NOR SCARS FROM THE PAST."

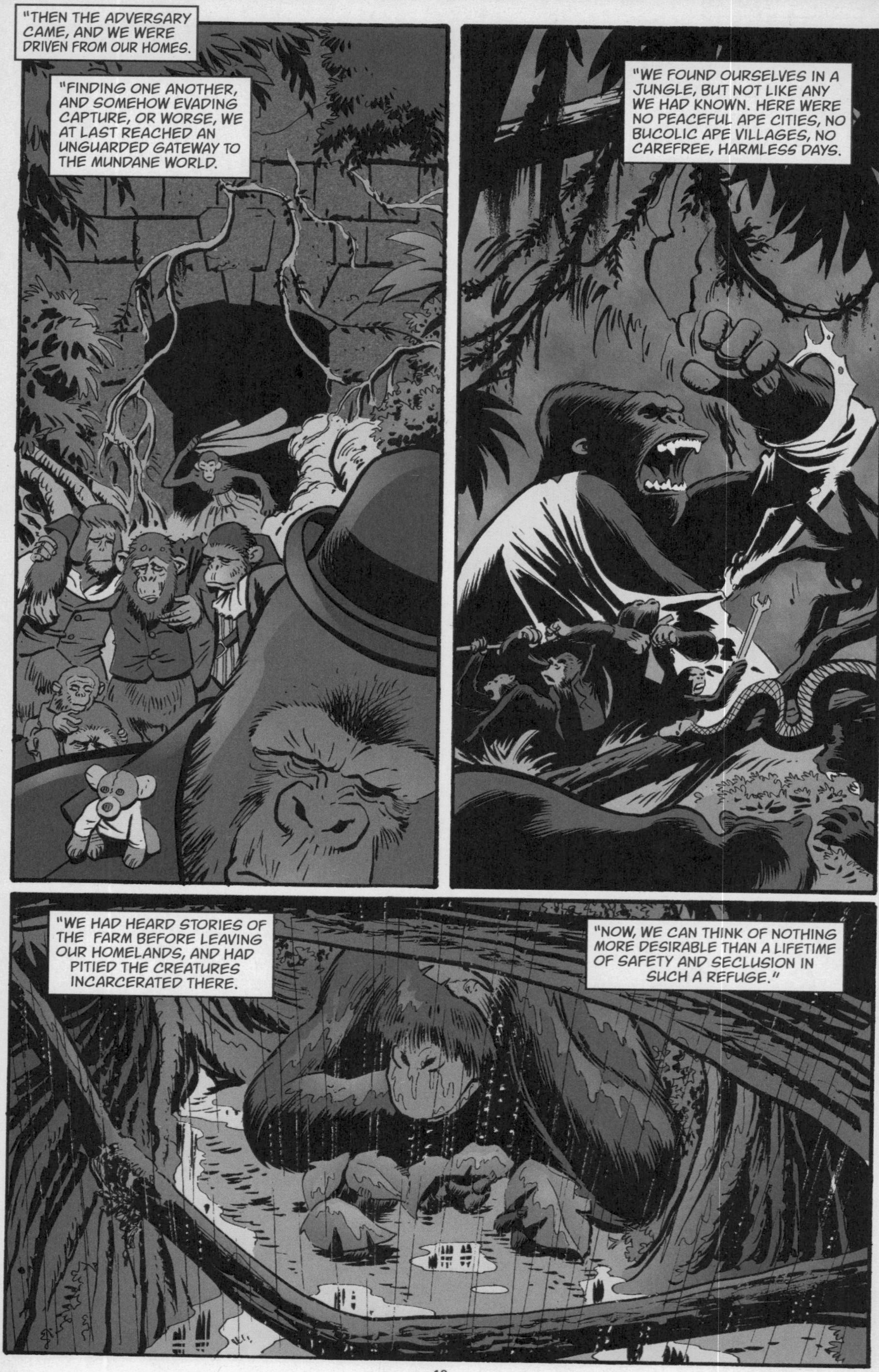
"THEN THE ADVERSARY CAME, AND WE WERE DRIVEN FROM OUR HOMES.
"FINDING ONE ANOTHER, AND SOMEHOW EVADING CAPTURE, OR WORSE, WE AT LAST REACHED AN UNGUARDED GATEWAY TO THE MUNDANE WORLD.
"WE FOUND OURSELVES IN A JUNGLE, BUT NOT LIKE ANY WE HAD KNOWN. HERE WERE NO PEACEFUL APE CITIES, NO BUCOLIC APE VILLAGES, NO CAREFREE, HARMLESS DAYS.
"WE HAD HEARD STORIES OF THE FARM BEFORE LEAVING OUR HOMELANDS, AND HAD PITIED THE CREATURES INCARCERATED THERE.
"NOW, WE CAN THINK OF NOTHING MORE DESIRABLE THAN A LIFETIME OF SAFETY AND SECLUSION IN SUCH A REFUGE."

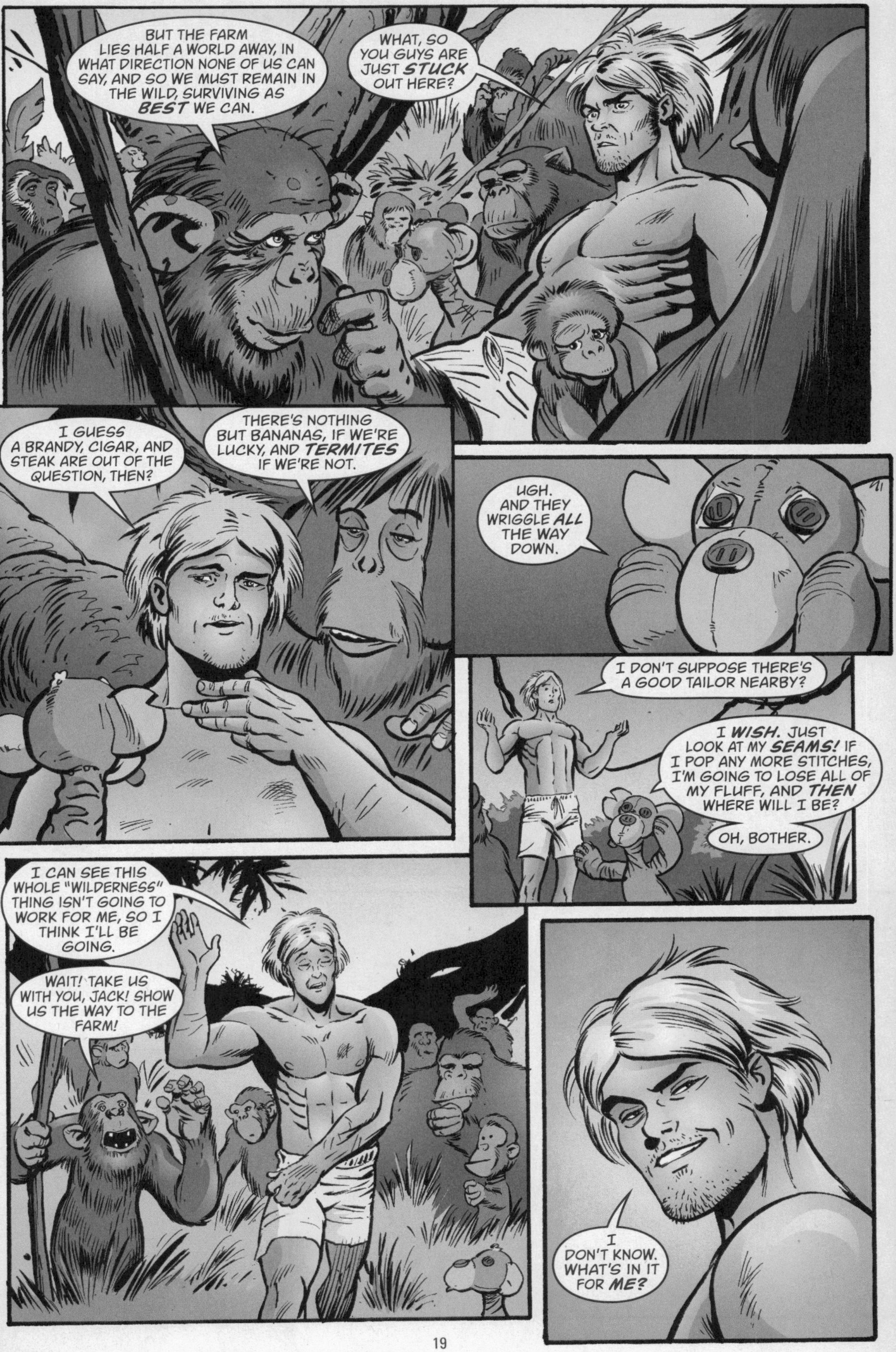
BUT THE FARM LIES HALF A WORLD AWAY, IN WHAT DIRECTION NONE OF US CAN SAY, AND SO WE MUST REMAIN IN THE WILD, SURVIVING AS BEST WE CAN.
WHAT, SO YOU GUYS ARE JUST STUCK OUT HERE?
I GUESS A BRANDY, CIGAR, AND STEAK ARE OUT OF THE QUESTION, THEN?
THERE'S NOTHING BUT BANANAS, IF WE'RE LUCKY, AND TERMITES IF WE'RE NOT.
UGH. AND THEY WRIGGLE ALL THE WAY DOWN.
I DON'T SUPPOSE THERE'S A GOOD TAILOR NEARBY?
I WISH. JUST LOOK AT MY SEAMS! IF I POP ANY MORE STITCHES, I'M GOING TO LOSE ALL OF MY FLUFF, AND THEN WHERE WILL I BE?
OH, BOTHER.
I CAN SEE THIS WHOLE "WILDERNESS" THING ISN'T GOING TO WORK FOR ME, SO I THINK I'LL BE GOING.
WAIT! TAKE US WITH YOU, JACK! SHOW US THE WAY TO THE FARM!
I DON'T KNOW. WHAT'S IN IT FOR ME?

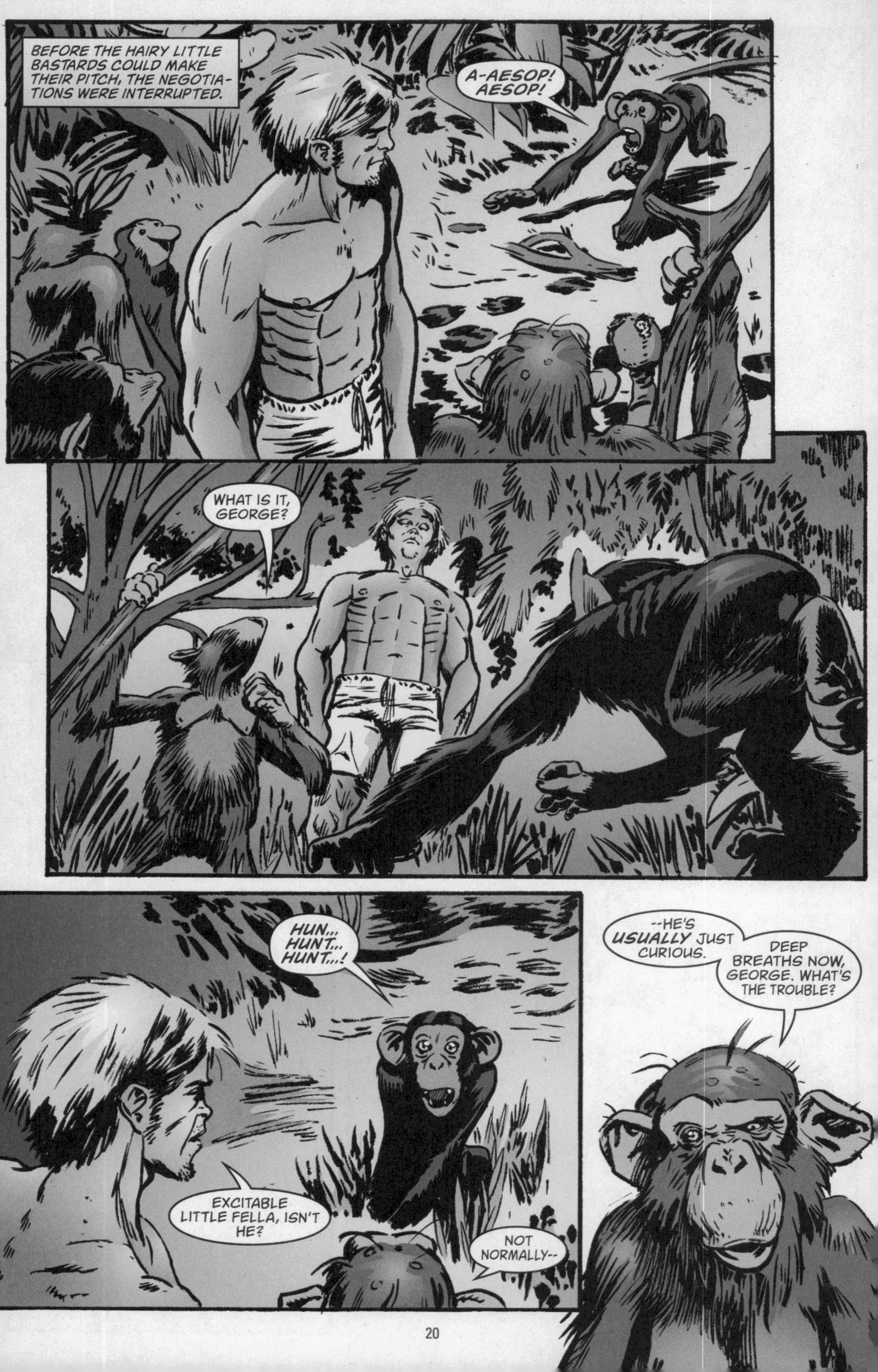
BEFORE THE HAIRY LITTLE BASTARDS COULD MAKE THEIR PITCH, THE NEGOTIATIONS WERE INTERRUPTED.
A-AESOP! AESOP!
WHAT IS IT, GEORGE?
HUN... HUNT... HUNT...!
EXCITABLE LITTLE FELLA, ISN'T HE?
NOT NORMALLY--
--HE'S USUALLY JUST CURIOUS.
DEEP BREATHS NOW, GEORGE. WHAT'S THE TROUBLE?

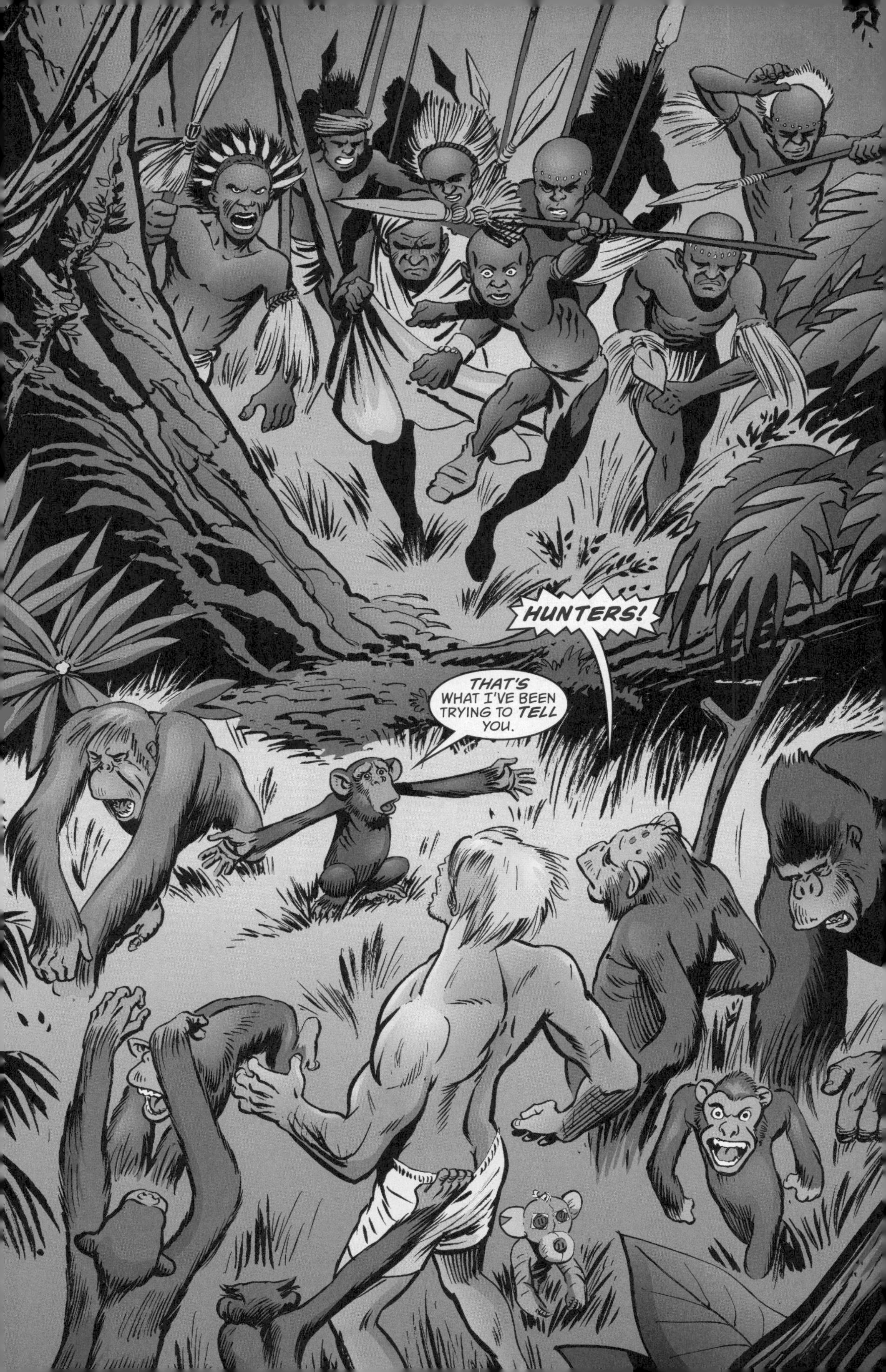
HUNTERS!
THAT'S WHAT I'VE BEEN TRYING TO TELL YOU.

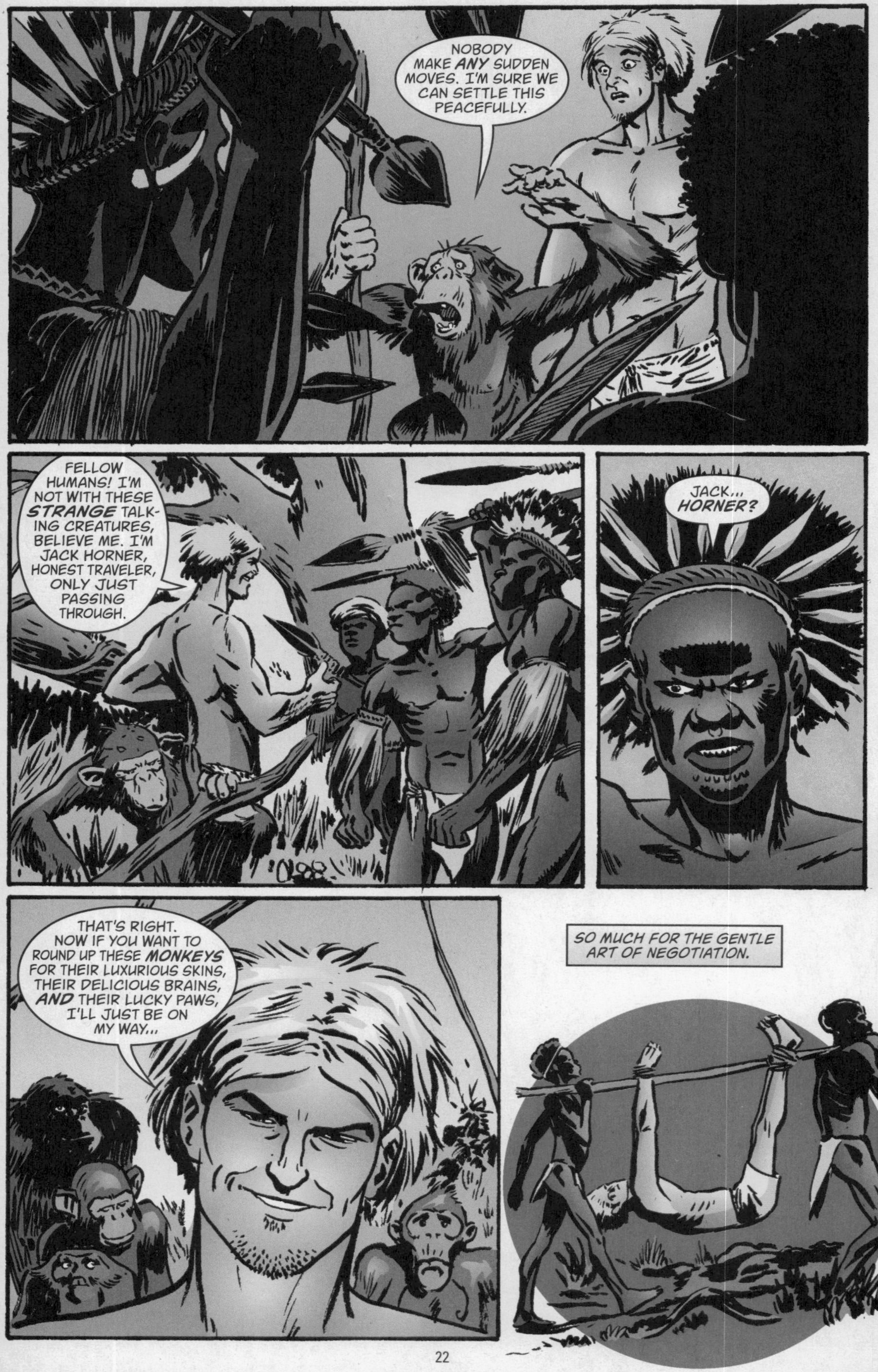
NOBODY MAKE ANY SUDDEN MOVES. I'M SURE WE CAN SETTLE THIS PEACEFULLY.
FELLOW HUMANS! I'M NOT WITH THESE STRANGE TALKING CREATURES, BELIEVE ME. I'M JACK HORNER, HONEST TRAVELER, ONLY JUST PASSING THROUGH.
JACK... HORNER?
THAT'S RIGHT. NOW IF YOU WANT TO ROUND UP THESE MONKEYS FOR THEIR LUXURIOUS SKINS, THEIR DELICIOUS BRAINS, AND THEIR LUCKY PAWS, I'LL JUST BE ON MY WAY...
SO MUCH FOR THE GENTLE ART OF NEGOTIATION.

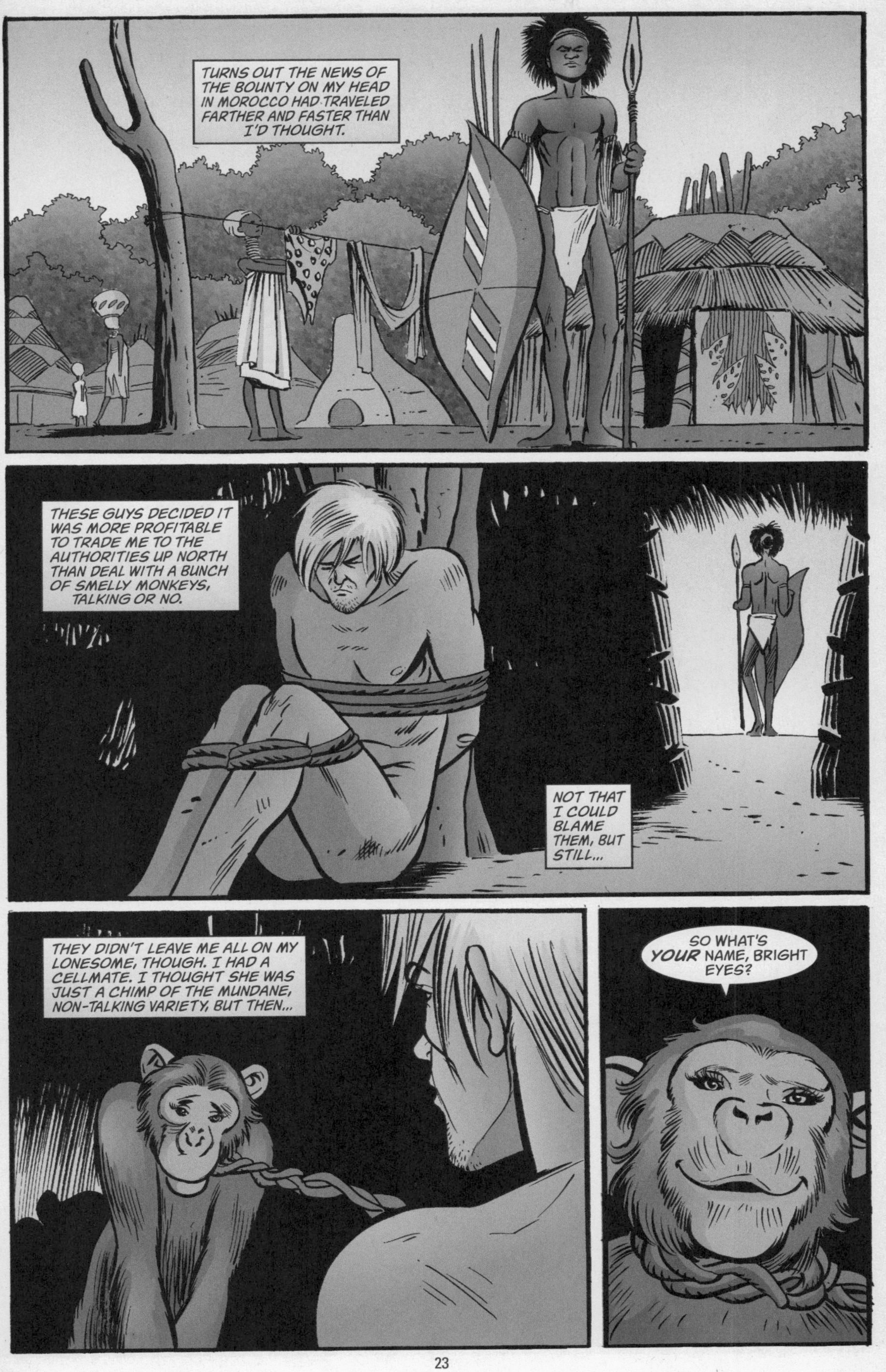
TURNS OUT THE NEWS OF THE BOUNTY ON MY HEAD IN MOROCCO HAD TRAVELED FARTHER AND FASTER THAN I'D THOUGHT.
THESE GUYS DECIDED IT WAS MORE PROFITABLE TO TRADE ME TO THE AUTHORITIES UP NORTH THAN DEAL WITH A BUNCH OF SMELLY MONKEYS, TALKING OR NO.
NOT THAT I COULD BLAME THEM, BUT STILL...
THEY DIDN'T LEAVE ME ALL ON MY LONESOME, THOUGH. I HAD A CELLMATE. I THOUGHT SHE WAS JUST A CHIMP OF THE MUNDANE, NON-TALKING VARIETY, BUT THEN...
SO WHAT'S **YOUR** NAME, BRIGHT EYES?

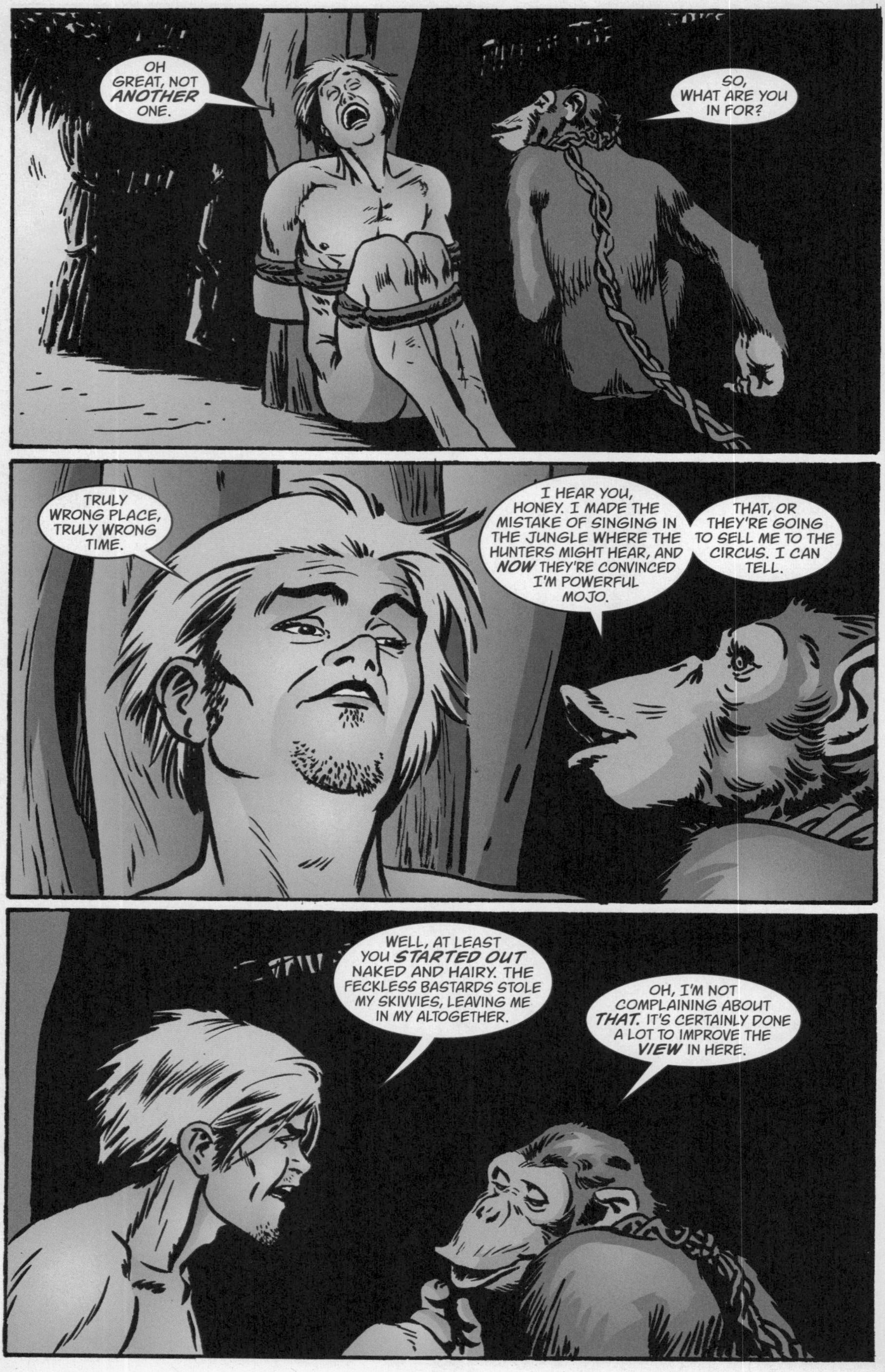
OH GREAT, NOT ANOTHER ONE.
SO, WHAT ARE YOU IN FOR?
TRULY WRONG PLACE, TRULY WRONG TIME.
I HEAR YOU, HONEY. I MADE THE MISTAKE OF SINGING IN THE JUNGLE WHERE THE HUNTERS MIGHT HEAR, AND NOW THEY'RE CONVINCED I'M POWERFUL MOJO.
THAT, OR THEY'RE GOING TO SELL ME TO THE CIRCUS. I CAN TELL.
WELL, AT LEAST YOU STARTED OUT NAKED AND HAIRY. THE FECKLESS BASTARDS STOLE MY SKIVVIES, LEAVING ME IN MY ALTOGETHER.
OH, I'M NOT COMPLAINING ABOUT THAT. IT'S CERTAINLY DONE A LOT TO IMPROVE THE VIEW IN HERE.

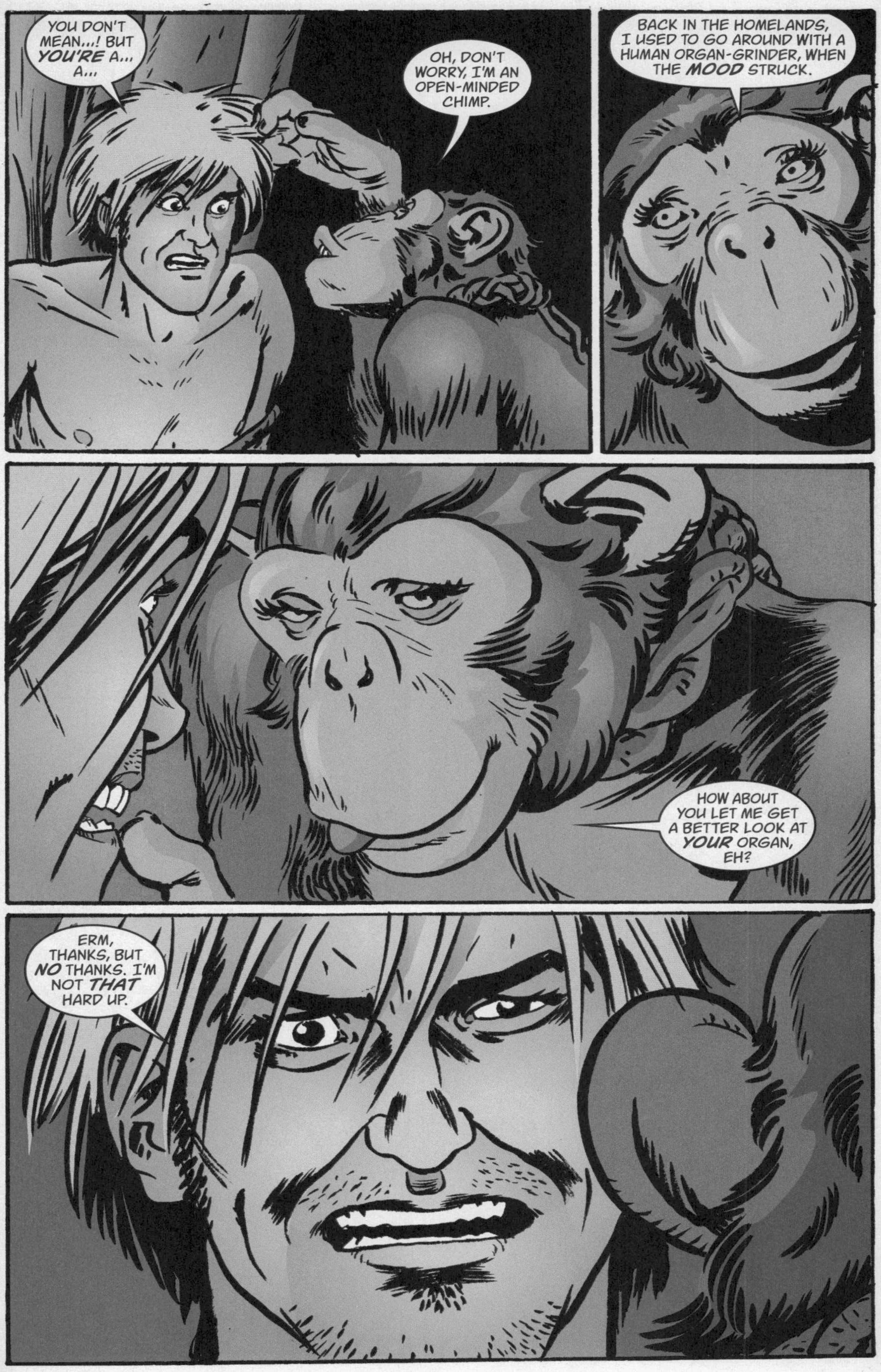
YOU DON'T MEAN...! BUT YOU'RE A... A...
OH, DON'T WORRY, I'M AN OPEN-MINDED CHIMP.
BACK IN THE HOMELANDS, I USED TO GO AROUND WITH A HUMAN ORGAN-GRINDER, WHEN THE MOOD STRUCK.
HOW ABOUT YOU LET ME GET A BETTER LOOK AT YOUR ORGAN, EH?
ERM, THANKS, BUT NO THANKS. I'M NOT THAT HARD UP.

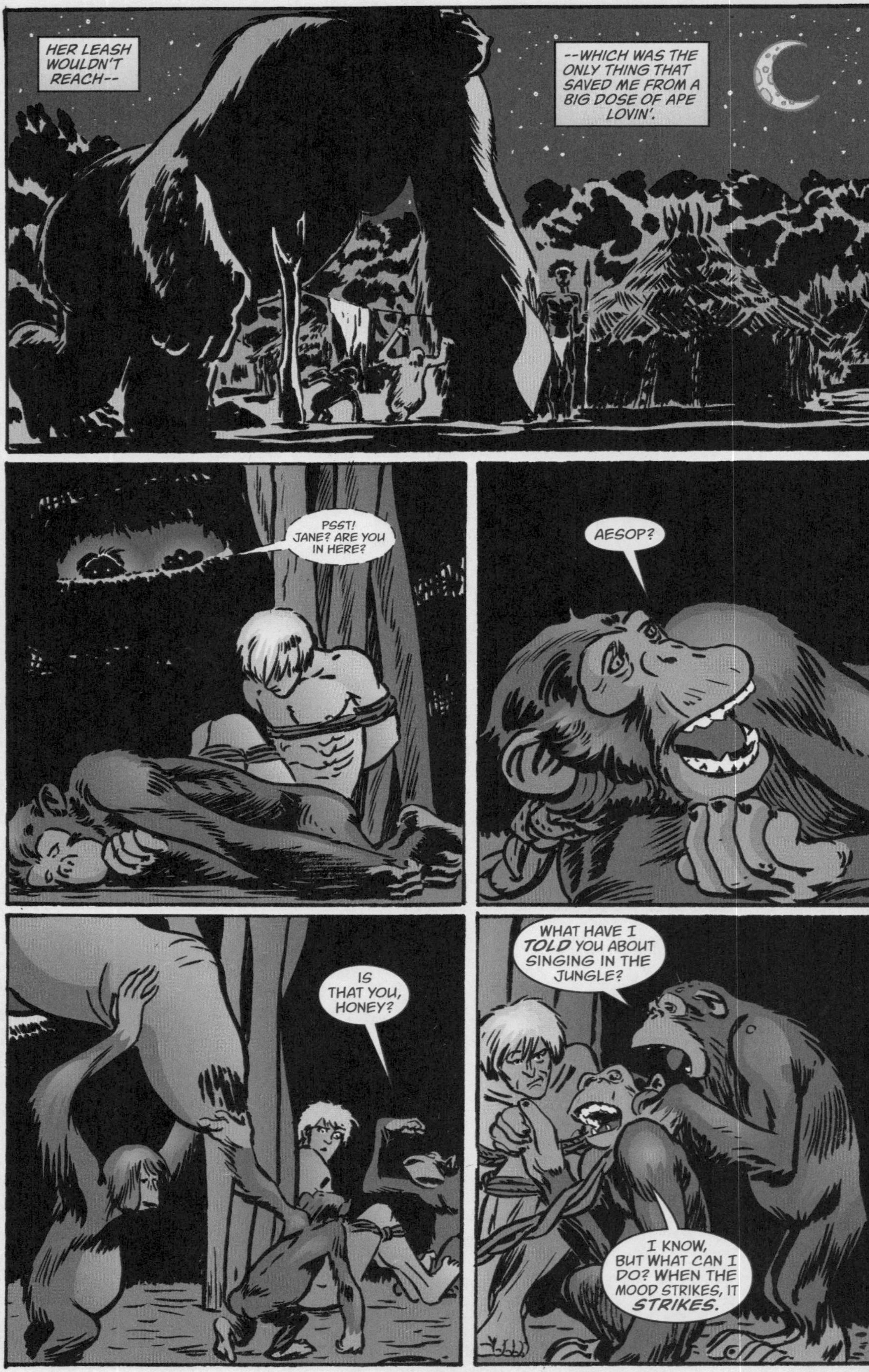
HER LEASH WOULDN'T REACH--
--WHICH WAS THE ONLY THING THAT SAVED ME FROM A BIG DOSE OF APE LOVIN'.
PSST! JANE? ARE YOU IN HERE?
AESOP?
IS THAT YOU, HONEY?
WHAT HAVE I TOLD YOU ABOUT SINGING IN THE JUNGLE?
I KNOW, BUT WHAT CAN I DO? WHEN THE MOOD STRIKES, IT STRIKES.

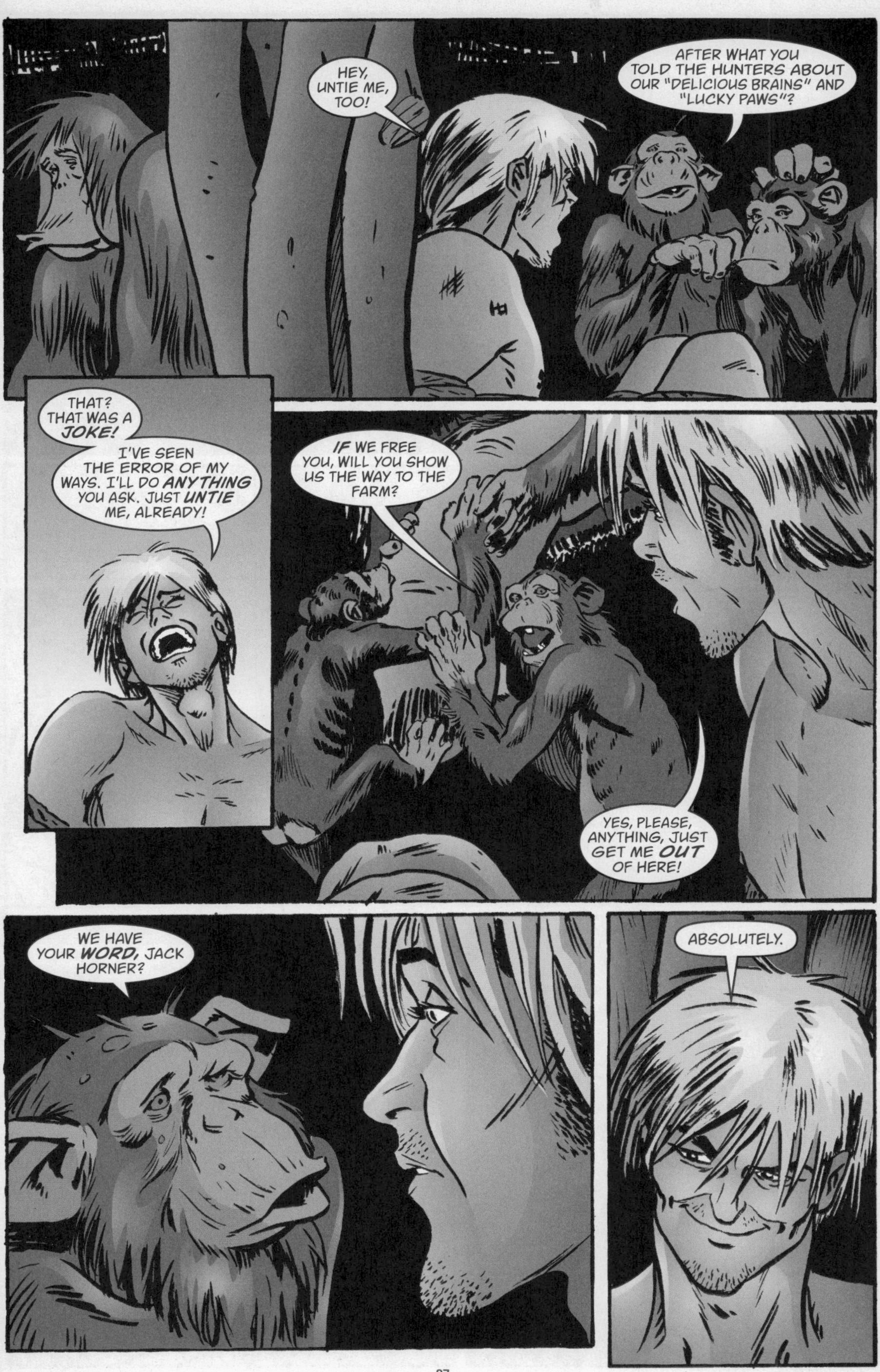
HEY, UNTIE ME, TOO!
AFTER WHAT YOU TOLD THE HUNTERS ABOUT OUR "DELICIOUS BRAINS" AND "LUCKY PAWS"?
THAT? THAT WAS A JOKE!
I'VE SEEN THE ERROR OF MY WAYS. I'LL DO ANYTHING YOU ASK. JUST UNTIE ME, ALREADY!
IF WE FREE YOU, WILL YOU SHOW US THE WAY TO THE FARM?
YES, PLEASE, ANYTHING, JUST GET ME OUT OF HERE!
WE HAVE YOUR WORD, JACK HORNER?
ABSOLUTELY.

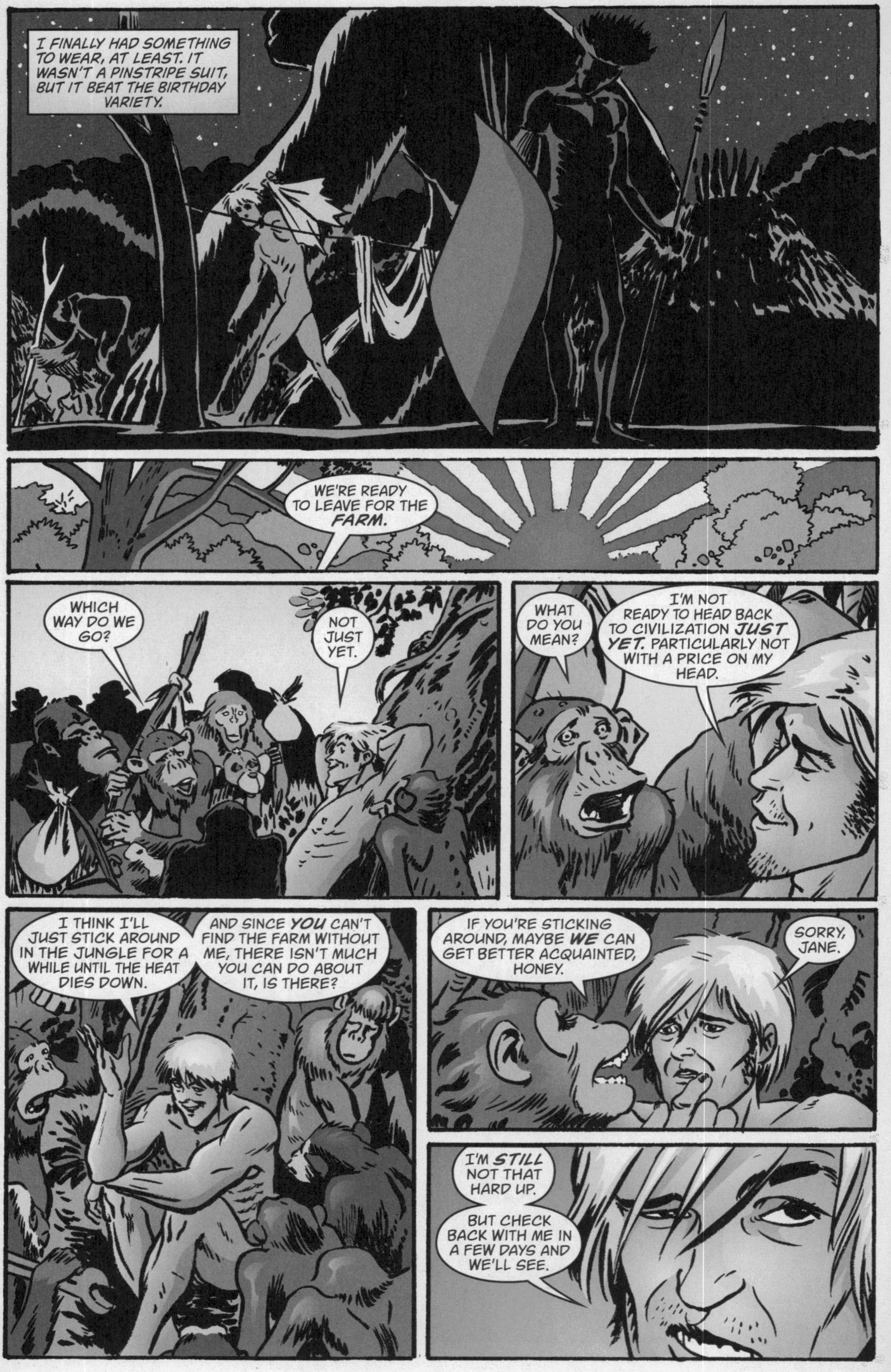
I FINALLY HAD SOMETHING TO WEAR, AT LEAST. IT WASN'T A PINSTRIPE SUIT, BUT IT BEAT THE BIRTHDAY VARIETY.
WE'RE READY TO LEAVE FOR THE FARM.
WHICH WAY DO WE GO?
NOT JUST YET.
WHAT DO YOU MEAN?
I'M NOT READY TO HEAD BACK TO CIVILIZATION JUST YET. PARTICULARLY NOT WITH A PRICE ON MY HEAD.
I THINK I'LL JUST STICK AROUND IN THE JUNGLE FOR A WHILE UNTIL THE HEAT DIES DOWN.
AND SINCE YOU CAN'T FIND THE FARM WITHOUT ME, THERE ISN'T MUCH YOU CAN DO ABOUT IT, IS THERE?
IF YOU'RE STICKING AROUND, MAYBE WE CAN GET BETTER ACQUAINTED, HONEY.
SORRY, JANE.
I'M STILL NOT THAT HARD UP.
BUT CHECK BACK WITH ME IN A FEW DAYS AND WE'LL SEE.

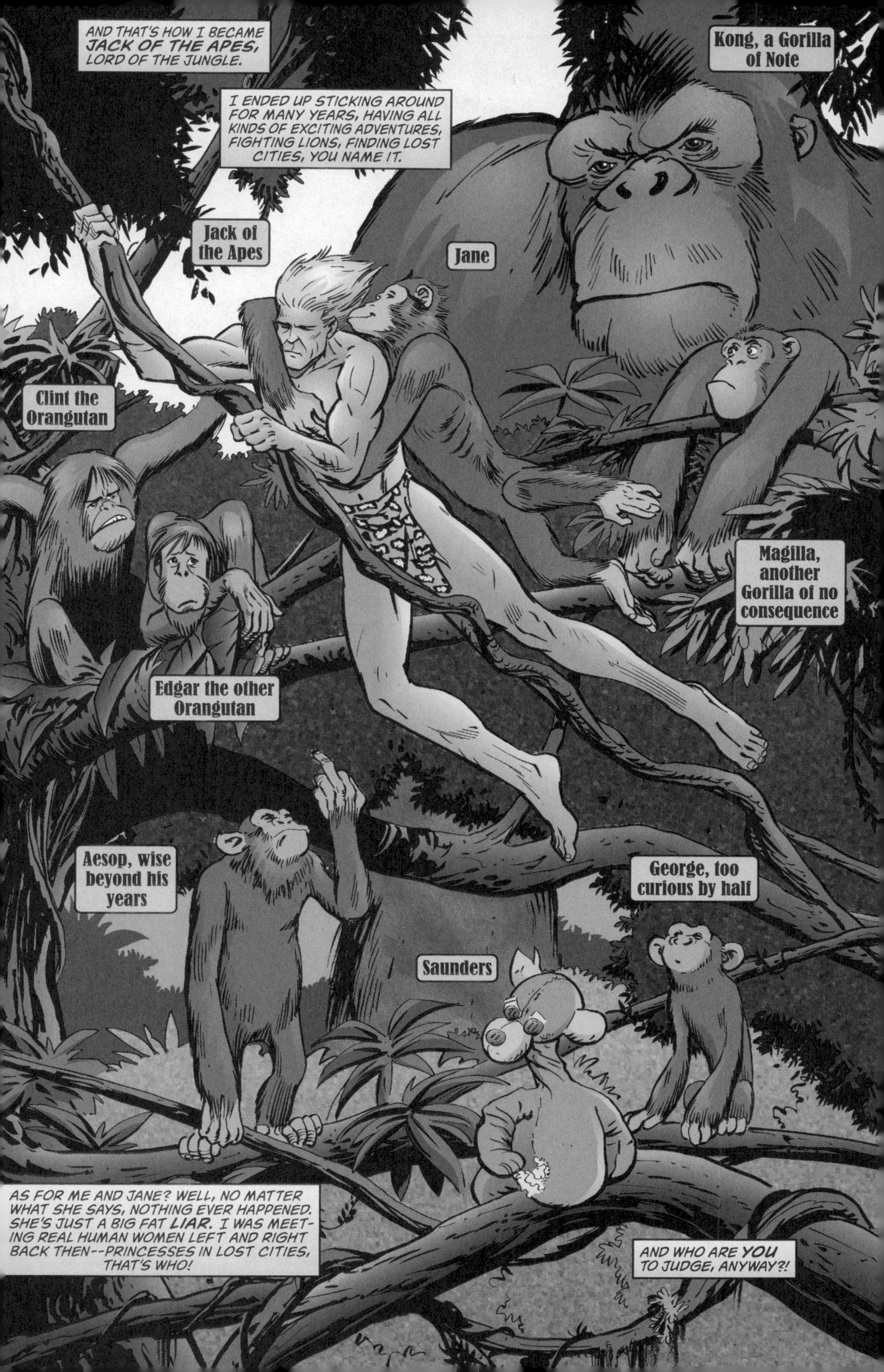

AND THAT'S HOW I BECAME JACK OF THE APES, LORD OF THE JUNGLE.
Kong, a Gorilla of Note
I ENDED UP STICKING AROUND FOR MANY YEARS, HAVING ALL KINDS OF EXCITING ADVENTURES, FIGHTING LIONS, FINDING LOST CITIES, YOU NAME IT.
Jack of the Apes
Jane
Clint the Orangutan
Magilla, another Gorilla of no consequence
Edgar the other Orangutan
Aesop, wise beyond his years
George, too curious by half
Saunders
AS FOR ME AND JANE? WELL, NO MATTER WHAT SHE SAYS, NOTHING EVER HAPPENED. SHE'S JUST A BIG FAT LIAR. I WAS MEETING REAL HUMAN WOMEN LEFT AND RIGHT BACK THEN--PRINCESSES IN LOST CITIES, THAT'S WHO!
AND WHO ARE YOU TO JUDGE, ANYWAY?!

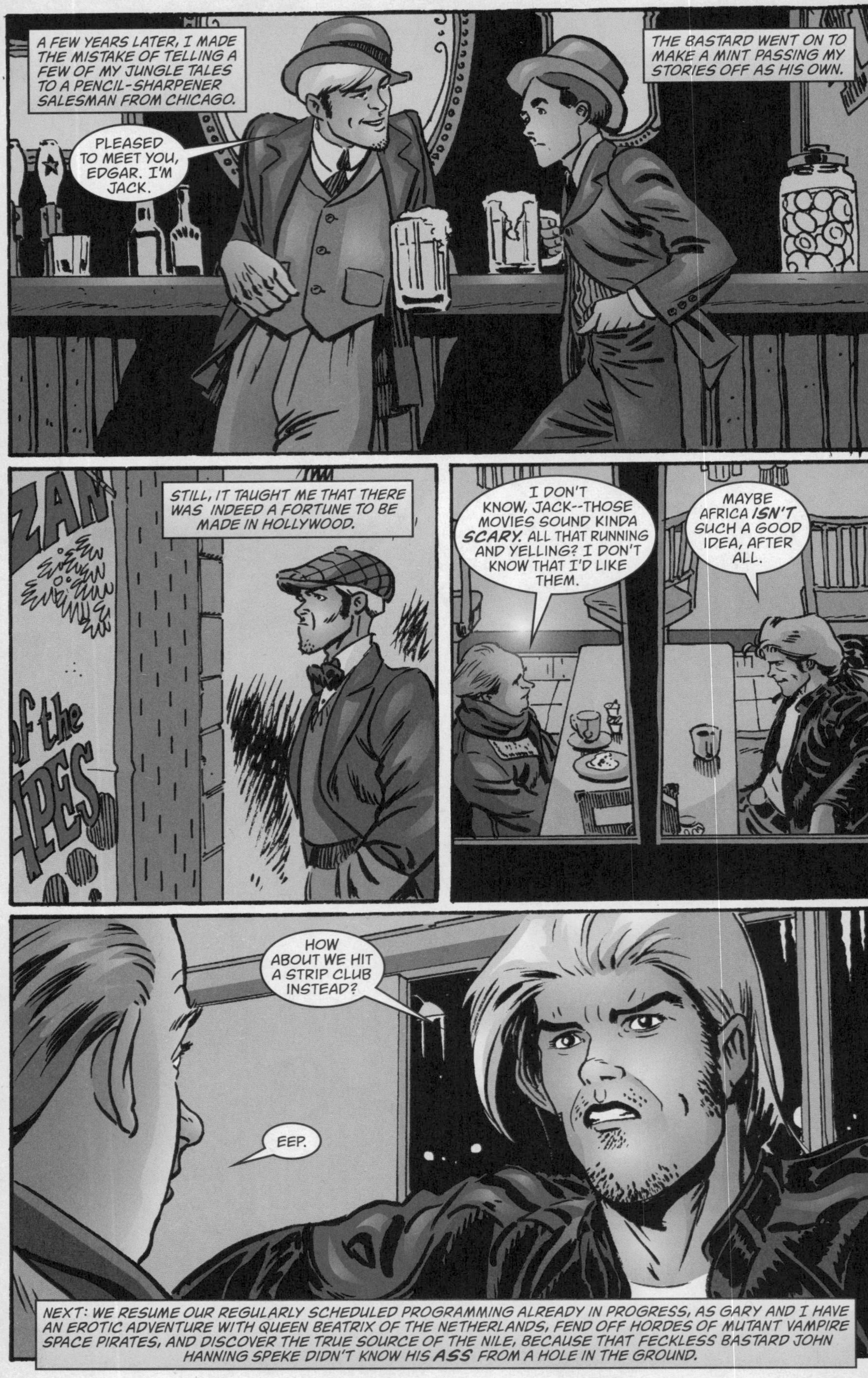
A FEW YEARS LATER, I MADE THE MISTAKE OF TELLING A FEW OF MY JUNGLE TALES TO A PENCIL-SHARPENER SALESMAN FROM CHICAGO.
PLEASED TO MEET YOU, EDGAR. I'M JACK.
THE BASTARD WENT ON TO MAKE A MINT PASSING MY STORIES OFF AS HIS OWN.
STILL, IT TAUGHT ME THAT THERE WAS INDEED A FORTUNE TO BE MADE IN HOLLYWOOD.
I DON'T KNOW, JACK--THOSE MOVIES SOUND KINDA SCARY. ALL THAT RUNNING AND YELLING? I DON'T KNOW THAT I'D LIKE THEM.
MAYBE AFRICA ISN'T SUCH A GOOD IDEA, AFTER ALL.
HOW ABOUT WE HIT A STRIP CLUB INSTEAD?
EEP.
NEXT: WE RESUME OUR REGULARLY SCHEDULED PROGRAMMING ALREADY IN PROGRESS, AS GARY AND I HAVE AN EROTIC ADVENTURE WITH QUEEN BEATRIX OF THE NETHERLANDS, FEND OFF HORDES OF MUTANT VAMPIRE SPACE PIRATES, AND DISCOVER THE TRUE SOURCE OF THE NILE, BECAUSE THAT FECKLESS BASTARD JOHN HANNING SPEKE DIDN'T KNOW HIS ASS FROM A HOLE IN THE GROUND.

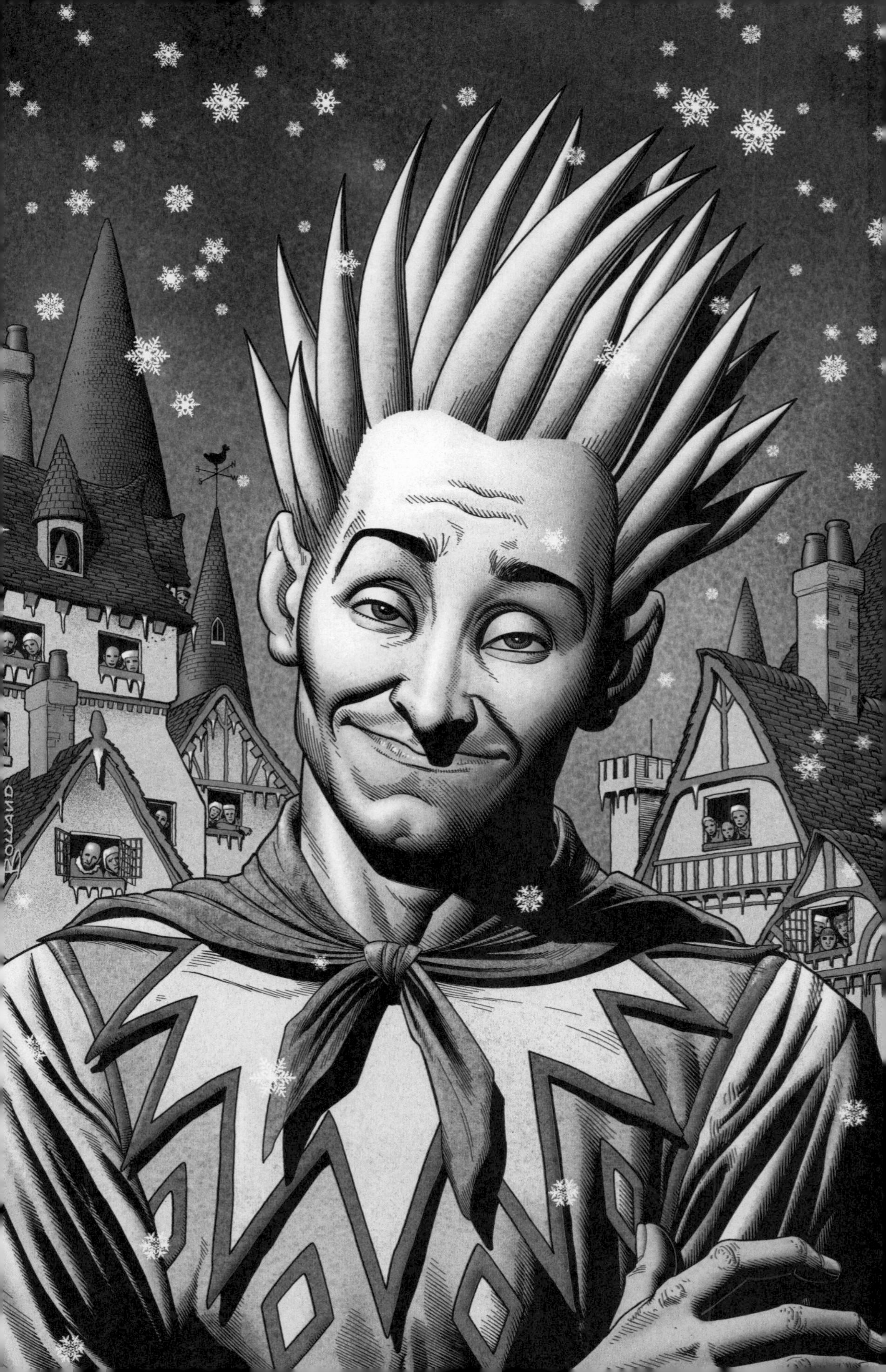
BOLLAND

"THE BASIC HEROIC IDEAL DIDN'T GET RUINED
JUST BECAUSE A **JACKASS** MADE USE OF IT."

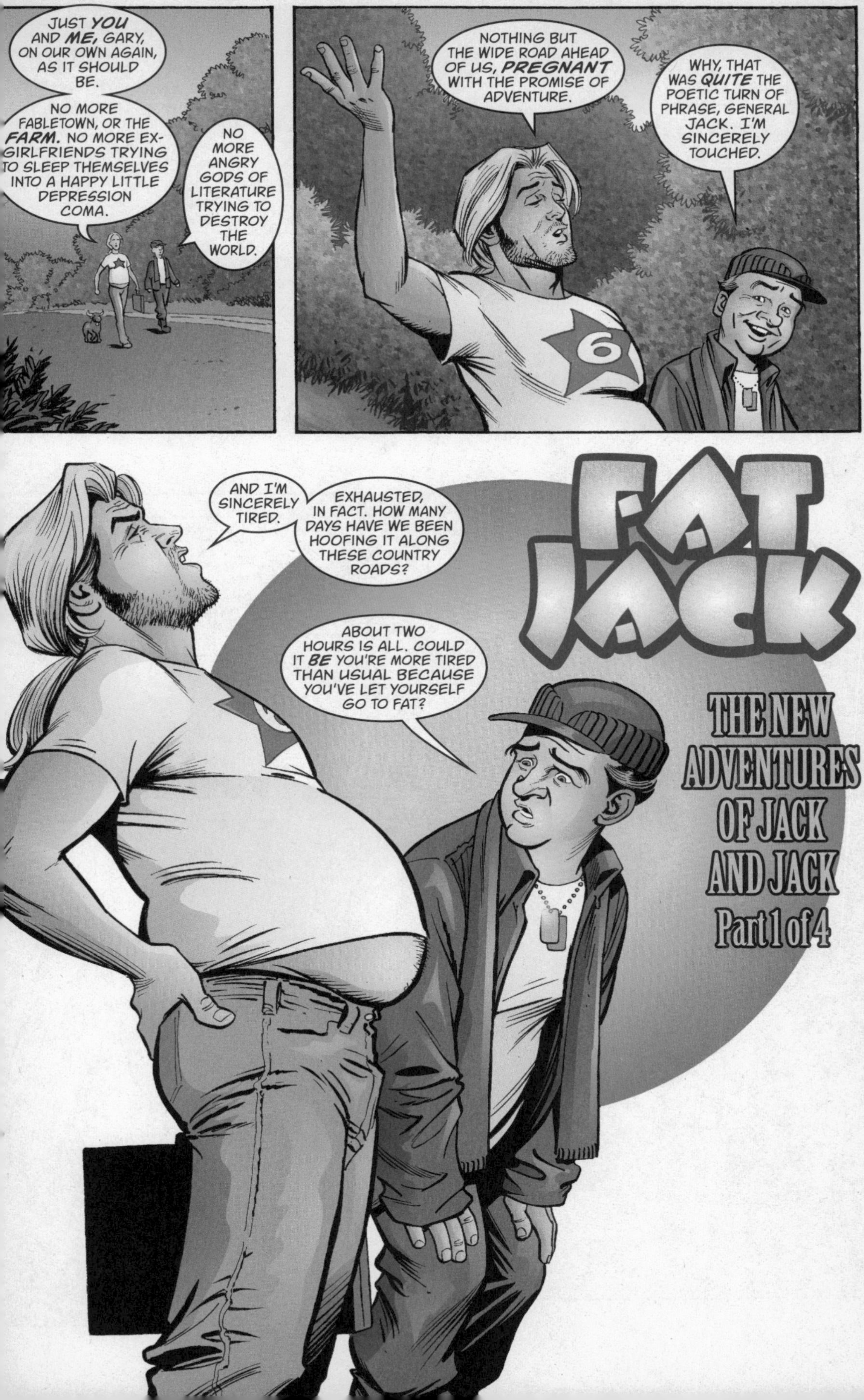
JUST YOU AND ME, GARY, ON OUR OWN AGAIN, AS IT SHOULD BE.
NO MORE FABLETOWN, OR THE FARM. NO MORE EX-GIRLFRIENDS TRYING TO SLEEP THEMSELVES INTO A HAPPY LITTLE DEPRESSION COMA.
NO MORE ANGRY GODS OF LITERATURE TRYING TO DESTROY THE WORLD.
NOTHING BUT THE WIDE ROAD AHEAD OF US, PREGNANT WITH THE PROMISE OF ADVENTURE.
WHY, THAT WAS QUITE THE POETIC TURN OF PHRASE, GENERAL JACK. I'M SINCERELY TOUCHED.
AND I'M SINCERELY TIRED.
EXHAUSTED, IN FACT. HOW MANY DAYS HAVE WE BEEN HOOFING IT ALONG THESE COUNTRY ROADS?
ABOUT TWO HOURS IS ALL. COULD IT BE YOU'RE MORE TIRED THAN USUAL BECAUSE YOU'VE LET YOURSELF GO TO FAT?
F.AT JACK
THE NEW ADVENTURES OF JACK AND JACK
Part 1 of 4

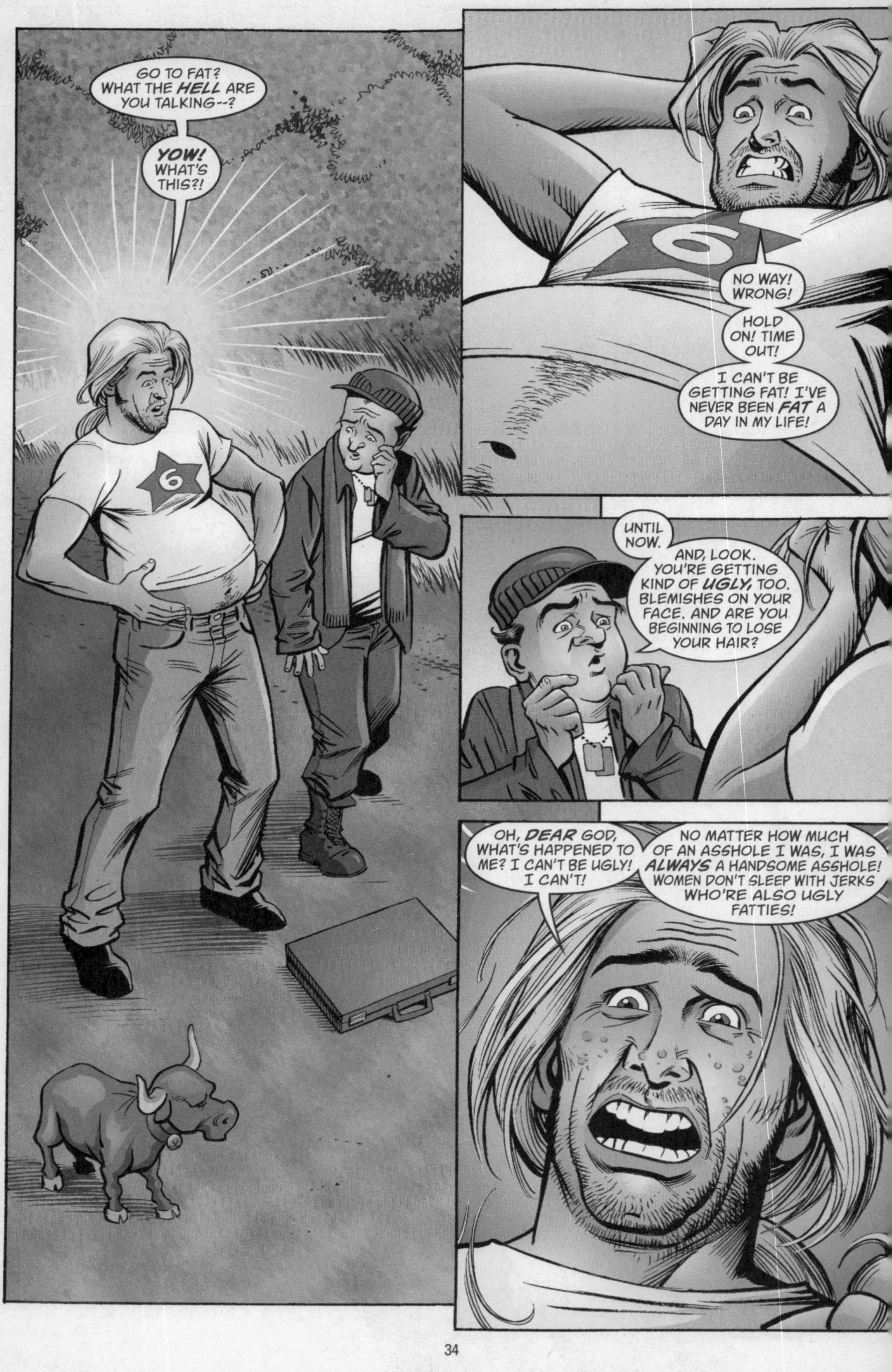
GO TO FAT? WHAT THE HELL ARE YOU TALKING--?
YOW! WHAT'S THIS?!
NO WAY! WRONG!
HOLD ON! TIME OUT!
I CAN'T BE GETTING FAT! I'VE NEVER BEEN FAT A DAY IN MY LIFE!
UNTIL NOW.
AND, LOOK. YOU'RE GETTING KIND OF UGLY, TOO. BLEMISHES ON YOUR FACE. AND ARE YOU BEGINNING TO LOSE YOUR HAIR?
OH, DEAR GOD, WHAT'S HAPPENED TO ME? I CAN'T BE UGLY! I CAN'T!
NO MATTER HOW MUCH OF AN ASSHOLE I WAS, I WAS ALWAYS A HANDSOME ASSHOLE! WOMEN DON'T SLEEP WITH JERKS WHO'RE ALSO UGLY FATTIES!

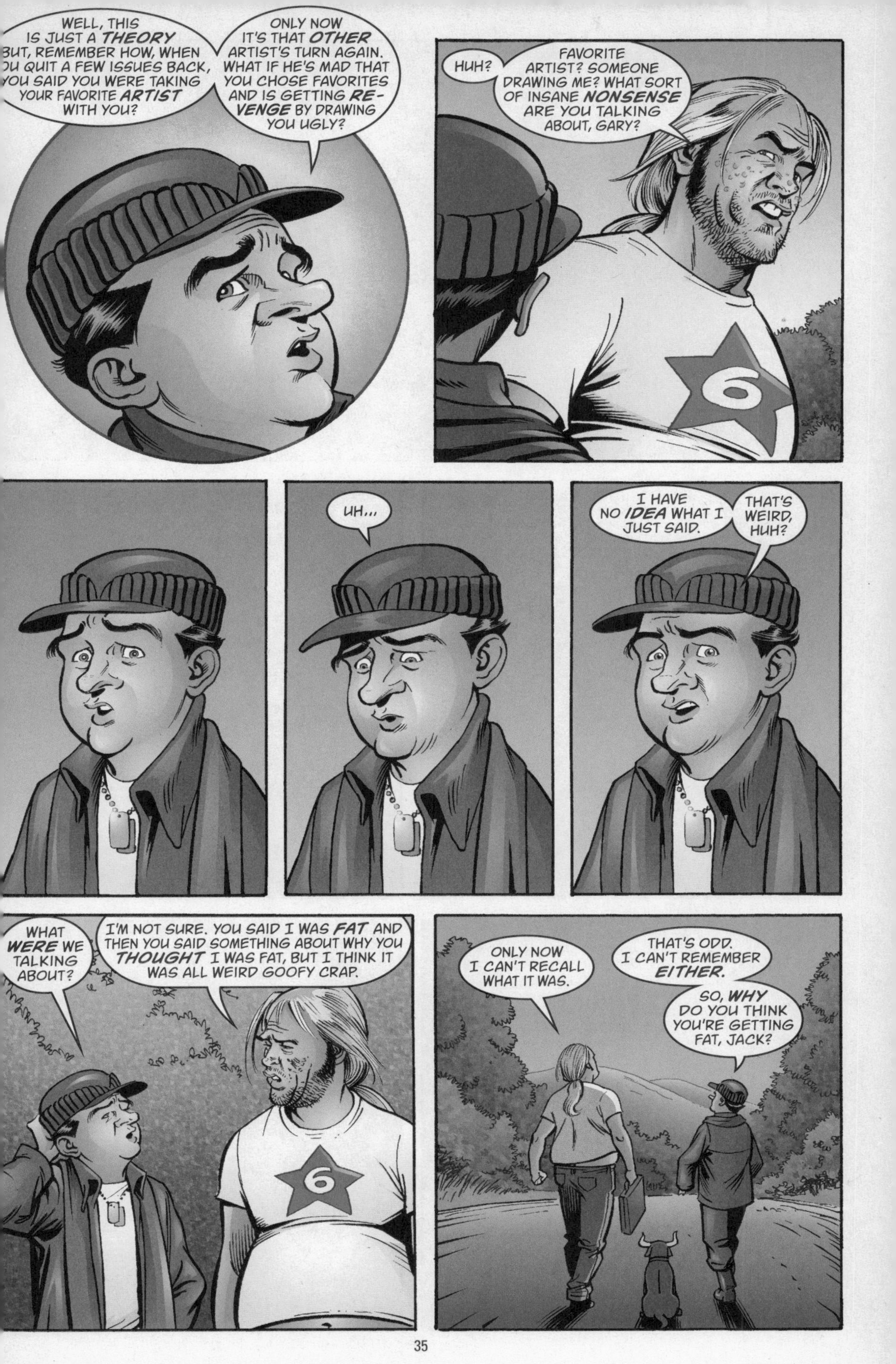

WELL, THIS IS JUST A THEORY BUT, REMEMBER HOW, WHEN YOU QUIT A FEW ISSUES BACK, YOU SAID YOU WERE TAKING YOUR FAVORITE ARTIST WITH YOU?
ONLY NOW IT'S THAT OTHER ARTIST'S TURN AGAIN. WHAT IF HE'S MAD THAT YOU CHOSE FAVORITES AND IS GETTING RE-VENGE BY DRAWING YOU UGLY?
HUH?
FAVORITE ARTIST? SOMEONE DRAWING ME? WHAT SORT OF INSANE NONSENSE ARE YOU TALKING ABOUT, GARY?
UH...
I HAVE NO IDEA WHAT I JUST SAID.
THAT'S WEIRD, HUH?
WHAT WERE WE TALKING ABOUT?
I'M NOT SURE. YOU SAID I WAS FAT AND THEN YOU SAID SOMETHING ABOUT WHY YOU THOUGHT I WAS FAT, BUT I THINK IT WAS ALL WEIRD GOOFY CRAP.
ONLY NOW I CAN'T RECALL WHAT IT WAS.
THAT'S ODD. I CAN'T REMEMBER EITHER.
SO, WHY DO YOU THINK YOU'RE GETTING FAT, JACK?

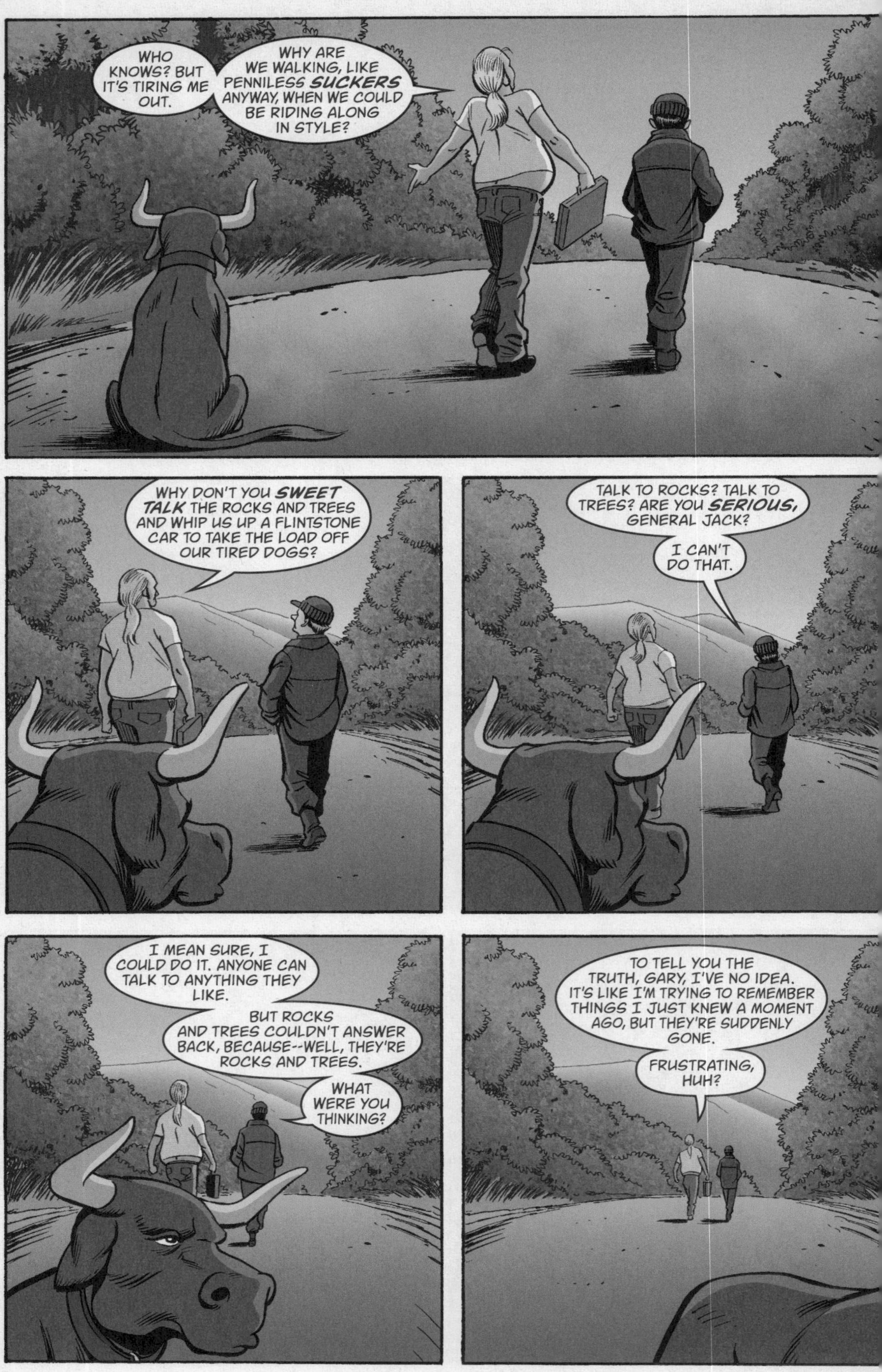
WHO KNOWS? BUT IT'S TIRING ME OUT.
WHY ARE WE WALKING, LIKE PENNILESS SUCKERS ANYWAY, WHEN WE COULD BE RIDING ALONG IN STYLE?
WHY DON'T YOU SWEET TALK THE ROCKS AND TREES AND WHIP US UP A FLINTSTONE CAR TO TAKE THE LOAD OFF OUR TIRED DOGS?
TALK TO ROCKS? TALK TO TREES? ARE YOU SERIOUS, GENERAL JACK?
I CAN'T DO THAT.
I MEAN SURE, I COULD DO IT. ANYONE CAN TALK TO ANYTHING THEY LIKE.
BUT ROCKS AND TREES COULDN'T ANSWER BACK, BECAUSE--WELL, THEY'RE ROCKS AND TREES.
WHAT WERE YOU THINKING?
TO TELL YOU THE TRUTH, GARY, I'VE NO IDEA. IT'S LIKE I'M TRYING TO REMEMBER THINGS I JUST KNEW A MOMENT AGO, BUT THEY'RE SUDDENLY GONE.
FRUSTRATING, HUH?

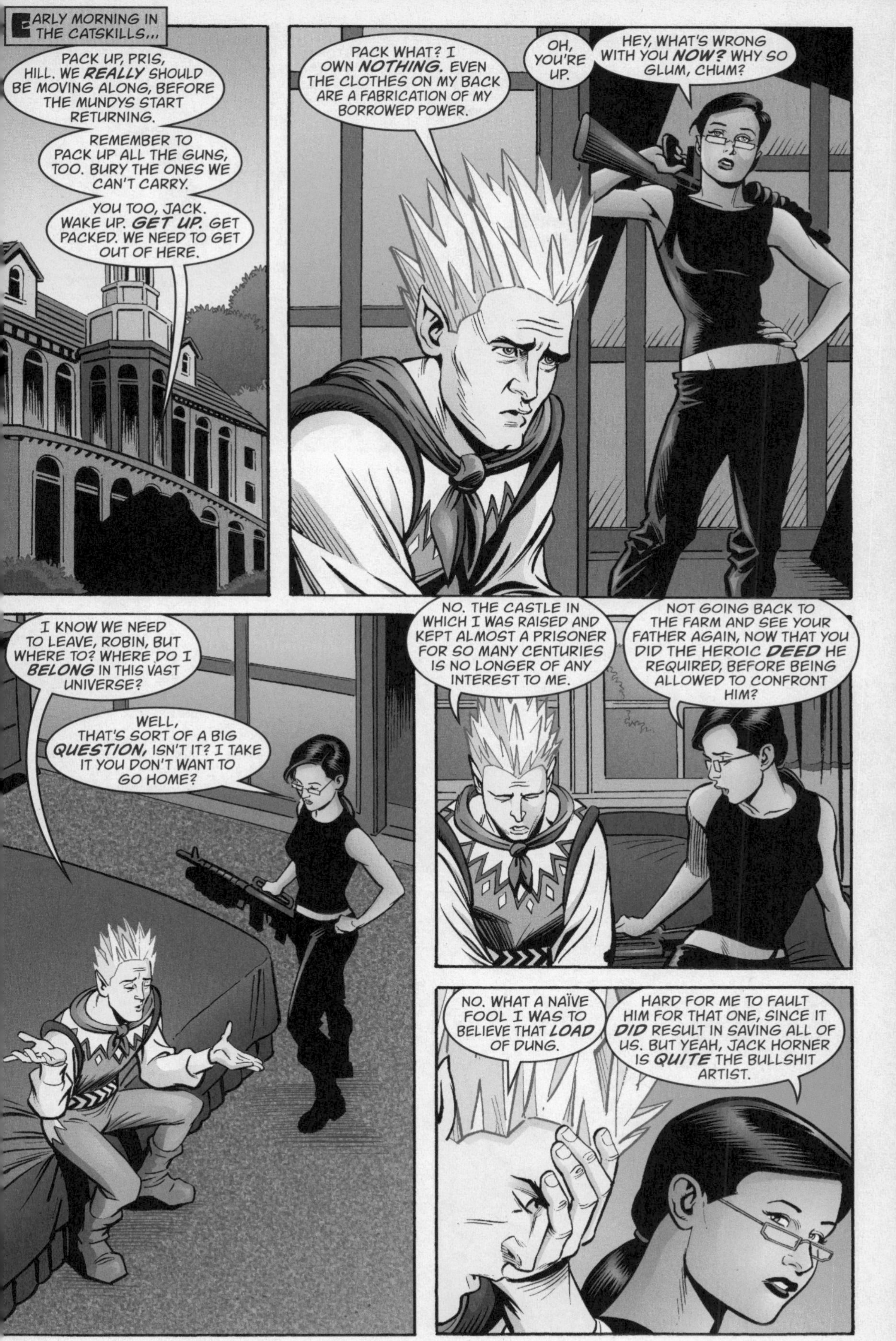
EARLY MORNING IN THE CATSKILLS...
PACK UP, PRIS, HILL. WE REALLY SHOULD BE MOVING ALONG, BEFORE THE MUNDYS START RETURNING.
REMEMBER TO PACK UP ALL THE GUNS, TOO. BURY THE ONES WE CAN'T CARRY.
YOU TOO, JACK. WAKE UP. GET UP. GET PACKED. WE NEED TO GET OUT OF HERE.
PACK WHAT? I OWN NOTHING. EVEN THE CLOTHES ON MY BACK ARE A FABRICATION OF MY BORROWED POWER.
OH, YOU'RE UP.
HEY, WHAT'S WRONG WITH YOU NOW? WHY SO GLUM, CHUM?
I KNOW WE NEED TO LEAVE, ROBIN, BUT WHERE TO? WHERE DO I BELONG IN THIS VAST UNIVERSE?
WELL, THAT'S SORT OF A BIG QUESTION, ISN'T IT? I TAKE IT YOU DON'T WANT TO GO HOME?
NO. THE CASTLE IN WHICH I WAS RAISED AND KEPT ALMOST A PRISONER FOR SO MANY CENTURIES IS NO LONGER OF ANY INTEREST TO ME.
NOT GOING BACK TO THE FARM AND SEE YOUR FATHER AGAIN, NOW THAT YOU DID THE HEROIC DEED HE REQUIRED, BEFORE BEING ALLOWED TO CONFRONT HIM?
NO. WHAT A NAÏVE FOOL I WAS TO BELIEVE THAT LOAD OF DUNG.
HARD FOR ME TO FAULT HIM FOR THAT ONE, SINCE IT DID RESULT IN SAVING ALL OF US. BUT YEAH, JACK HORNER IS QUITE THE BULLSHIT ARTIST.

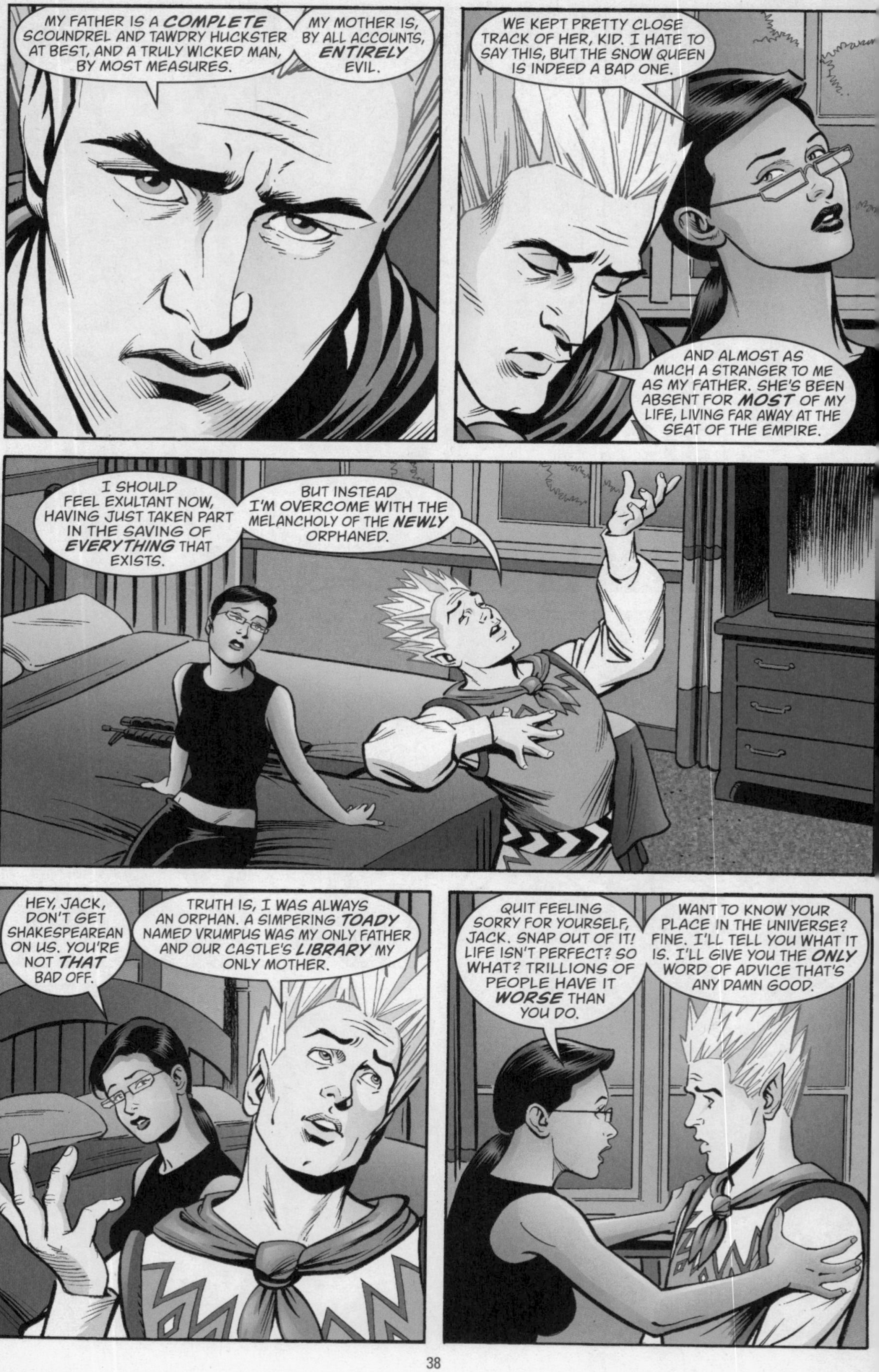

MY FATHER IS A COMPLETE SCOUNDREL AND TAWDRY HUCKSTER AT BEST, AND A TRULY WICKED MAN, BY MOST MEASURES.
MY MOTHER IS, BY ALL ACCOUNTS, ENTIRELY EVIL.
WE KEPT PRETTY CLOSE TRACK OF HER, KID. I HATE TO SAY THIS, BUT THE SNOW QUEEN IS INDEED A BAD ONE.
AND ALMOST AS MUCH A STRANGER TO ME AS MY FATHER. SHE'S BEEN ABSENT FOR MOST OF MY LIFE, LIVING FAR AWAY AT THE SEAT OF THE EMPIRE.
I SHOULD FEEL EXULTANT NOW, HAVING JUST TAKEN PART IN THE SAVING OF EVERYTHING THAT EXISTS.
BUT INSTEAD I'M OVERCOME WITH THE MELANCHOLY OF THE NEWLY ORPHANED.
HEY, JACK, DON'T GET SHAKESPEAREAN ON US. YOU'RE NOT THAT BAD OFF.
TRUTH IS, I WAS ALWAYS AN ORPHAN. A SIMPERING TOADY NAMED VRUMPUS WAS MY ONLY FATHER AND OUR CASTLE'S LIBRARY MY ONLY MOTHER.
QUIT FEELING SORRY FOR YOURSELF, JACK. SNAP OUT OF IT! LIFE ISN'T PERFECT? SO WHAT? TRILLIONS OF PEOPLE HAVE IT WORSE THAN YOU DO.
WANT TO KNOW YOUR PLACE IN THE UNIVERSE? FINE. I'LL TELL YOU WHAT IT IS. I'LL GIVE YOU THE ONLY WORD OF ADVICE THAT'S ANY DAMN GOOD.

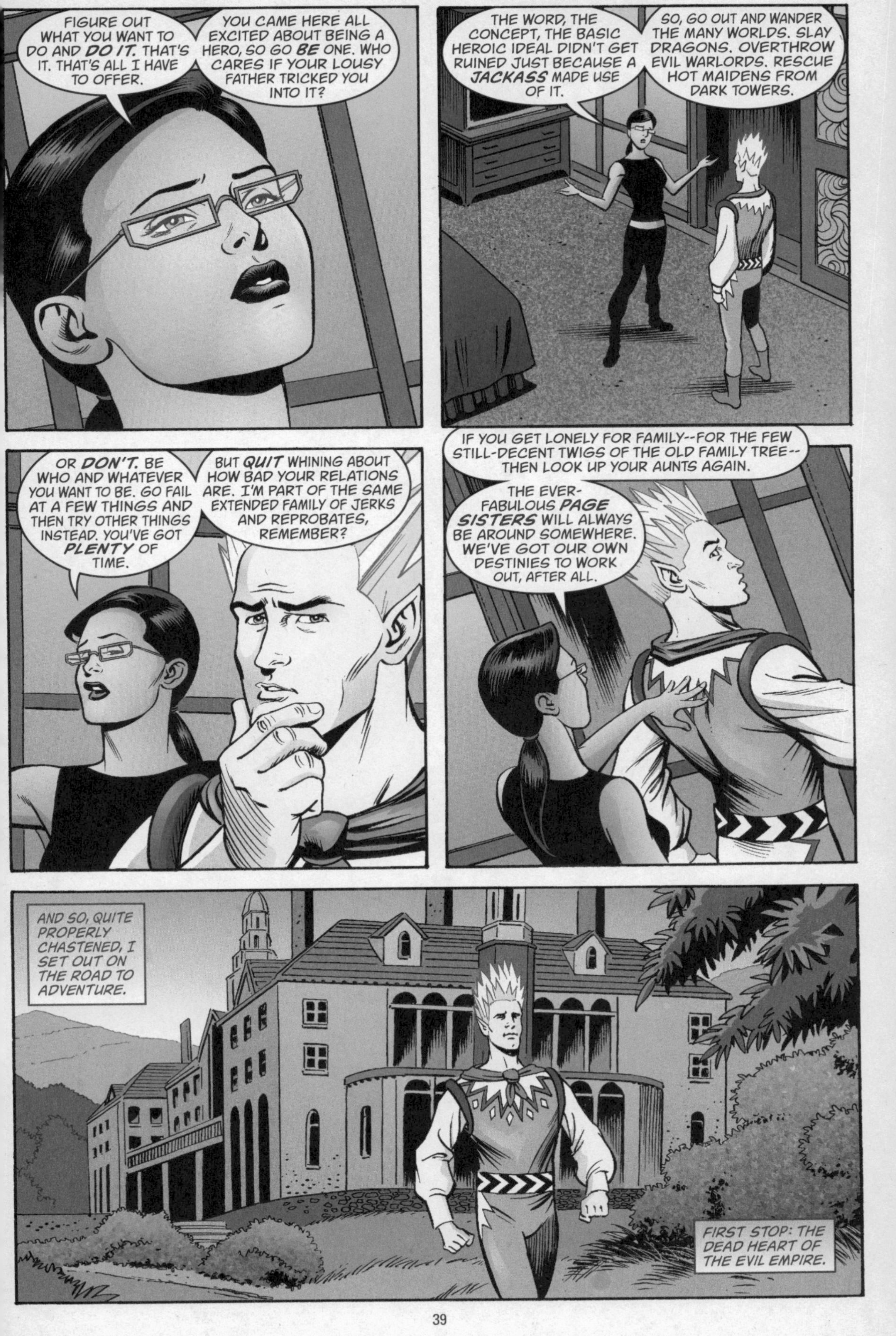
FIGURE OUT WHAT YOU WANT TO DO AND DO IT. THAT'S IT. THAT'S ALL I HAVE TO OFFER.
YOU CAME HERE ALL EXCITED ABOUT BEING A HERO, SO GO BE ONE. WHO CARES IF YOUR LOUSY FATHER TRICKED YOU INTO IT?
THE WORD, THE CONCEPT, THE BASIC HEROIC IDEAL DIDN'T GET RUINED JUST BECAUSE A JACKASS MADE USE OF IT.
SO, GO OUT AND WANDER THE MANY WORLDS. SLAY DRAGONS. OVERTHROW EVIL WARLORDS. RESCUE HOT MAIDENS FROM DARK TOWERS.
OR DON'T. BE WHO AND WHATEVER YOU WANT TO BE. GO FAIL AT A FEW THINGS AND THEN TRY OTHER THINGS INSTEAD. YOU'VE GOT PLENTY OF TIME.
BUT QUIT WHINING ABOUT HOW BAD YOUR RELATIONS ARE. I'M PART OF THE SAME EXTENDED FAMILY OF JERKS AND REPROBATES, REMEMBER?
IF YOU GET LONELY FOR FAMILY--FOR THE FEW STILL-DECENT TWIGS OF THE OLD FAMILY TREE--THEN LOOK UP YOUR AUNTS AGAIN.
THE EVER-FABULOUS PAGE SISTERS WILL ALWAYS BE AROUND SOMEWHERE. WE'VE GOT OUR OWN DESTINIES TO WORK OUT, AFTER ALL.
AND SO, QUITE PROPERLY CHASTENED, I SET OUT ON THE ROAD TO ADVENTURE.
FIRST STOP: THE DEAD HEART OF THE EVIL EMPIRE.

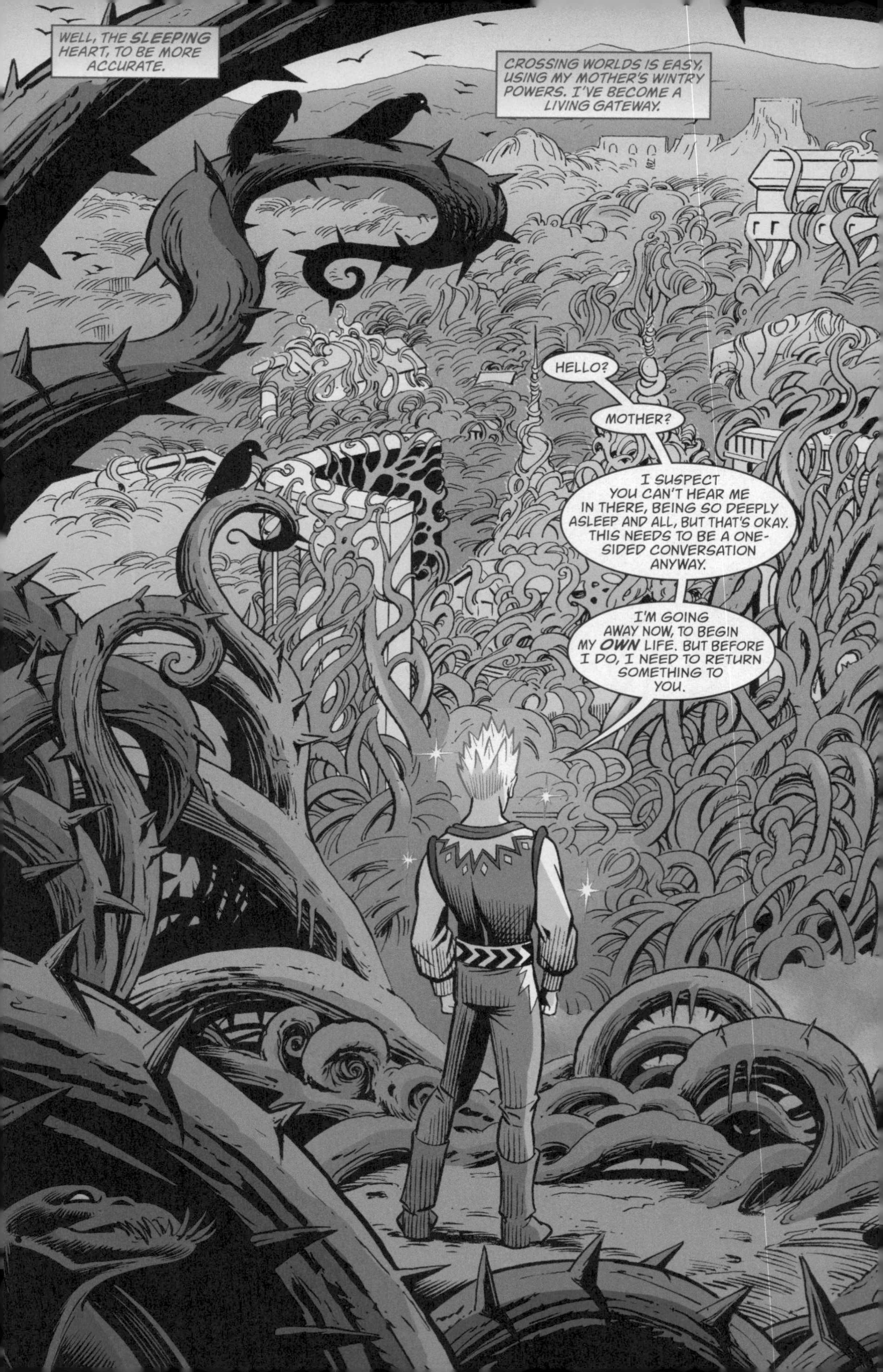
WELL, THE SLEEPING HEART, TO BE MORE ACCURATE.
CROSSING WORLDS IS EASY, USING MY MOTHER'S WINTRY POWERS. I'VE BECOME A LIVING GATEWAY.
HELLO?
MOTHER?
I SUSPECT YOU CAN'T HEAR ME IN THERE, BEING SO DEEPLY ASLEEP AND ALL, BUT THAT'S OKAY. THIS NEEDS TO BE A ONE-SIDED CONVERSATION ANYWAY.
I'M GOING AWAY NOW, TO BEGIN MY OWN LIFE. BUT BEFORE I DO, I NEED TO RETURN SOMETHING TO YOU.

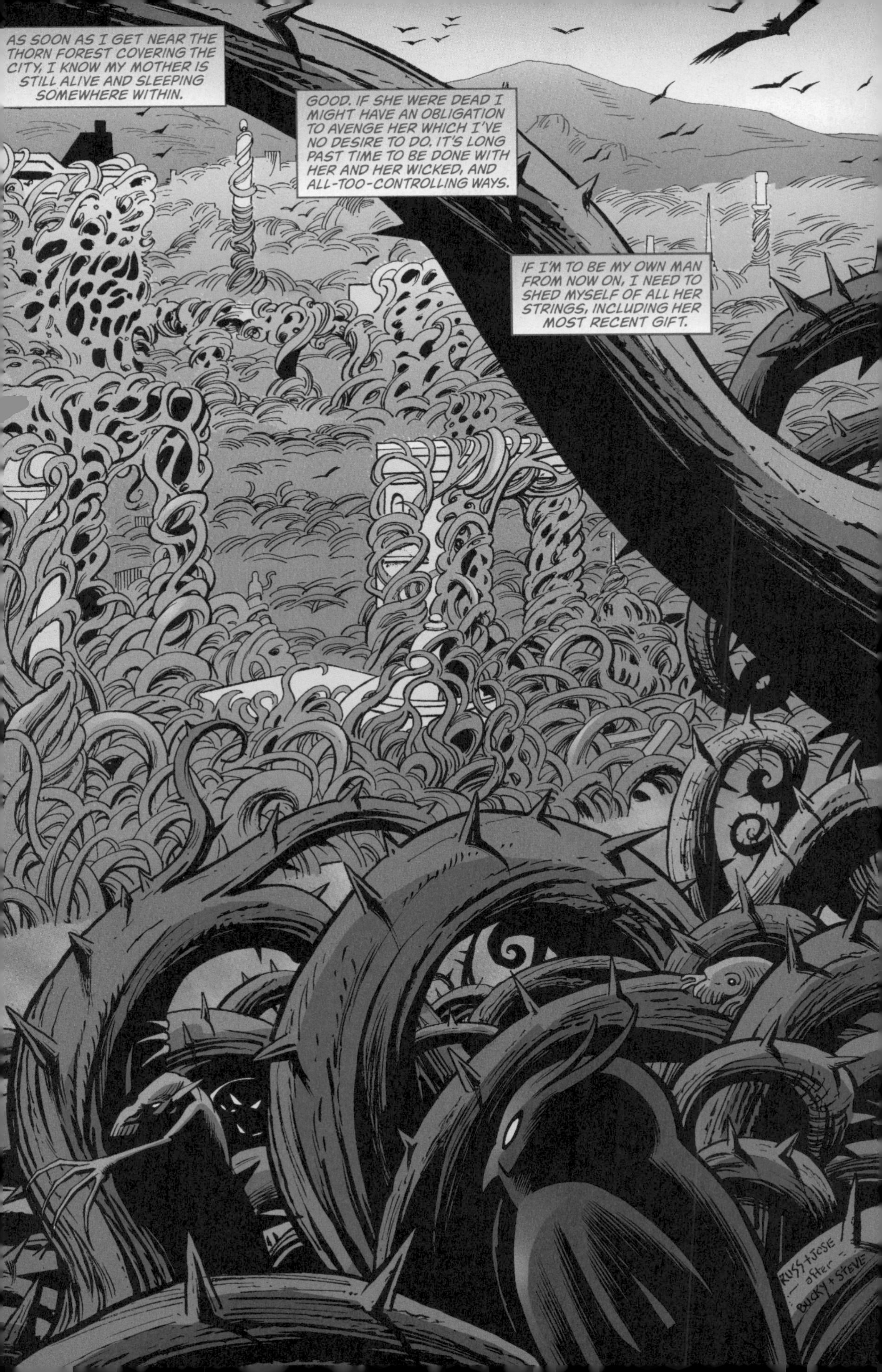
AS SOON AS I GET NEAR THE THORN FOREST COVERING THE CITY, I KNOW MY MOTHER IS STILL ALIVE AND SLEEPING SOMEWHERE WITHIN.
GOOD. IF SHE WERE DEAD I MIGHT HAVE AN OBLIGATION TO AVENGE HER WHICH I'VE NO DESIRE TO DO. IT'S LONG PAST TIME TO BE DONE WITH HER AND HER WICKED, AND ALL-TOO-CONTROLLING WAYS.
IF I'M TO BE MY OWN MAN FROM NOW ON, I NEED TO SHED MYSELF OF ALL HER STRINGS, INCLUDING HER MOST RECENT GIFT.
RUSS + JOSE after BUCKY + STEVE

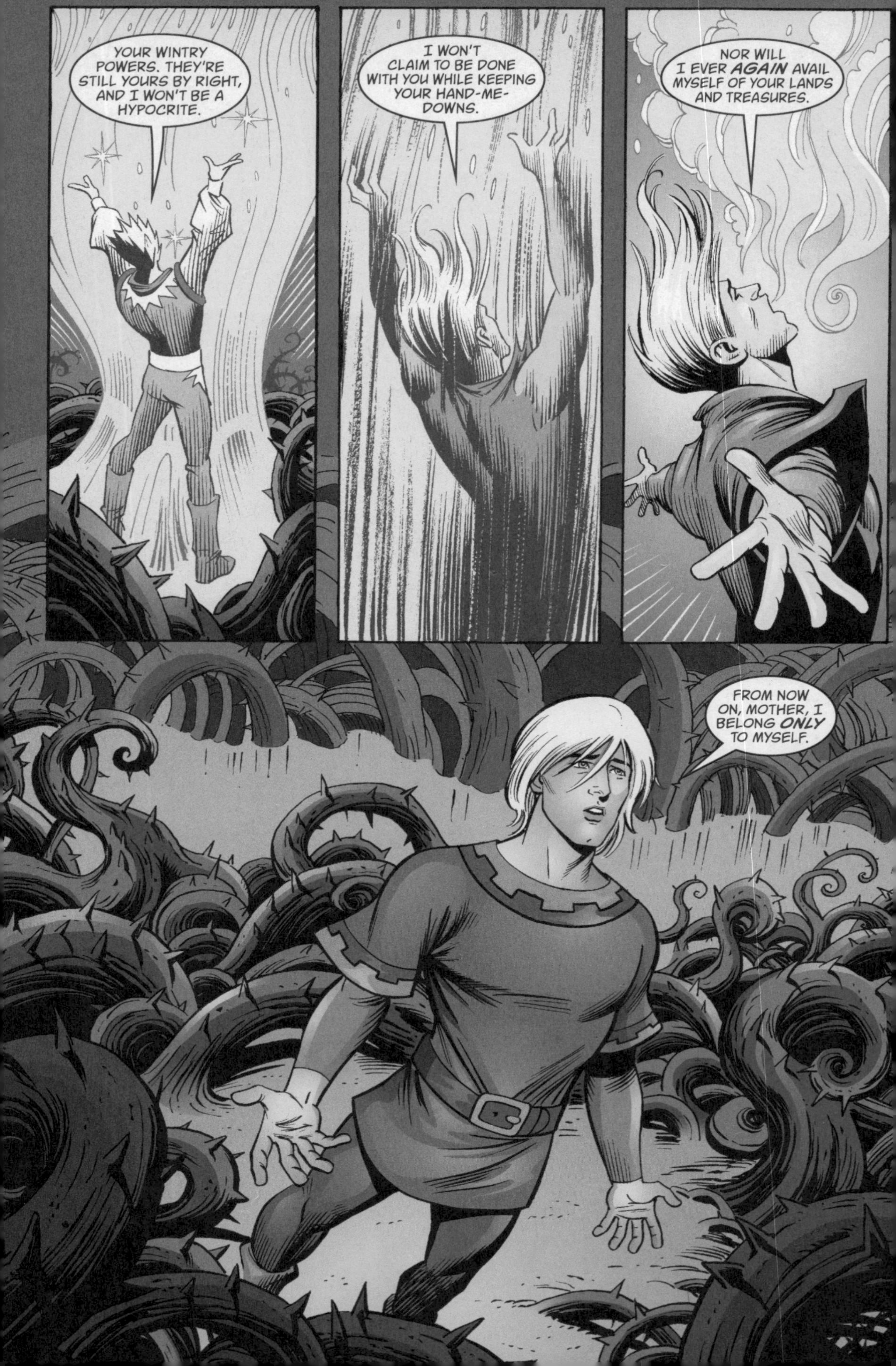
YOUR WINTRY POWERS. THEY'RE STILL YOURS BY RIGHT, AND I WON'T BE A HYPOCRITE.
I WON'T CLAIM TO BE DONE WITH YOU WHILE KEEPING YOUR HAND-ME-DOWNS.
NOR WILL I EVER AGAIN AVAIL MYSELF OF YOUR LANDS AND TREASURES.
FROM NOW ON, MOTHER, I BELONG ONLY TO MYSELF.

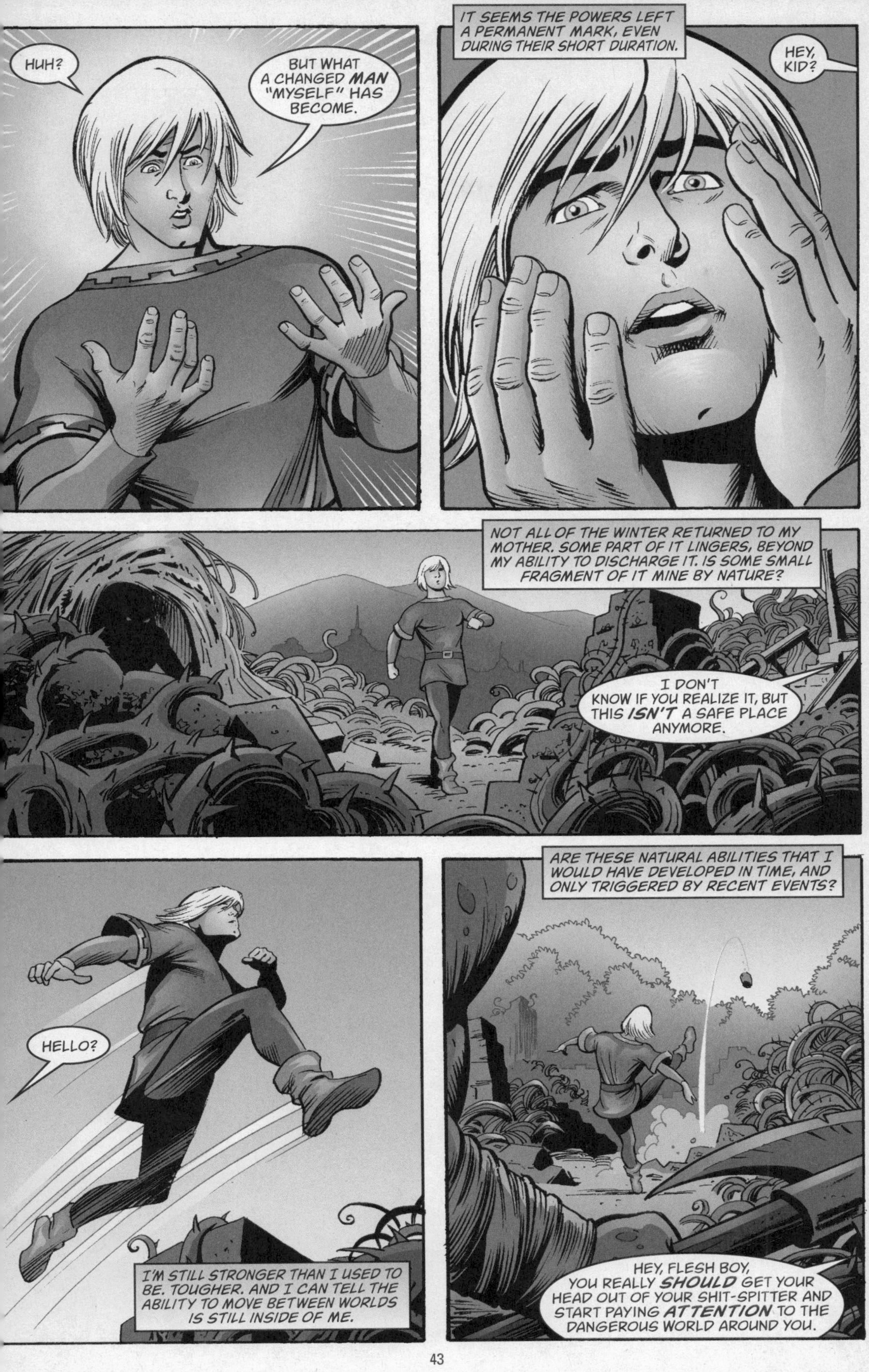
HUH?
BUT WHAT A CHANGED MAN "MYSELF" HAS BECOME.
IT SEEMS THE POWERS LEFT A PERMANENT MARK, EVEN DURING THEIR SHORT DURATION.
HEY, KID?
NOT ALL OF THE WINTER RETURNED TO MY MOTHER. SOME PART OF IT LINGERS, BEYOND MY ABILITY TO DISCHARGE IT. IS SOME SMALL FRAGMENT OF IT MINE BY NATURE?
I DON'T KNOW IF YOU REALIZE IT, BUT THIS ISN'T A SAFE PLACE ANYMORE.
HELLO?
I'M STILL STRONGER THAN I USED TO BE. TOUGHER. AND I CAN TELL THE ABILITY TO MOVE BETWEEN WORLDS IS STILL INSIDE OF ME.
ARE THESE NATURAL ABILITIES THAT I WOULD HAVE DEVELOPED IN TIME, AND ONLY TRIGGERED BY RECENT EVENTS?
HEY, FLESH BOY, YOU REALLY SHOULD GET YOUR HEAD OUT OF YOUR SHIT-SPITTER AND START PAYING ATTENTION TO THE DANGEROUS WORLD AROUND YOU.

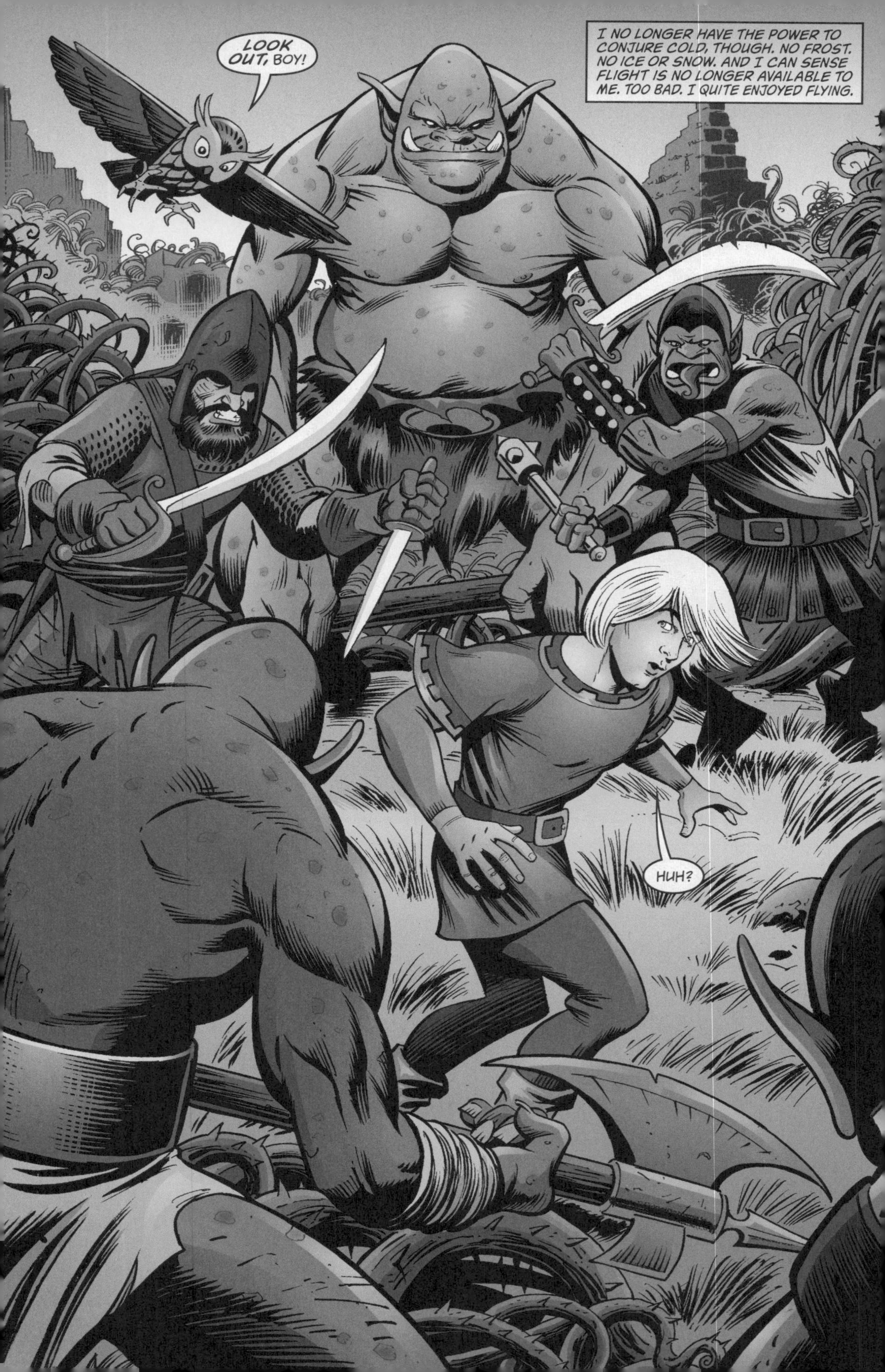
I NO LONGER HAVE THE POWER TO CONJURE COLD, THOUGH. NO FROST. NO ICE OR SNOW. AND I CAN SENSE FLIGHT IS NO LONGER AVAILABLE TO ME. TOO BAD. I QUITE ENJOYED FLYING.
LOOK OUT, BOY!
HUH?

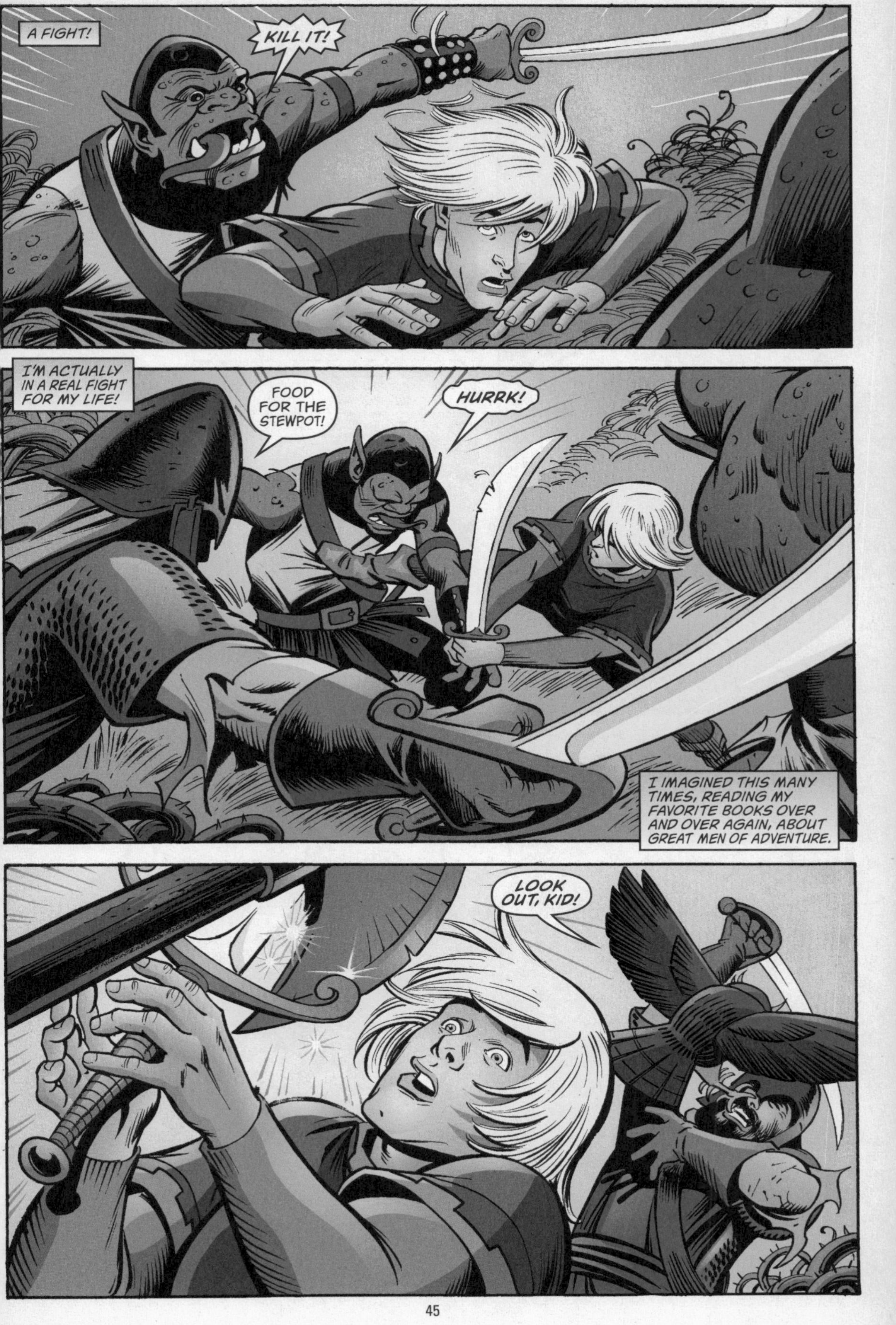
A FIGHT!
KILL IT!
I'M ACTUALLY IN A REAL FIGHT FOR MY LIFE!
FOOD FOR THE STEWPOT!
HURRK!
I IMAGINED THIS MANY TIMES, READING MY FAVORITE BOOKS OVER AND OVER AGAIN, ABOUT GREAT MEN OF ADVENTURE.
LOOK OUT, KID!

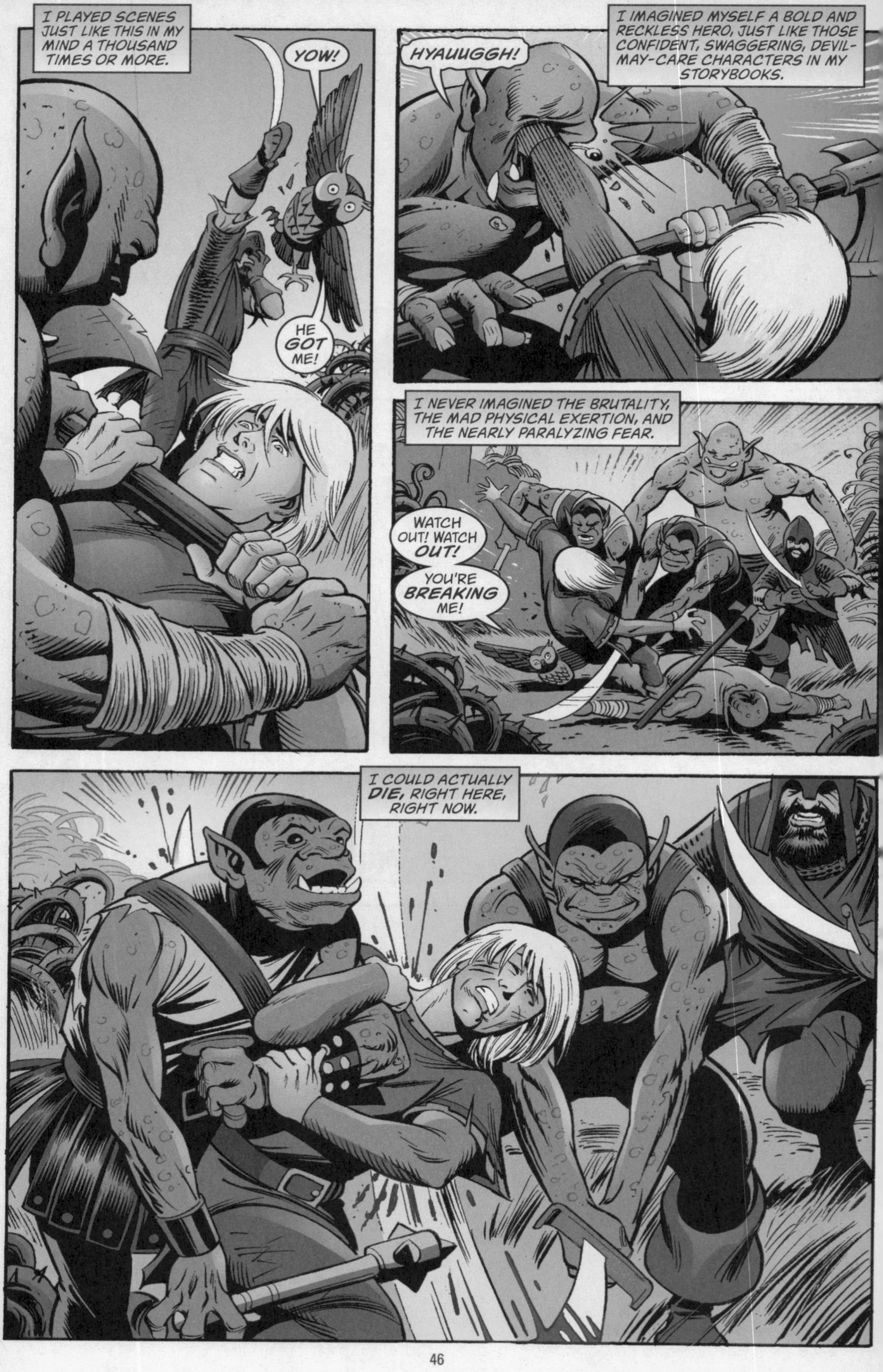

I PLAYED SCENES JUST LIKE THIS IN MY MIND A THOUSAND TIMES OR MORE.
YOW!
HE GOT ME!
I IMAGINED MYSELF A BOLD AND RECKLESS HERO, JUST LIKE THOSE CONFIDENT, SWAGGERING, DEVIL-MAY-CARE CHARACTERS IN MY STORYBOOKS.
HYAUUGGH!
I NEVER IMAGINED THE BRUTALITY, THE MAD PHYSICAL EXERTION, AND THE NEARLY PARALYZING FEAR.
WATCH OUT! WATCH OUT!
YOU'RE BREAKING ME!
I COULD ACTUALLY DIE, RIGHT HERE, RIGHT NOW.

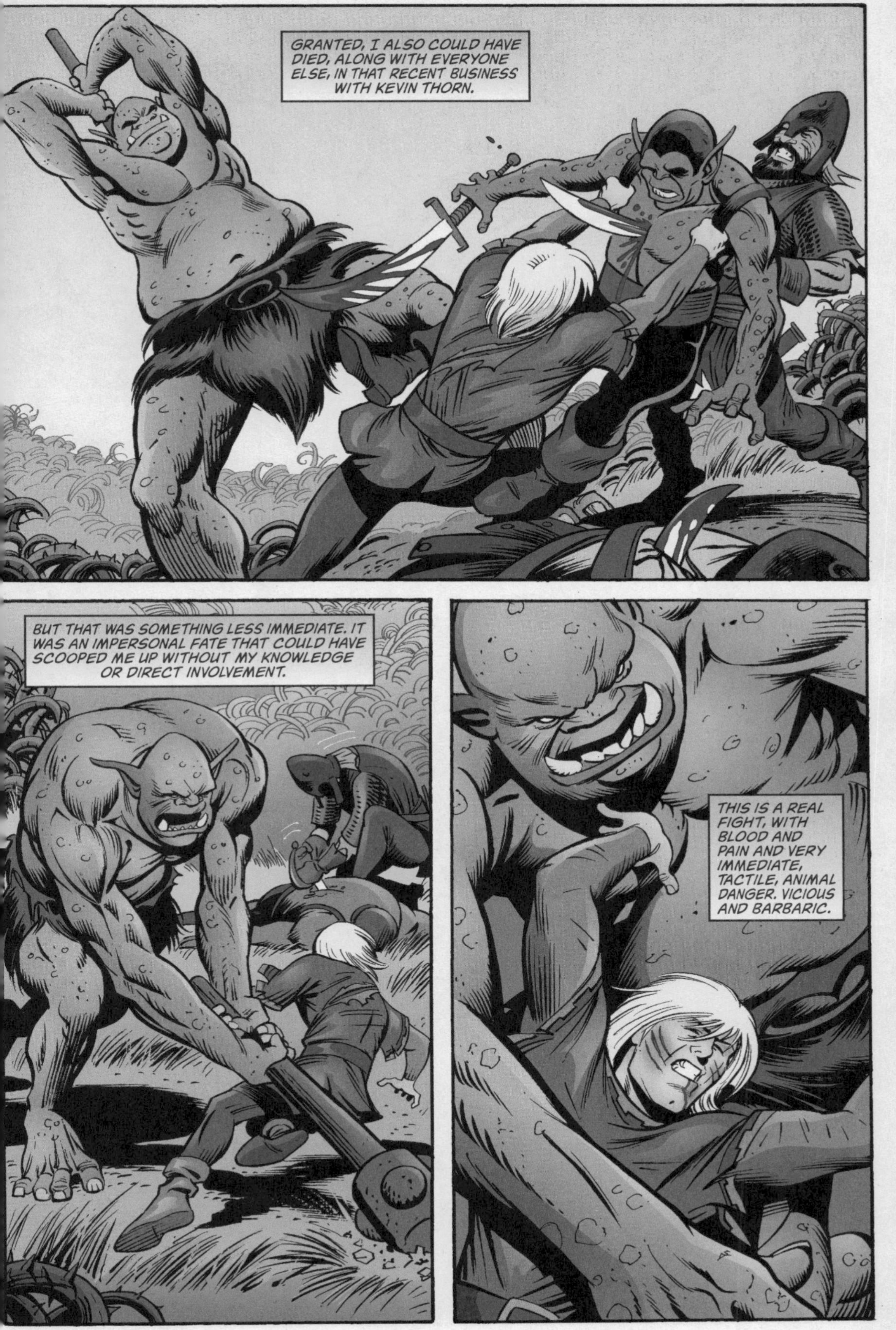
GRANTED, I ALSO COULD HAVE DIED, ALONG WITH EVERYONE ELSE, IN THAT RECENT BUSINESS WITH KEVIN THORN.
BUT THAT WAS SOMETHING LESS IMMEDIATE. IT WAS AN IMPERSONAL FATE THAT COULD HAVE SCOOPED ME UP WITHOUT MY KNOWLEDGE OR DIRECT INVOLVEMENT.
THIS IS A REAL FIGHT, WITH BLOOD AND PAIN AND VERY IMMEDIATE, TACTILE, ANIMAL DANGER. VICIOUS AND BARBARIC.

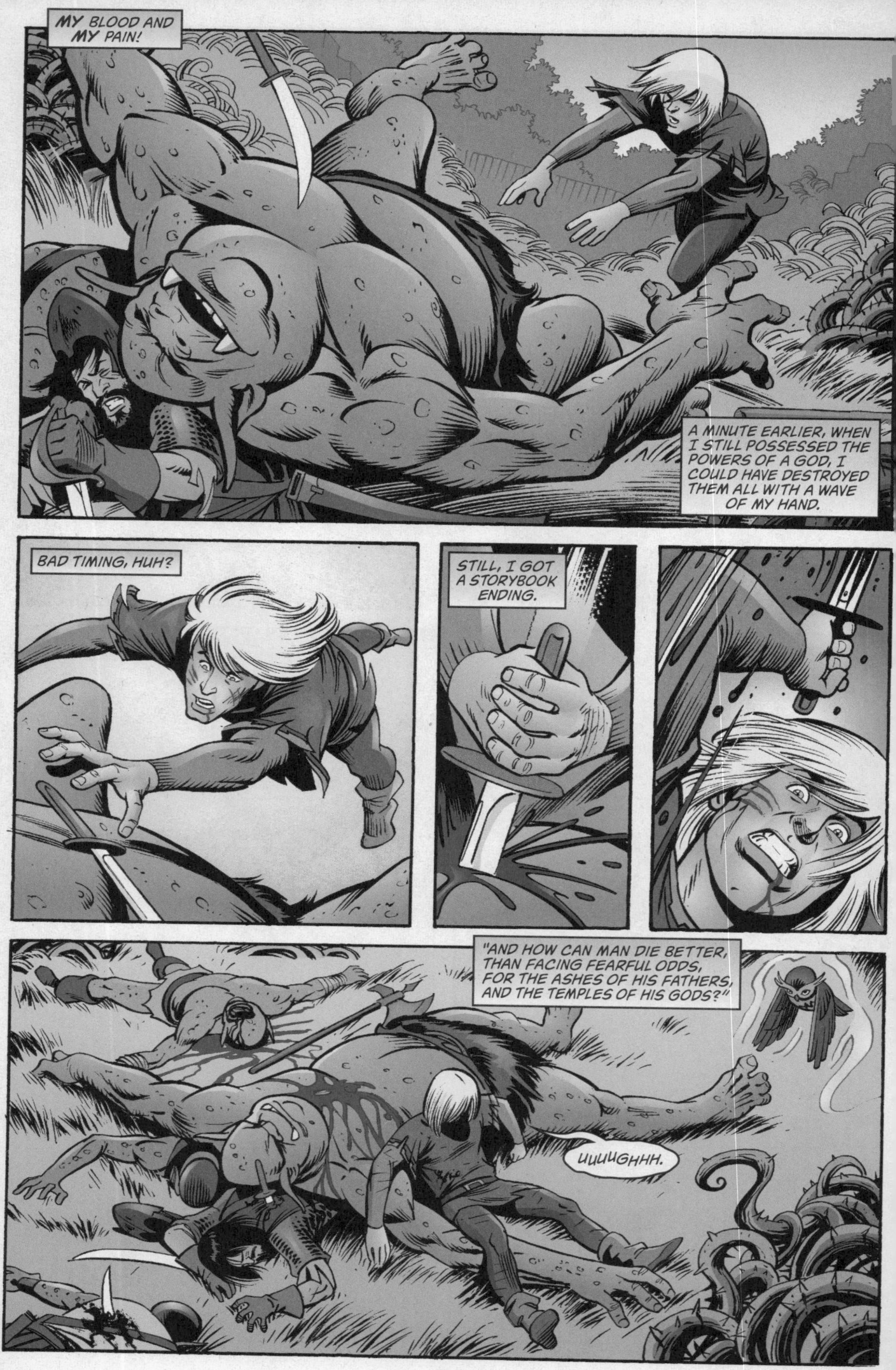
MY BLOOD AND MY PAIN!
A MINUTE EARLIER, WHEN I STILL POSSESSED THE POWERS OF A GOD, I COULD HAVE DESTROYED THEM ALL WITH A WAVE OF MY HAND.
BAD TIMING, HUH?
STILL, I GOT A STORYBOOK ENDING.
"AND HOW CAN MAN DIE BETTER, THAN FACING FEARFUL ODDS, FOR THE ASHES OF HIS FATHERS, AND THE TEMPLES OF HIS GODS?"
UUUUGHHH.

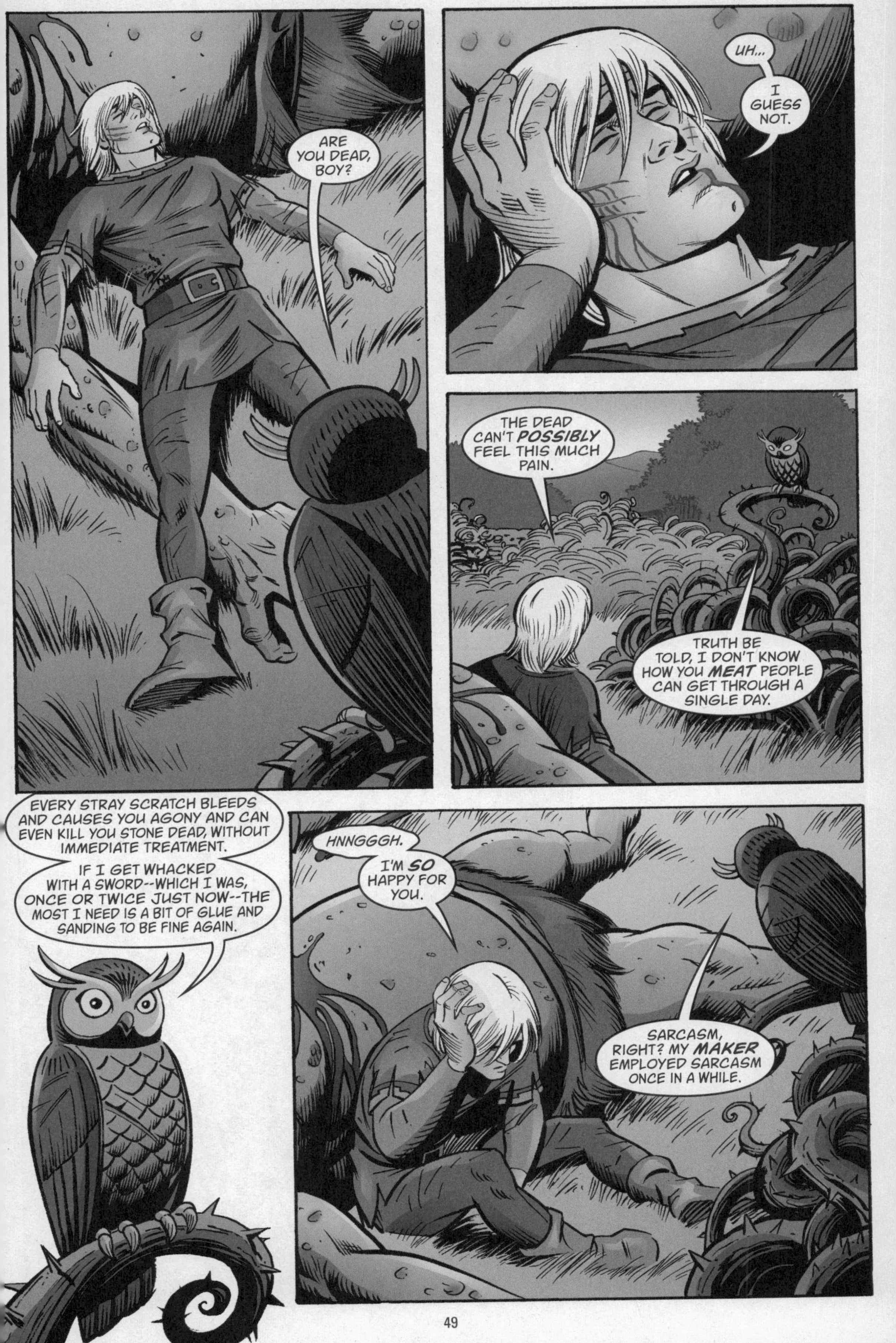
ARE YOU DEAD, BOY?
UH...
I GUESS NOT.
THE DEAD CAN'T **POSSIBLY** FEEL THIS MUCH PAIN.
TRUTH BE TOLD, I DON'T KNOW HOW YOU **MEAT** PEOPLE CAN GET THROUGH A SINGLE DAY.
EVERY STRAY SCRATCH BLEEDS AND CAUSES YOU AGONY AND CAN EVEN KILL YOU STONE DEAD, WITHOUT IMMEDIATE TREATMENT.
IF I GET WHACKED WITH A SWORD--WHICH I WAS, ONCE OR TWICE JUST NOW--THE MOST I NEED IS A BIT OF GLUE AND SANDING TO BE FINE AGAIN.
HNNGGGH.
I'M **SO** HAPPY FOR YOU.
SARCASM, RIGHT? MY **MAKER** EMPLOYED SARCASM ONCE IN A WHILE.

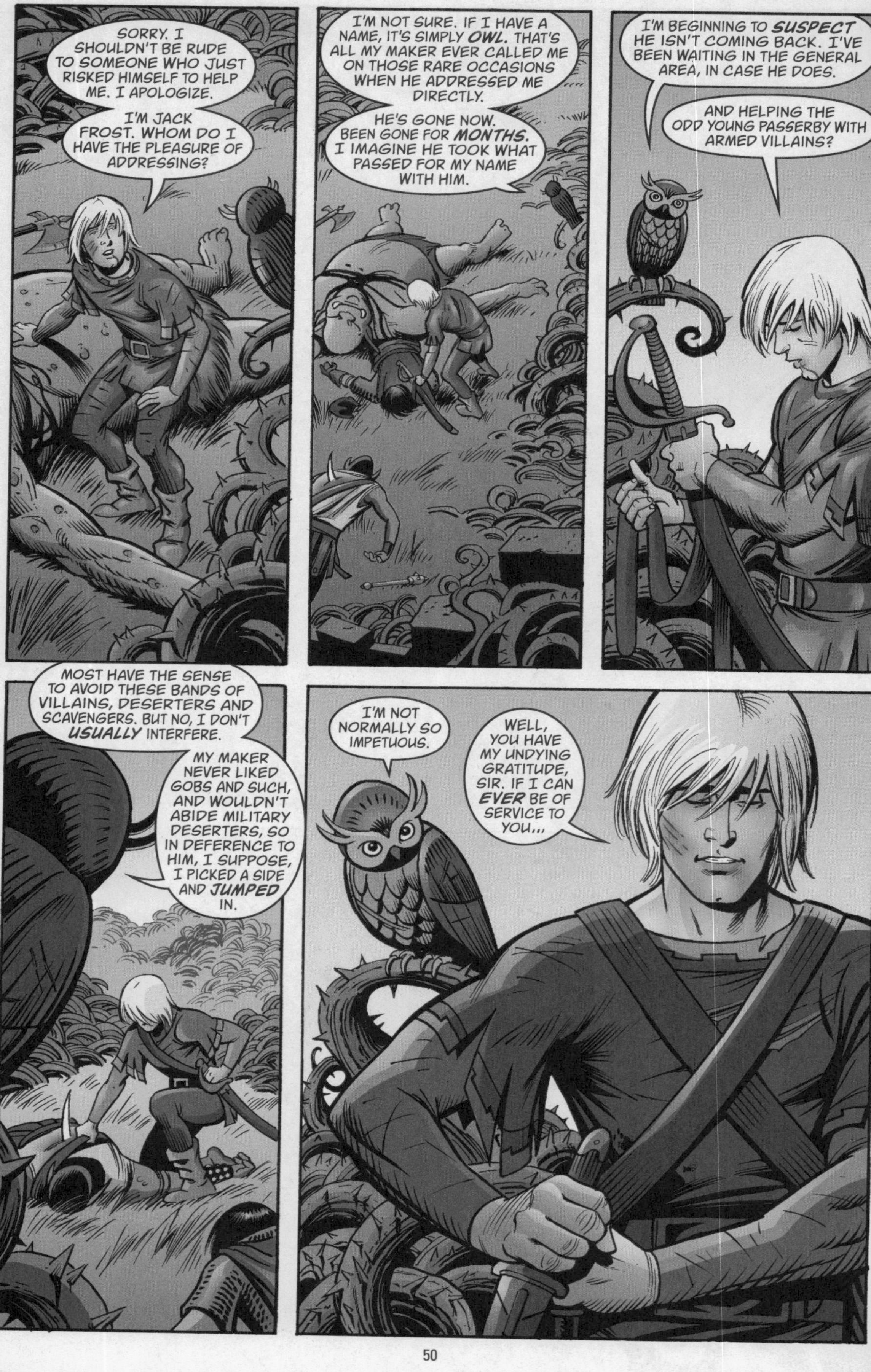
SORRY. I SHOULDN'T BE RUDE TO SOMEONE WHO JUST RISKED HIMSELF TO HELP ME. I APOLOGIZE.
I'M JACK FROST. WHOM DO I HAVE THE PLEASURE OF ADDRESSING?
I'M NOT SURE. IF I HAVE A NAME, IT'S SIMPLY OWL. THAT'S ALL MY MAKER EVER CALLED ME ON THOSE RARE OCCASIONS WHEN HE ADDRESSED ME DIRECTLY.
HE'S GONE NOW. BEEN GONE FOR MONTHS. I IMAGINE HE TOOK WHAT PASSED FOR MY NAME WITH HIM.
I'M BEGINNING TO SUSPECT HE ISN'T COMING BACK. I'VE BEEN WAITING IN THE GENERAL AREA, IN CASE HE DOES.
AND HELPING THE ODD YOUNG PASSERBY WITH ARMED VILLAINS?
MOST HAVE THE SENSE TO AVOID THESE BANDS OF VILLAINS, DESERTERS AND SCAVENGERS. BUT NO, I DON'T USUALLY INTERFERE.
MY MAKER NEVER LIKED GOBS AND SUCH, AND WOULDN'T ABIDE MILITARY DESERTERS, SO IN DEFERENCE TO HIM, I SUPPOSE, I PICKED A SIDE AND JUMPED IN.
I'M NOT NORMALLY SO IMPETUOUS.
WELL, YOU HAVE MY UNDYING GRATITUDE, SIR. IF I CAN EVER BE OF SERVICE TO YOU...

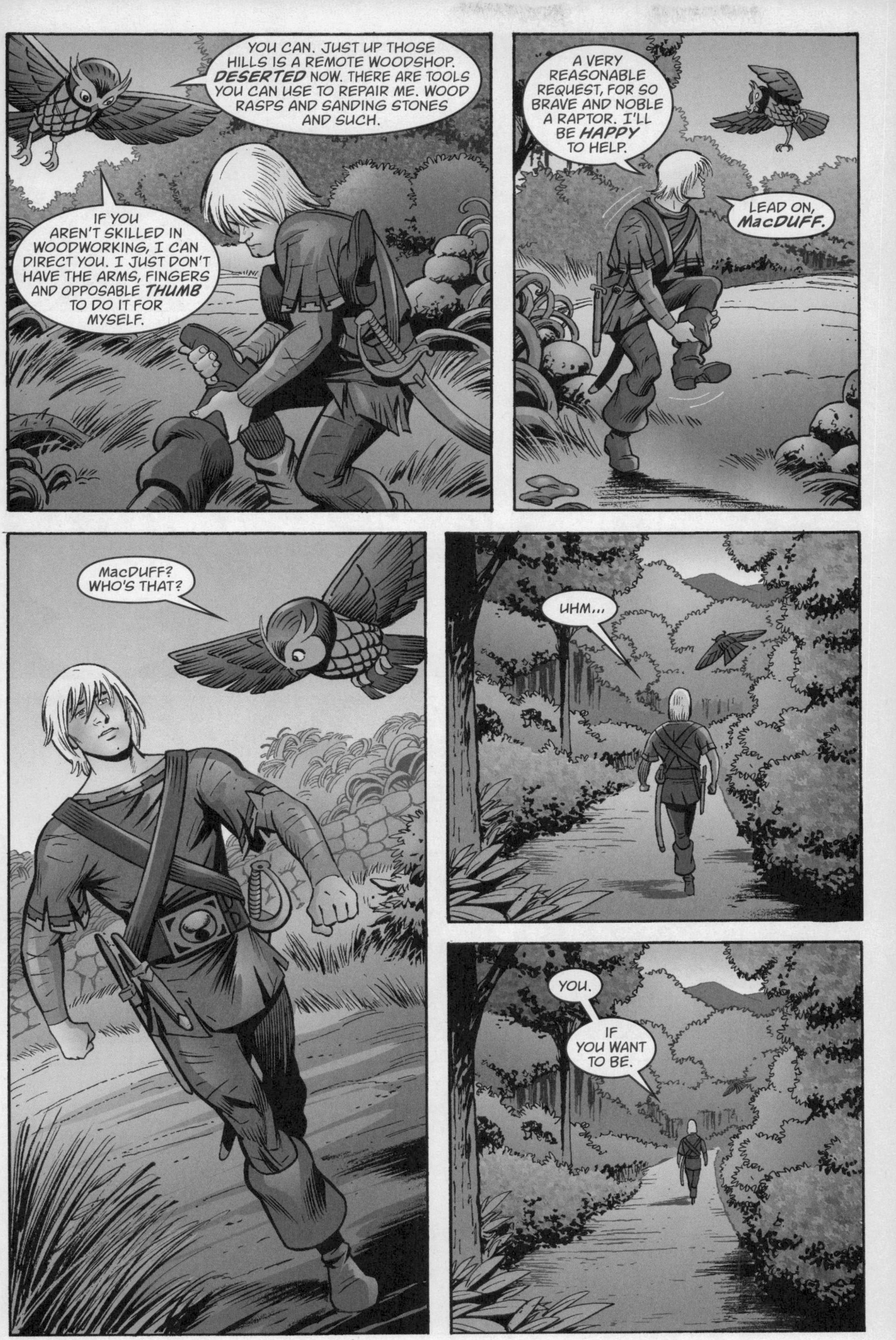
YOU CAN. JUST UP THOSE HILLS IS A REMOTE WOODSHOP. DESERTED NOW. THERE ARE TOOLS YOU CAN USE TO REPAIR ME. WOOD RASPS AND SANDING STONES AND SUCH.
IF YOU AREN'T SKILLED IN WOODWORKING, I CAN DIRECT YOU. I JUST DON'T HAVE THE ARMS, FINGERS AND OPPOSABLE THUMB TO DO IT FOR MYSELF.
A VERY REASONABLE REQUEST, FOR SO BRAVE AND NOBLE A RAPTOR. I'LL BE HAPPY TO HELP.
LEAD ON, MacDUFF.
MacDUFF? WHO'S THAT?
UHM...
YOU.
IF YOU WANT TO BE.

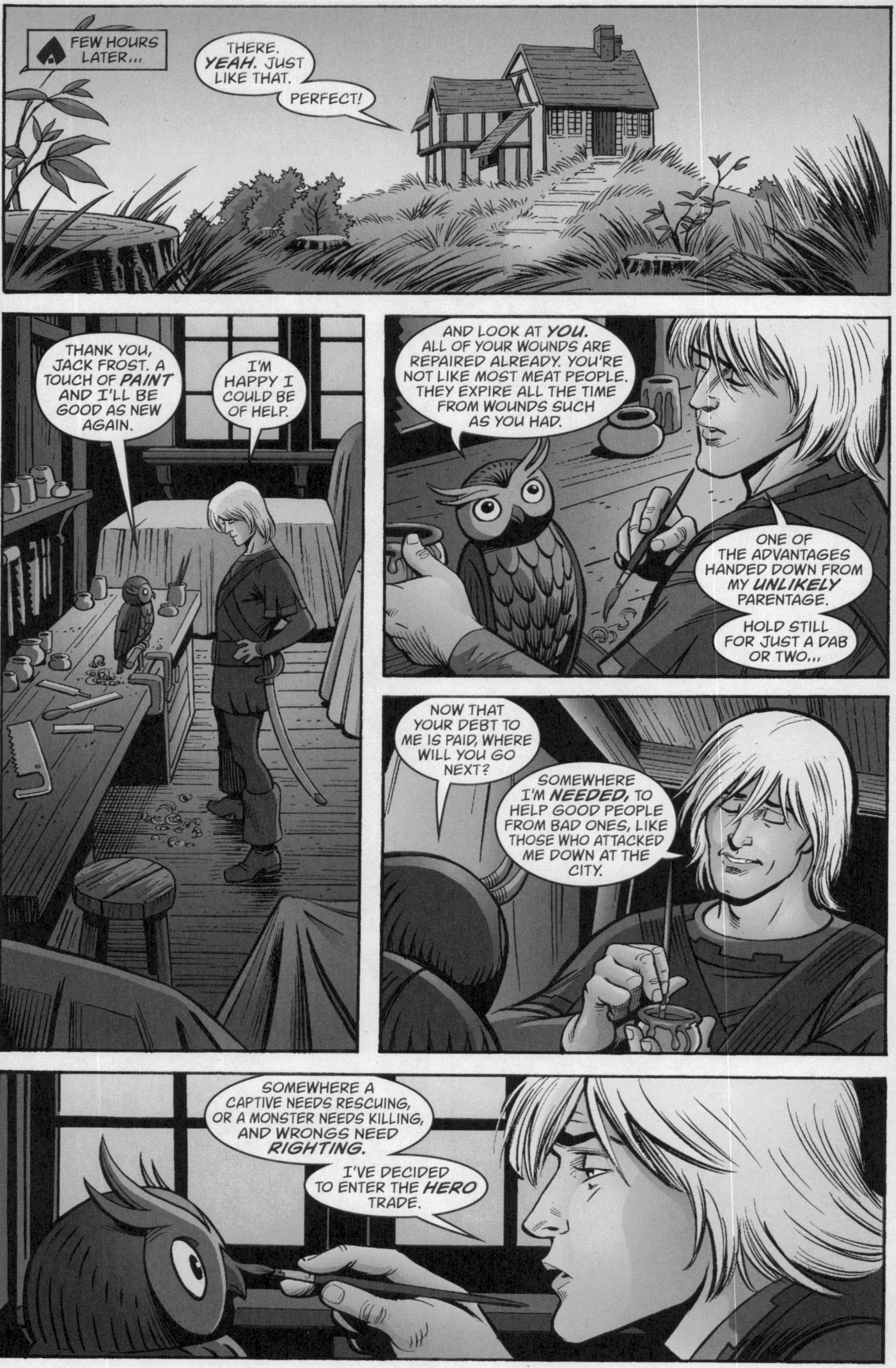
FEW HOURS LATER...
THERE. YEAH. JUST LIKE THAT.
PERFECT!
THANK YOU, JACK FROST. A TOUCH OF PAINT AND I'LL BE GOOD AS NEW AGAIN.
I'M HAPPY I COULD BE OF HELP.
AND LOOK AT YOU. ALL OF YOUR WOUNDS ARE REPAIRED ALREADY. YOU'RE NOT LIKE MOST MEAT PEOPLE. THEY EXPIRE ALL THE TIME FROM WOUNDS SUCH AS YOU HAD.
ONE OF THE ADVANTAGES HANDED DOWN FROM MY UNLIKELY PARENTAGE.
HOLD STILL FOR JUST A DAB OR TWO...
NOW THAT YOUR DEBT TO ME IS PAID, WHERE WILL YOU GO NEXT?
SOMEWHERE I'M NEEDED, TO HELP GOOD PEOPLE FROM BAD ONES, LIKE THOSE WHO ATTACKED ME DOWN AT THE CITY.
SOMEWHERE A CAPTIVE NEEDS RESCUING, OR A MONSTER NEEDS KILLING, AND WRONGS NEED RIGHTING.
I'VE DECIDED TO ENTER THE HERO TRADE.

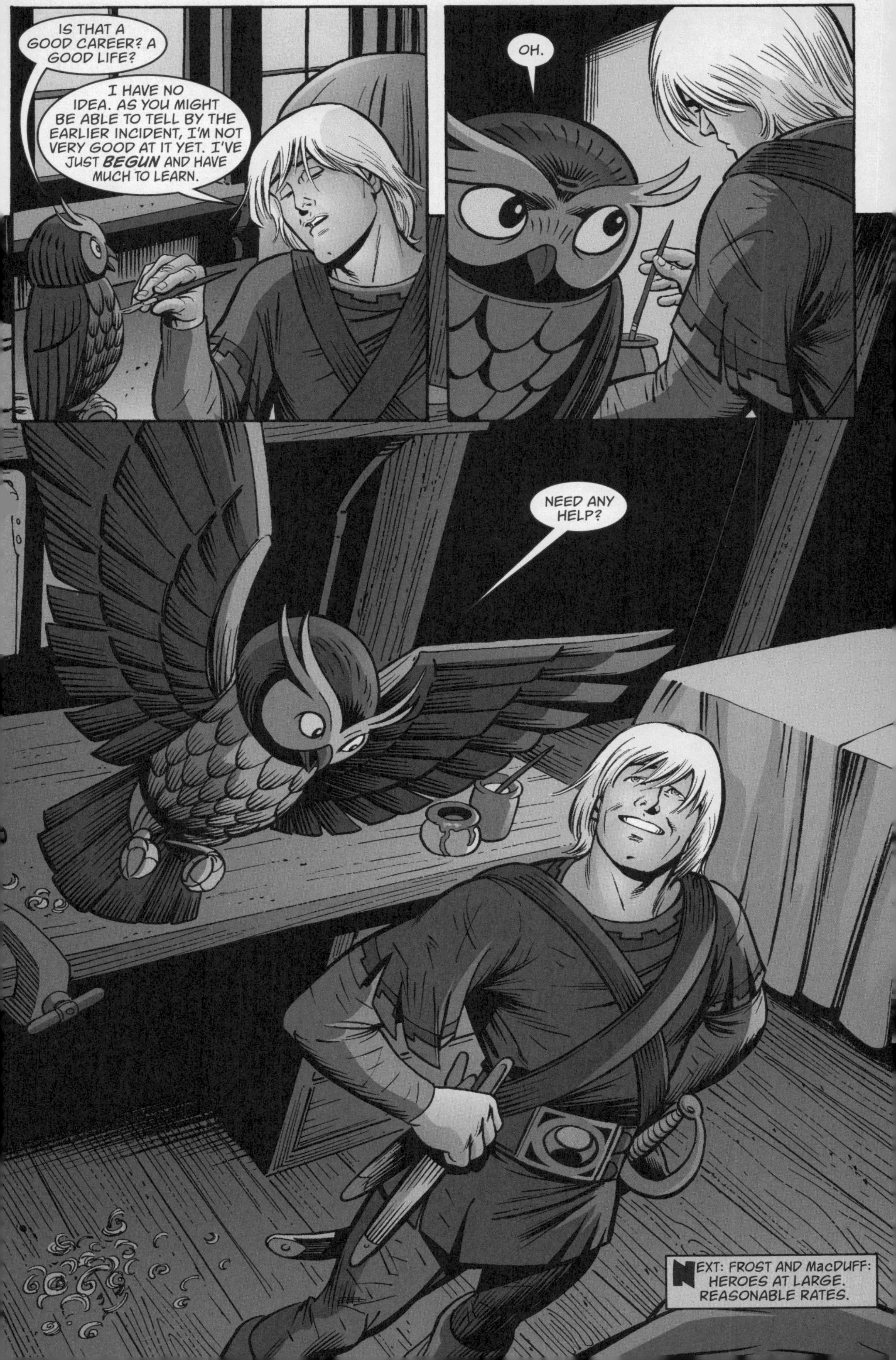
IS THAT A GOOD CAREER? A GOOD LIFE?
I HAVE NO IDEA. AS YOU MIGHT BE ABLE TO TELL BY THE EARLIER INCIDENT, I'M NOT VERY GOOD AT IT YET. I'VE JUST BEGUN AND HAVE MUCH TO LEARN.
OH.
NEED ANY HELP?
NEXT: FROST AND MacDUFF: HEROES AT LARGE. REASONABLE RATES.

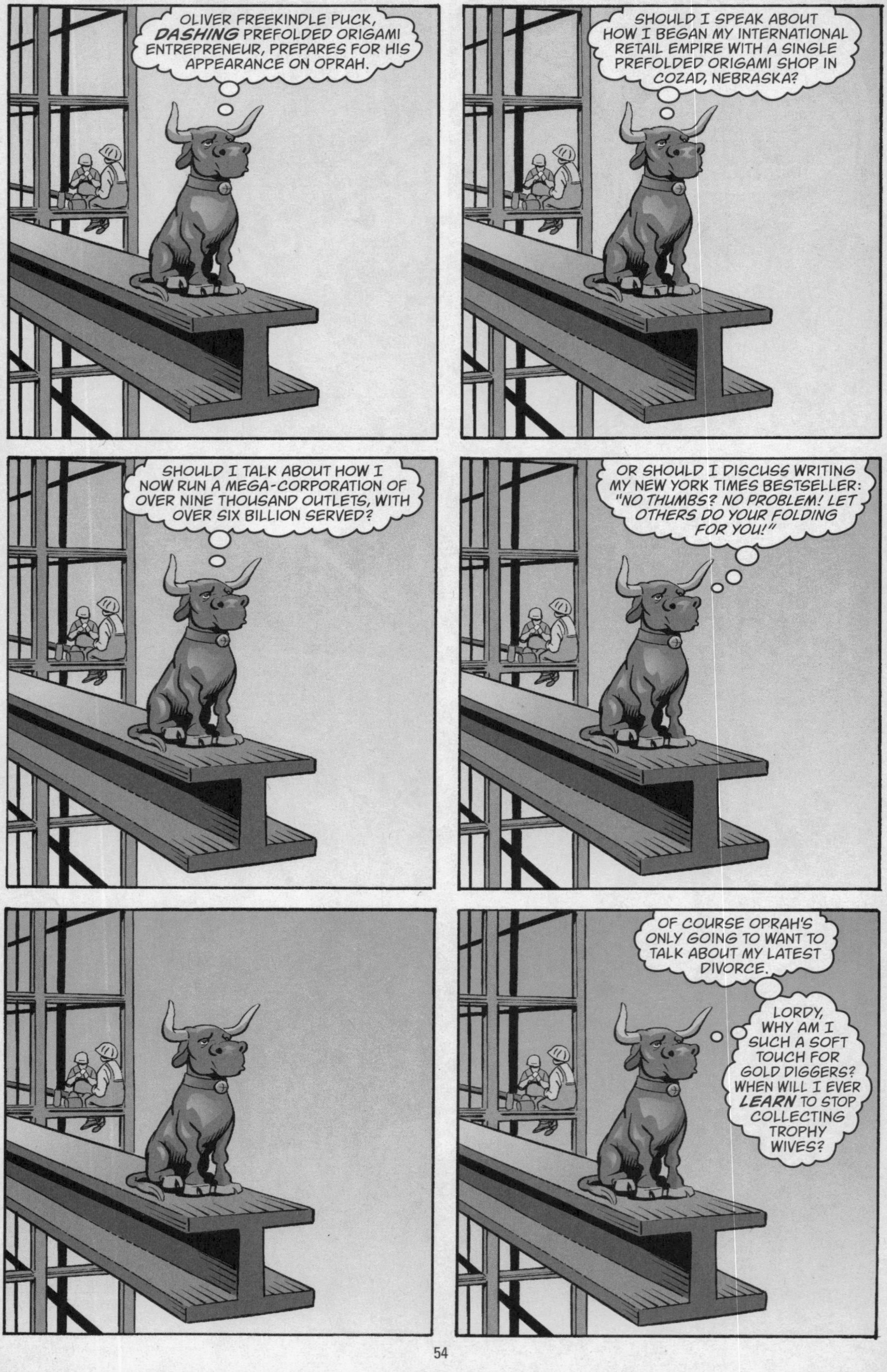
OLIVER FREEKINDLE PUCK, DASHING PREFOLDED ORIGAMI ENTREPRENEUR, PREPARES FOR HIS APPEARANCE ON OPRAH.
SHOULD I SPEAK ABOUT HOW I BEGAN MY INTERNATIONAL RETAIL EMPIRE WITH A SINGLE PREFOLDED ORIGAMI SHOP IN COZAD, NEBRASKA?
SHOULD I TALK ABOUT HOW I NOW RUN A MEGA-CORPORATION OF OVER NINE THOUSAND OUTLETS, WITH OVER SIX BILLION SERVED?
OR SHOULD I DISCUSS WRITING MY NEW YORK TIMES BESTSELLER: "NO THUMBS? NO PROBLEM! LET OTHERS DO YOUR FOLDING FOR YOU!"
OF COURSE OPRAH'S ONLY GOING TO WANT TO TALK ABOUT MY LATEST DIVORCE.
LORDY, WHY AM I SUCH A SOFT TOUCH FOR GOLD DIGGERS? WHEN WILL I EVER LEARN TO STOP COLLECTING TROPHY WIVES?

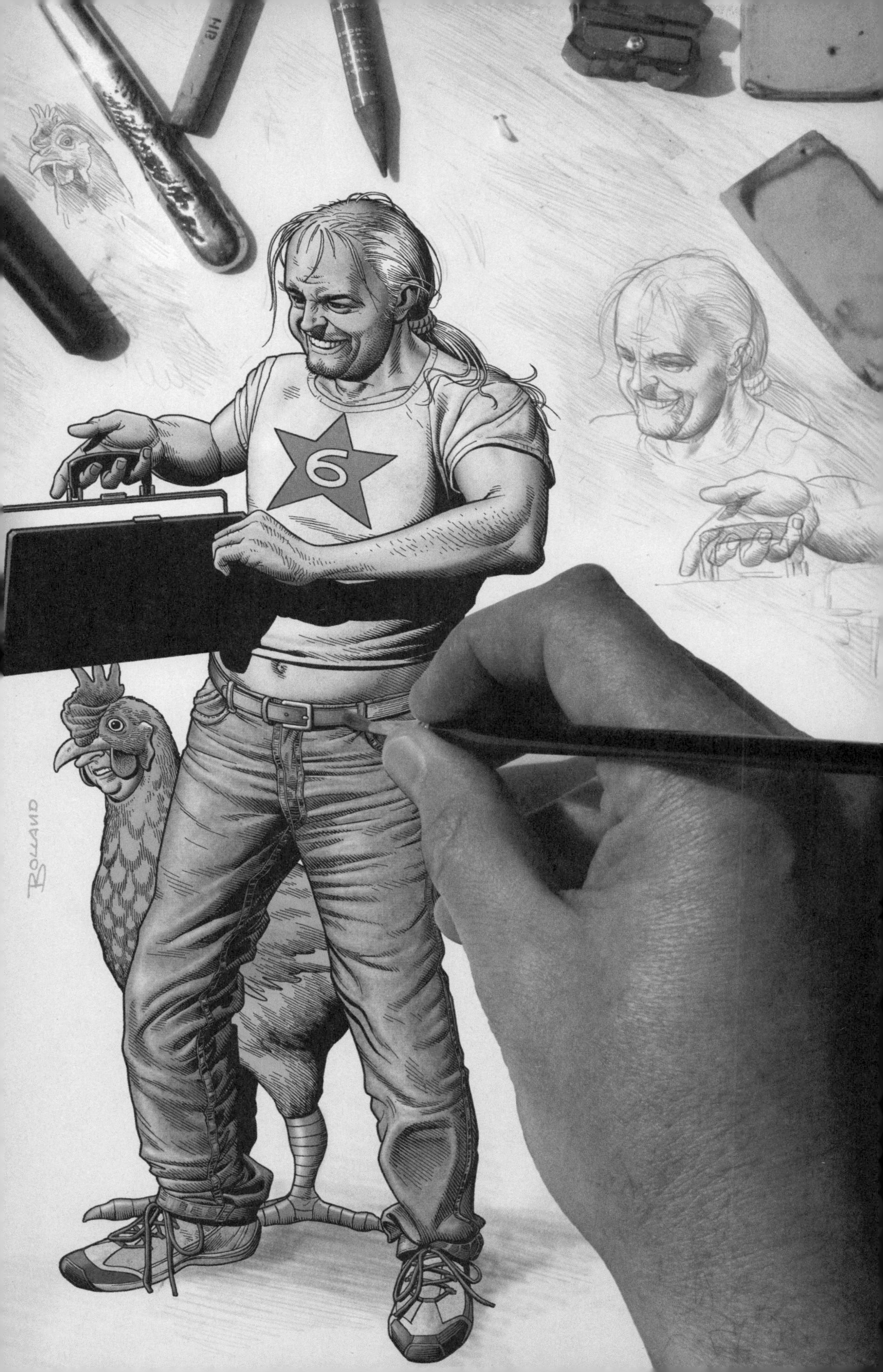
BOLLAND

"MY PARTNER AND I ARE **VERY** SERIOUS
ABOUT THE HERO PROFESSION."

Following the incident at the great city of thorns, Jack and his new companion set off on foot for the rural districts northeast of the imperial capital. Most Jack scholars set this period as the beginning of his career, universally discounting his occasional mentions of an incident in the American Adirondacks as a fabrication.

– From: "A Probable Outline of Jack Frost's Life and Adventures" by Wulf Alondair Lathe

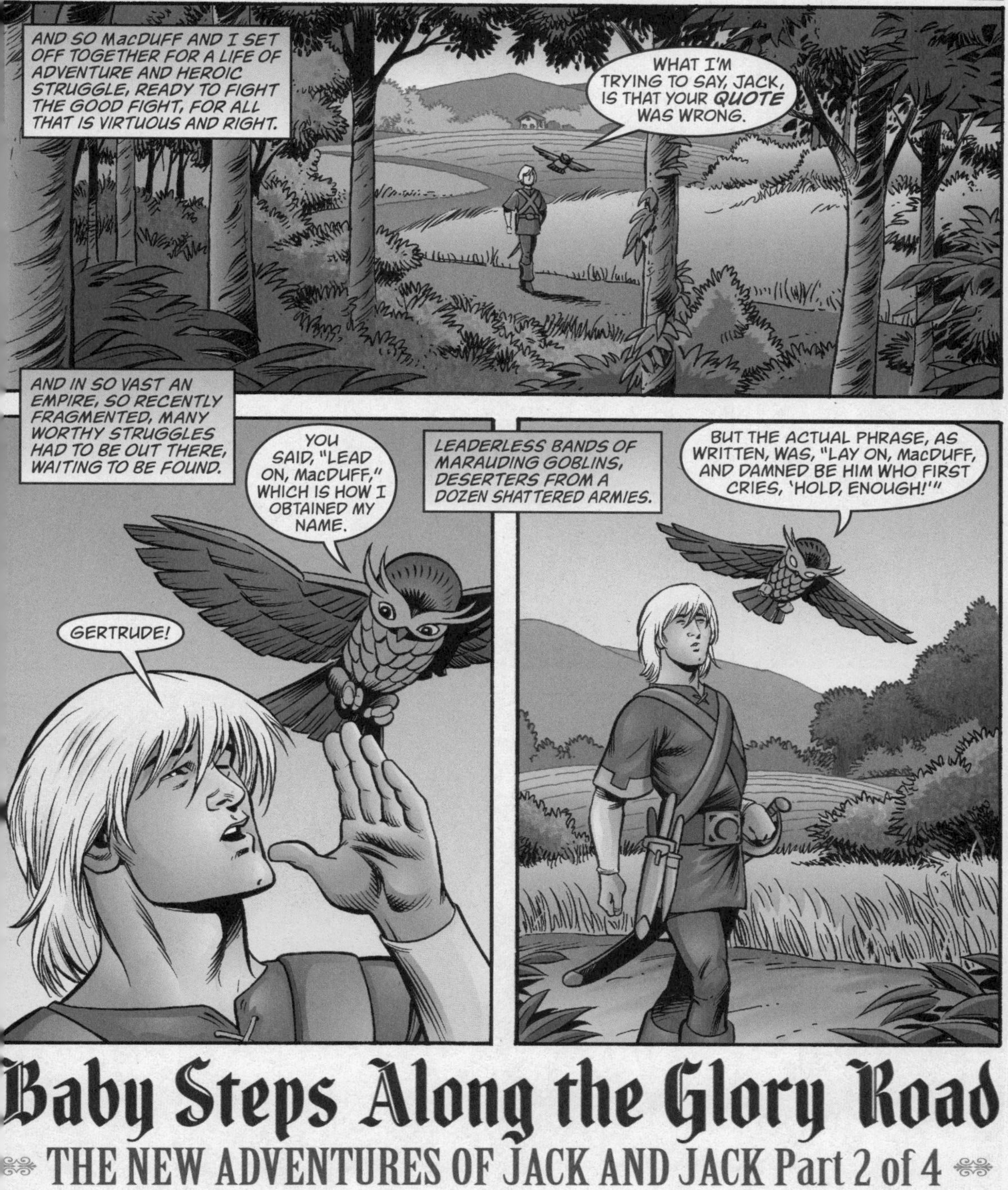

AND SO MacDUFF AND I SET OFF TOGETHER FOR A LIFE OF ADVENTURE AND HEROIC STRUGGLE, READY TO FIGHT THE GOOD FIGHT, FOR ALL THAT IS VIRTUOUS AND RIGHT.
WHAT I'M TRYING TO SAY, JACK, IS THAT YOUR QUOTE WAS WRONG.
AND IN SO VAST AN EMPIRE, SO RECENTLY FRAGMENTED, MANY WORTHY STRUGGLES HAD TO BE OUT THERE, WAITING TO BE FOUND.
YOU SAID, "LEAD ON, MacDUFF," WHICH IS HOW I OBTAINED MY NAME.
GERTRUDE!
LEADERLESS BANDS OF MARAUDING GOBLINS, DESERTERS FROM A DOZEN SHATTERED ARMIES.
BUT THE ACTUAL PHRASE, AS WRITTEN, WAS, "LAY ON, MacDUFF, AND DAMNED BE HIM WHO FIRST CRIES, 'HOLD, ENOUGH!'"

Baby Steps Along the Glory Road

THE NEW ADVENTURES OF JACK AND JACK Part 2 of 4

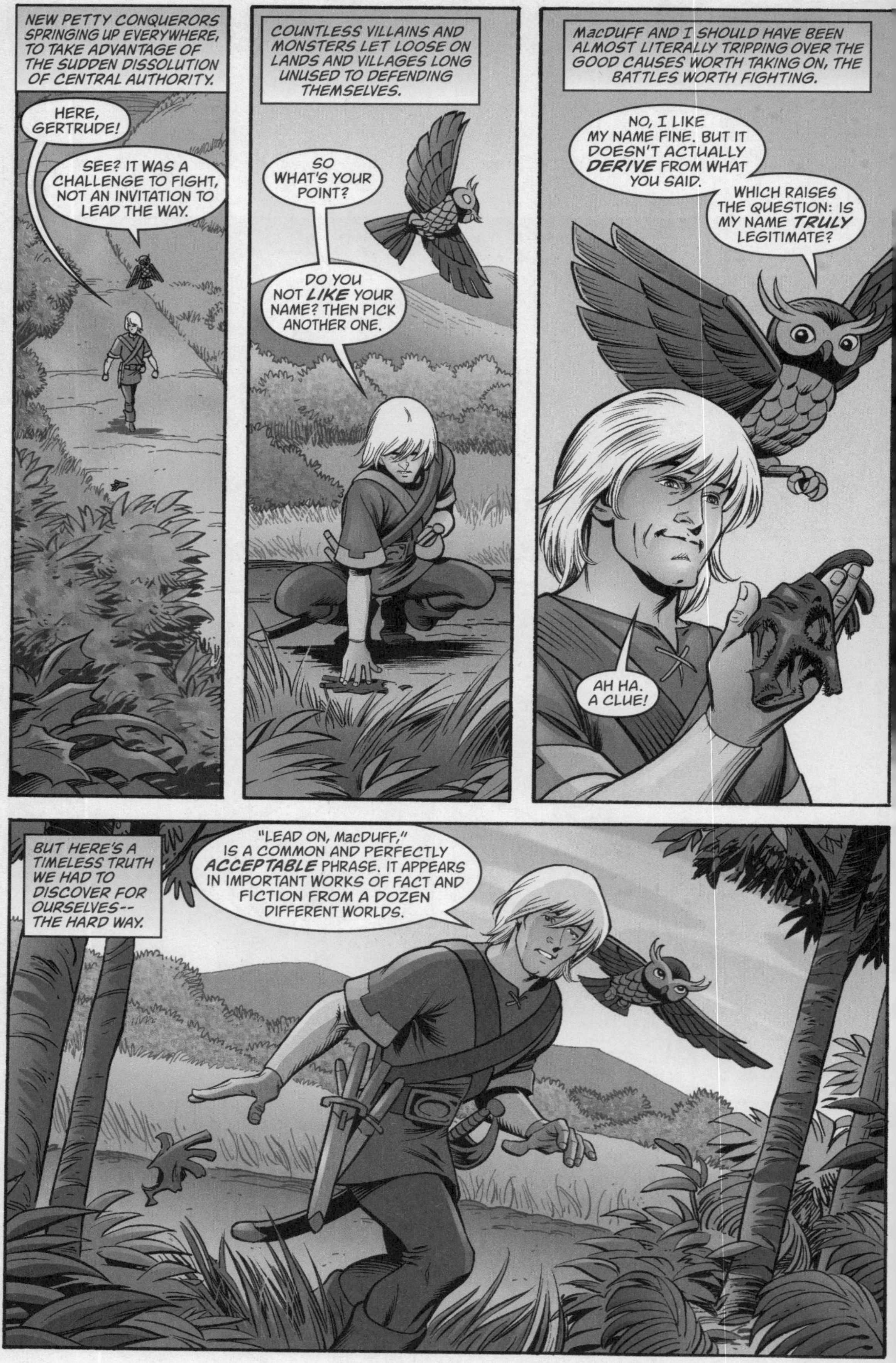
NEW PETTY CONQUERORS SPRINGING UP EVERYWHERE, TO TAKE ADVANTAGE OF THE SUDDEN DISSOLUTION OF CENTRAL AUTHORITY.
HERE, GERTRUDE!
SEE? IT WAS A CHALLENGE TO FIGHT, NOT AN INVITATION TO LEAD THE WAY.
COUNTLESS VILLAINS AND MONSTERS LET LOOSE ON LANDS AND VILLAGES LONG UNUSED TO DEFENDING THEMSELVES.
SO WHAT'S YOUR POINT?
DO YOU NOT LIKE YOUR NAME? THEN PICK ANOTHER ONE.
MacDUFF AND I SHOULD HAVE BEEN ALMOST LITERALLY TRIPPING OVER THE GOOD CAUSES WORTH TAKING ON, THE BATTLES WORTH FIGHTING.
NO, I LIKE MY NAME FINE. BUT IT DOESN'T ACTUALLY DERIVE FROM WHAT YOU SAID.
WHICH RAISES THE QUESTION: IS MY NAME TRULY LEGITIMATE?
AH HA. A CLUE!
BUT HERE'S A TIMELESS TRUTH WE HAD TO DISCOVER FOR OURSELVES-- THE HARD WAY.
"LEAD ON, MacDUFF," IS A COMMON AND PERFECTLY ACCEPTABLE PHRASE. IT APPEARS IN IMPORTANT WORKS OF FACT AND FICTION FROM A DOZEN DIFFERENT WORLDS.

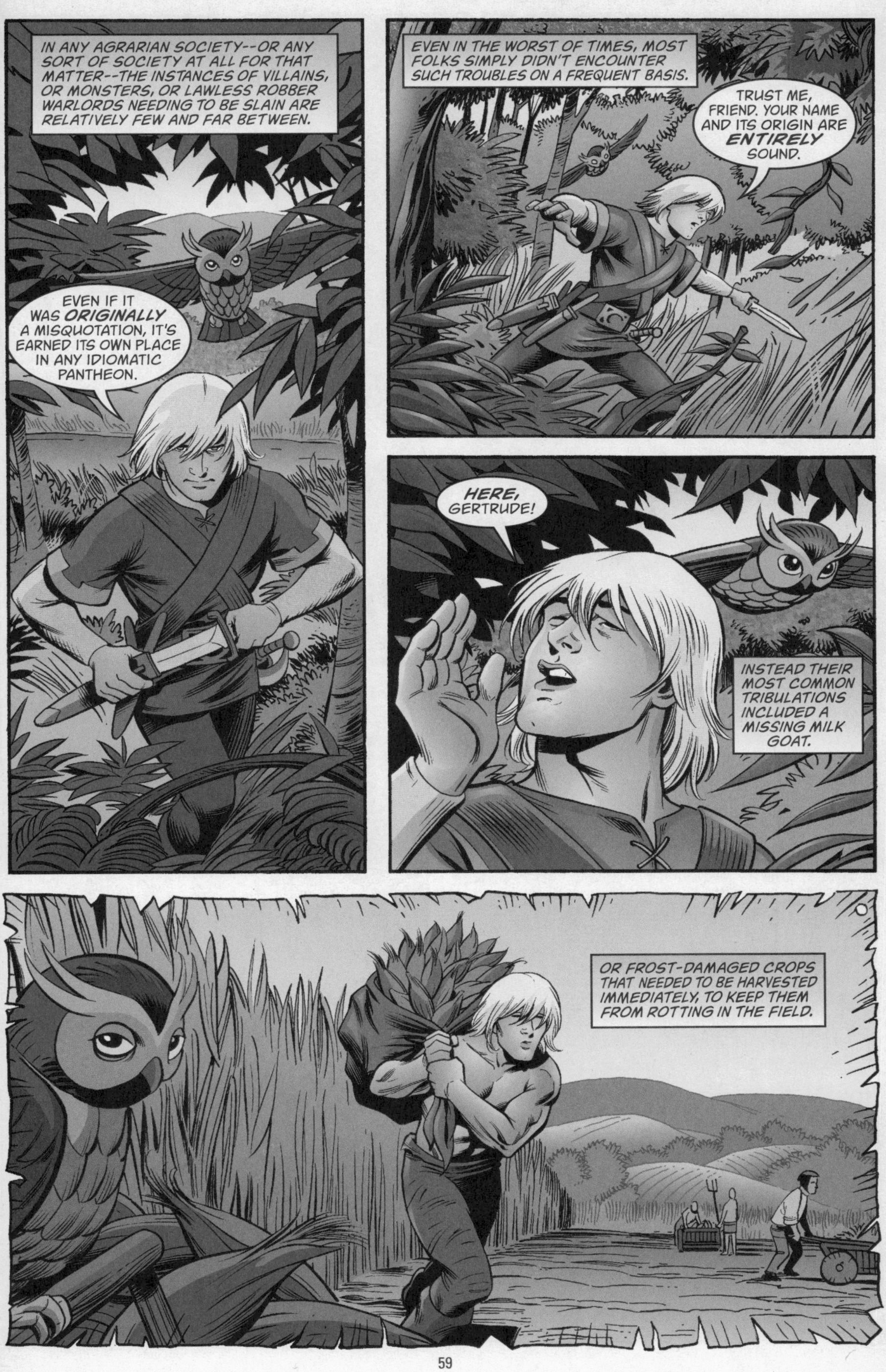
IN ANY AGRARIAN SOCIETY--OR ANY SORT OF SOCIETY AT ALL FOR THAT MATTER--THE INSTANCES OF VILLAINS, OR MONSTERS, OR LAWLESS ROBBER WARLORDS NEEDING TO BE SLAIN ARE RELATIVELY FEW AND FAR BETWEEN.
EVEN IF IT WAS ORIGINALLY A MISQUOTATION, IT'S EARNED ITS OWN PLACE IN ANY IDIOMATIC PANTHEON.
EVEN IN THE WORST OF TIMES, MOST FOLKS SIMPLY DIDN'T ENCOUNTER SUCH TROUBLES ON A FREQUENT BASIS.
TRUST ME, FRIEND. YOUR NAME AND ITS ORIGIN ARE ENTIRELY SOUND.
HERE, GERTRUDE!
INSTEAD THEIR MOST COMMON TRIBULATIONS INCLUDED A MISSING MILK GOAT.
OR FROST-DAMAGED CROPS THAT NEEDED TO BE HARVESTED IMMEDIATELY, TO KEEP THEM FROM ROTTING IN THE FIELD.

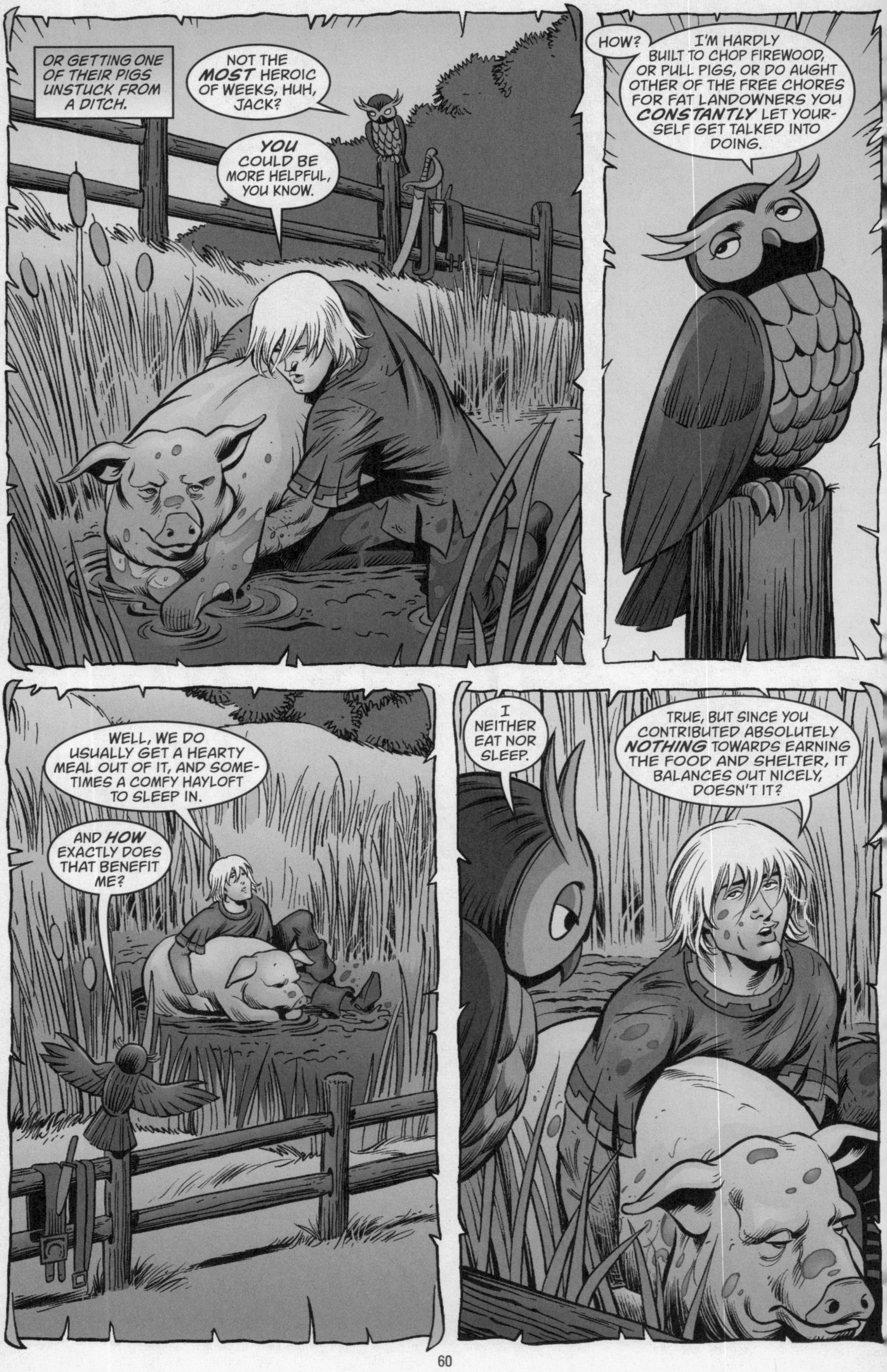
OR GETTING ONE OF THEIR PIGS UNSTUCK FROM A DITCH.
NOT THE **MOST** HEROIC OF WEEKS, HUH, JACK?
YOU COULD BE MORE HELPFUL, YOU KNOW.
HOW?
I'M HARDLY BUILT TO CHOP FIREWOOD, OR PULL PIGS, OR DO AUGHT OTHER OF THE FREE CHORES FOR FAT LANDOWNERS YOU **CONSTANTLY** LET YOURSELF GET TALKED INTO DOING.
WELL, WE DO USUALLY GET A HEARTY MEAL OUT OF IT, AND SOMETIMES A COMFY HAYLOFT TO SLEEP IN.
AND **HOW** EXACTLY DOES THAT BENEFIT ME?
I NEITHER EAT NOR SLEEP.
TRUE, BUT SINCE YOU CONTRIBUTED ABSOLUTELY **NOTHING** TOWARDS EARNING THE FOOD AND SHELTER, IT BALANCES OUT NICELY, DOESN'T IT?

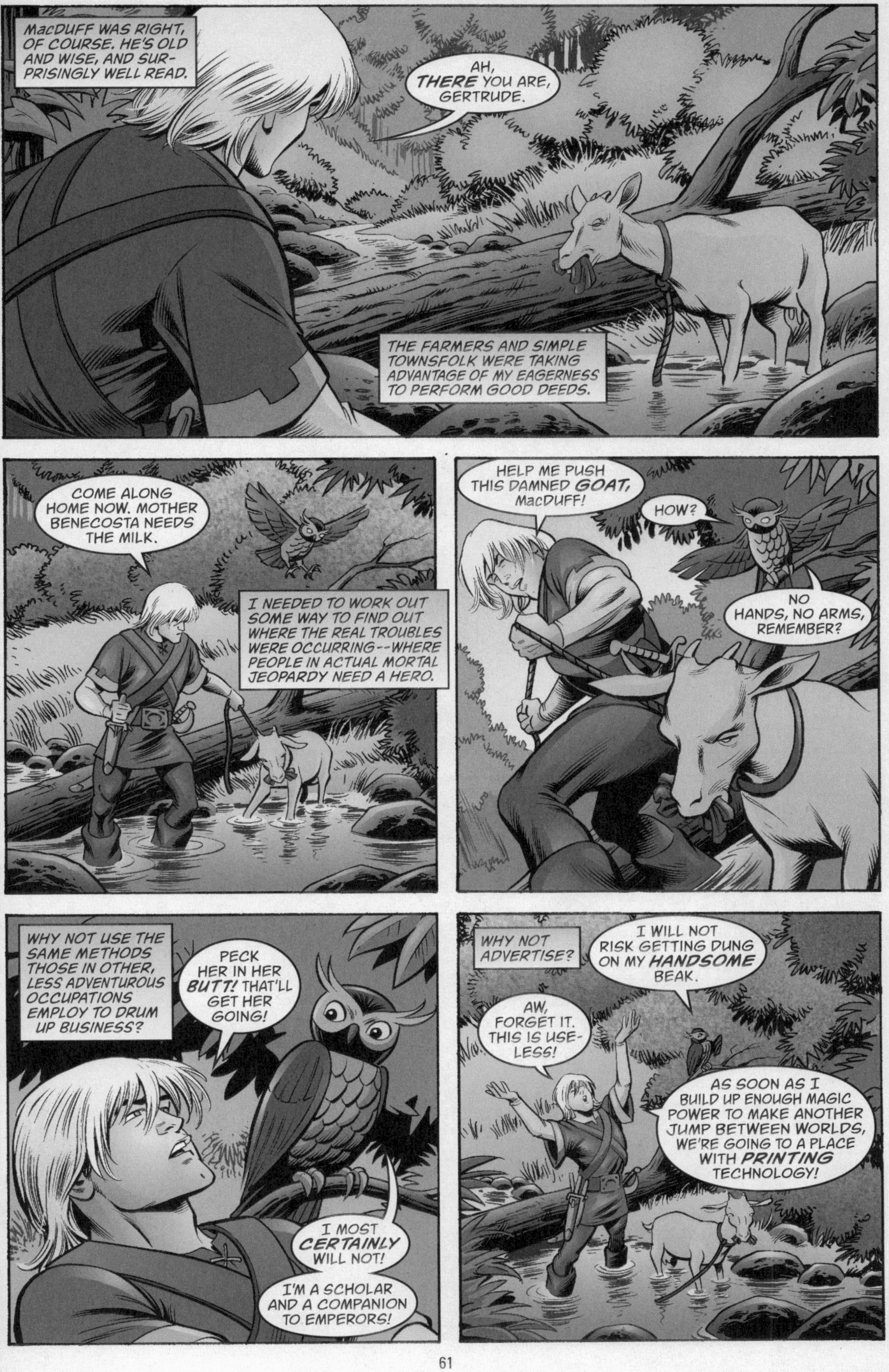
MacDUFF WAS RIGHT, OF COURSE. HE'S OLD AND WISE, AND SURPRISINGLY WELL READ.
AH, THERE YOU ARE, GERTRUDE.
THE FARMERS AND SIMPLE TOWNSFOLK WERE TAKING ADVANTAGE OF MY EAGERNESS TO PERFORM GOOD DEEDS.
COME ALONG HOME NOW. MOTHER BENECOSTA NEEDS THE MILK.
I NEEDED TO WORK OUT SOME WAY TO FIND OUT WHERE THE REAL TROUBLES WERE OCCURRING--WHERE PEOPLE IN ACTUAL MORTAL JEOPARDY NEED A HERO.
HELP ME PUSH THIS DAMNED GOAT, MacDUFF!
HOW?
NO HANDS, NO ARMS, REMEMBER?
WHY NOT USE THE SAME METHODS THOSE IN OTHER, LESS ADVENTUROUS OCCUPATIONS EMPLOY TO DRUM UP BUSINESS?
PECK HER IN HER BUTT! THAT'LL GET HER GOING!
I MOST CERTAINLY WILL NOT!
I'M A SCHOLAR AND A COMPANION TO EMPERORS!
WHY NOT ADVERTISE?
I WILL NOT RISK GETTING DUNG ON MY HANDSOME BEAK.
AW, FORGET IT. THIS IS USELESS!
AS SOON AS I BUILD UP ENOUGH MAGIC POWER TO MAKE ANOTHER JUMP BETWEEN WORLDS, WE'RE GOING TO A PLACE WITH PRINTING TECHNOLOGY!

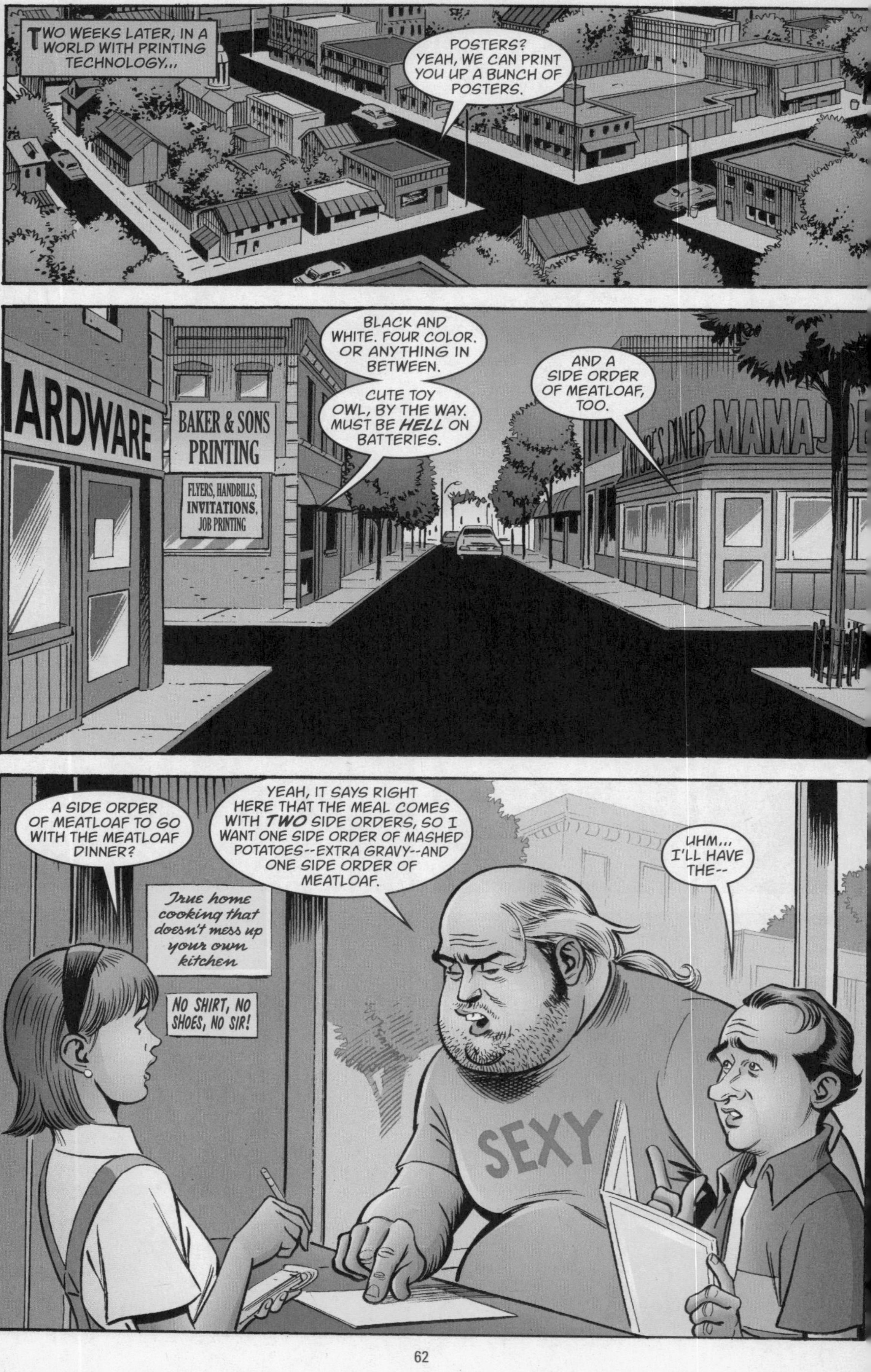
TWO WEEKS LATER, IN A WORLD WITH PRINTING TECHNOLOGY...
POSTERS? YEAH, WE CAN PRINT YOU UP A BUNCH OF POSTERS.
BAKER & SONS PRINTING
FLYERS, HANDBILLS, INVITATIONS, JOB PRINTING
BLACK AND WHITE. FOUR COLOR. OR ANYTHING IN BETWEEN.
CUTE TOY OWL, BY THE WAY. MUST BE HELL ON BATTERIES.
AND A SIDE ORDER OF MEATLOAF, TOO.
A SIDE ORDER OF MEATLOAF TO GO WITH THE MEATLOAF DINNER?
YEAH, IT SAYS RIGHT HERE THAT THE MEAL COMES WITH TWO SIDE ORDERS, SO I WANT ONE SIDE ORDER OF MASHED POTATOES--EXTRA GRAVY--AND ONE SIDE ORDER OF MEATLOAF.
UHM... I'LL HAVE THE--
True home cooking that doesn't mess up your own kitchen
NO SHIRT, NO SHOES, NO SIR!
SEXY

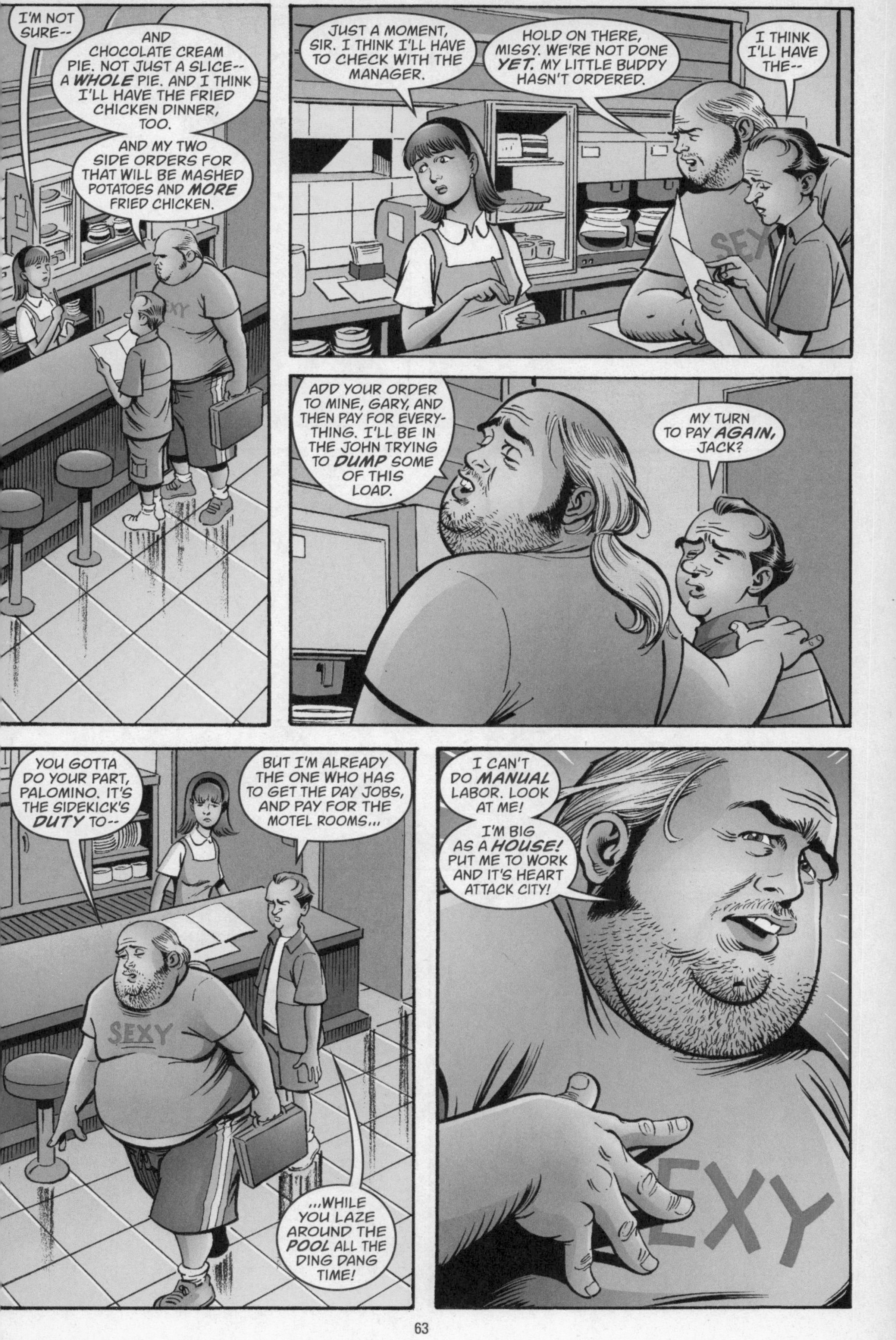
I'M NOT SURE--
AND CHOCOLATE CREAM PIE. NOT JUST A SLICE-- A WHOLE PIE. AND I THINK I'LL HAVE THE FRIED CHICKEN DINNER, TOO.
AND MY TWO SIDE ORDERS FOR THAT WILL BE MASHED POTATOES AND MORE FRIED CHICKEN.
SEXY
JUST A MOMENT, SIR. I THINK I'LL HAVE TO CHECK WITH THE MANAGER.
HOLD ON THERE, MISSY. WE'RE NOT DONE YET. MY LITTLE BUDDY HASN'T ORDERED.
I THINK I'LL HAVE THE--
SEX
ADD YOUR ORDER TO MINE, GARY, AND THEN PAY FOR EVERY-THING. I'LL BE IN THE JOHN TRYING TO DUMP SOME OF THIS LOAD.
MY TURN TO PAY AGAIN, JACK?
YOU GOTTA DO YOUR PART, PALOMINO. IT'S THE SIDEKICK'S DUTY TO--
BUT I'M ALREADY THE ONE WHO HAS TO GET THE DAY JOBS, AND PAY FOR THE MOTEL ROOMS...
SEXY
...WHILE YOU LAZE AROUND THE POOL ALL THE DING DANG TIME!
I CAN'T DO MANUAL LABOR. LOOK AT ME!
I'M BIG AS A HOUSE! PUT ME TO WORK AND IT'S HEART ATTACK CITY!
EXY

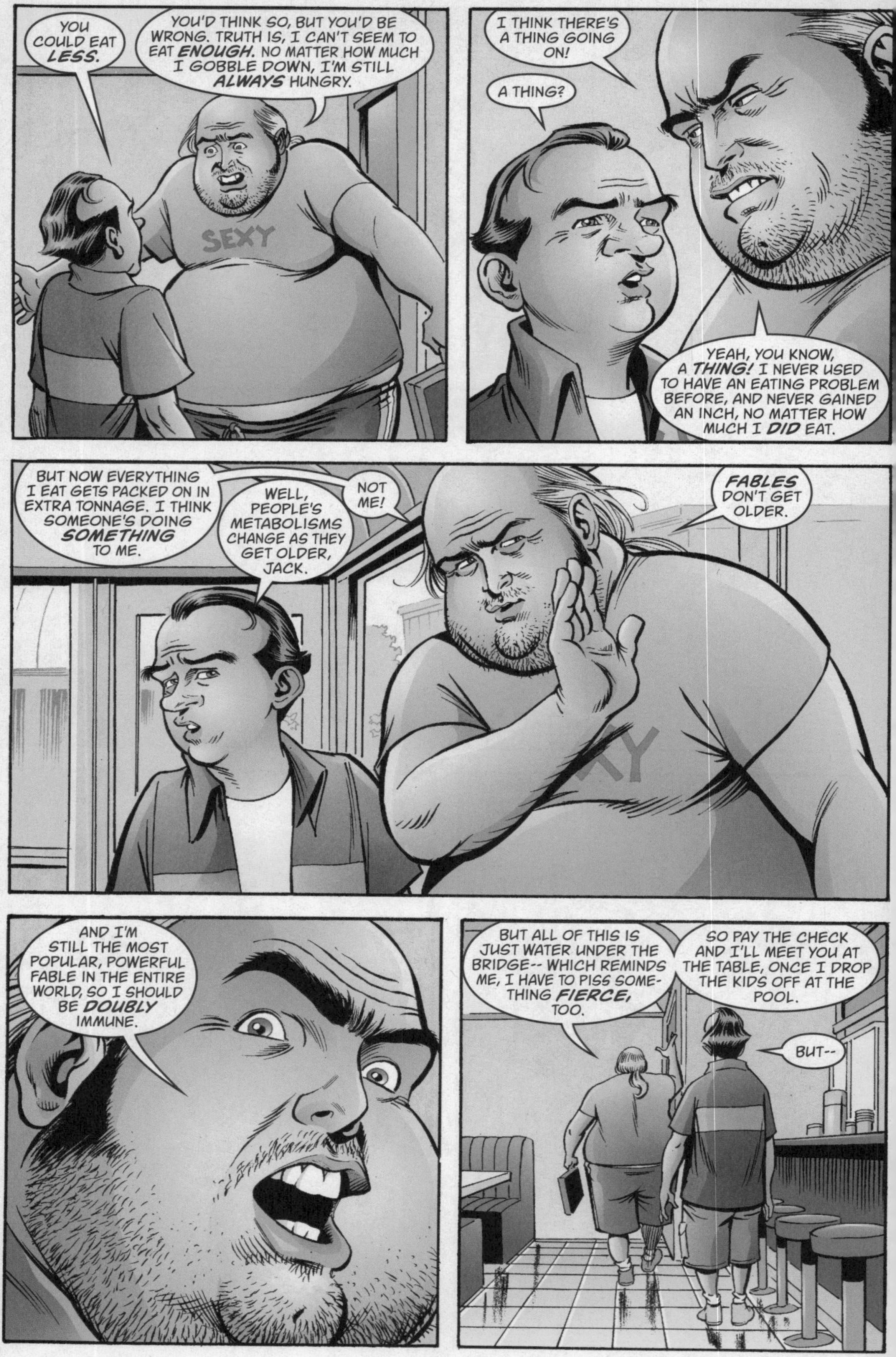
YOU COULD EAT LESS.
YOU'D THINK SO, BUT YOU'D BE WRONG. TRUTH IS, I CAN'T SEEM TO EAT ENOUGH. NO MATTER HOW MUCH I GOBBLE DOWN, I'M STILL ALWAYS HUNGRY.
SEXY
I THINK THERE'S A THING GOING ON!
A THING?
YEAH, YOU KNOW, A THING! I NEVER USED TO HAVE AN EATING PROBLEM BEFORE, AND NEVER GAINED AN INCH, NO MATTER HOW MUCH I DID EAT.
BUT NOW EVERYTHING I EAT GETS PACKED ON IN EXTRA TONNAGE. I THINK SOMEONE'S DOING SOMETHING TO ME.
WELL, PEOPLE'S METABOLISMS CHANGE AS THEY GET OLDER, JACK.
NOT ME!
FABLES DON'T GET OLDER.
AND I'M STILL THE MOST POPULAR, POWERFUL FABLE IN THE ENTIRE WORLD, SO I SHOULD BE DOUBLY IMMUNE.
BUT ALL OF THIS IS JUST WATER UNDER THE BRIDGE-- WHICH REMINDS ME, I HAVE TO PISS SOMETHING FIERCE, TOO.
SO PAY THE CHECK AND I'LL MEET YOU AT THE TABLE, ONCE I DROP THE KIDS OFF AT THE POOL.
BUT--

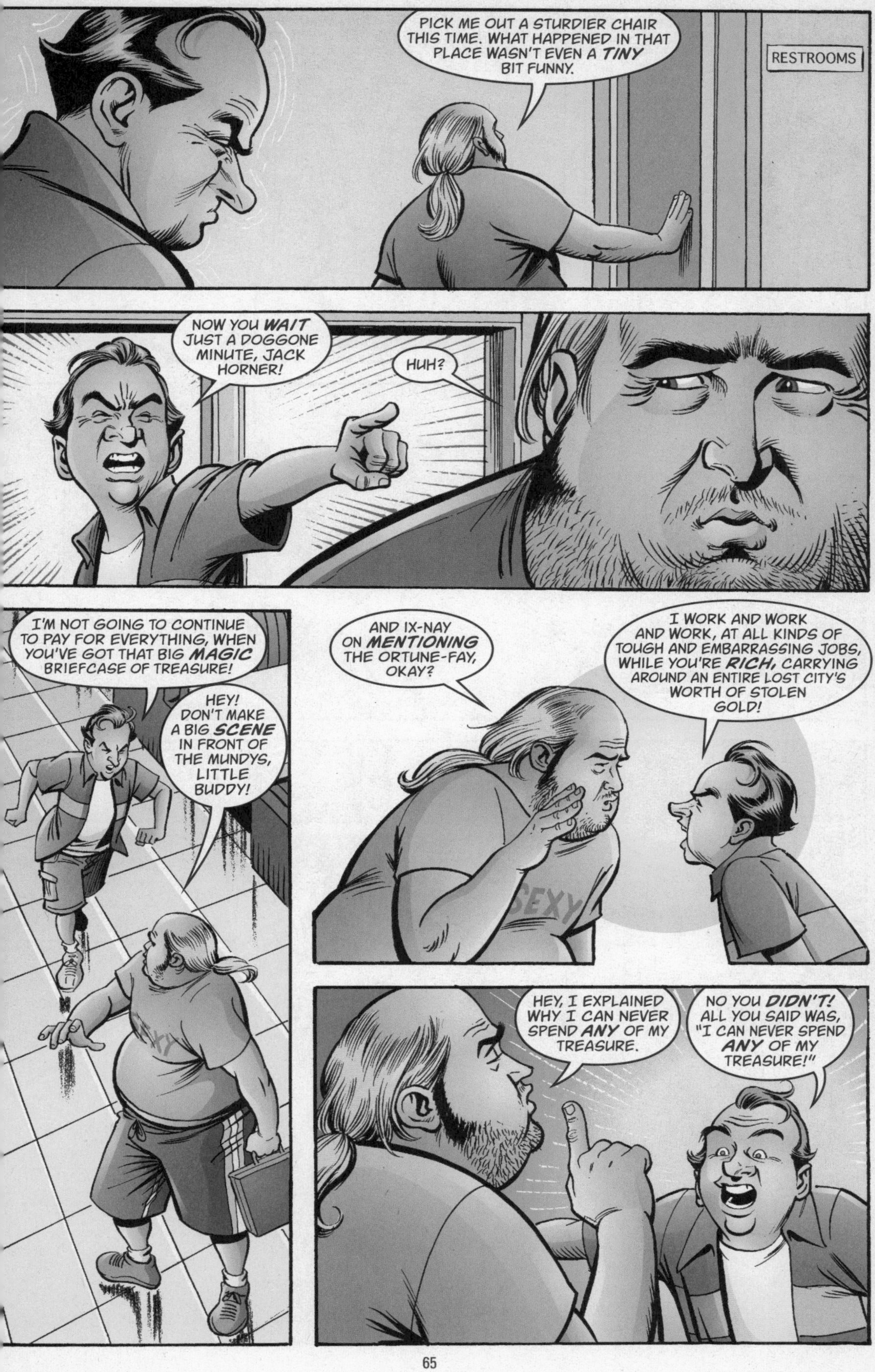
PICK ME OUT A STURDIER CHAIR THIS TIME. WHAT HAPPENED IN THAT PLACE WASN'T EVEN A TINY BIT FUNNY.
RESTROOMS
NOW YOU WAIT JUST A DOGGONE MINUTE, JACK HORNER!
HUH?
I'M NOT GOING TO CONTINUE TO PAY FOR EVERYTHING, WHEN YOU'VE GOT THAT BIG MAGIC BRIEFCASE OF TREASURE!
HEY! DON'T MAKE A BIG SCENE IN FRONT OF THE MUNDYS, LITTLE BUDDY!
AND IX-NAY ON MENTIONING THE ORTUNE-FAY, OKAY?
I WORK AND WORK AND WORK, AT ALL KINDS OF TOUGH AND EMBARRASSING JOBS, WHILE YOU'RE RICH, CARRYING AROUND AN ENTIRE LOST CITY'S WORTH OF STOLEN GOLD!
SEXY
HEY, I EXPLAINED WHY I CAN NEVER SPEND ANY OF MY TREASURE.
NO YOU DIDN'T! ALL YOU SAID WAS, "I CAN NEVER SPEND ANY OF MY TREASURE!"

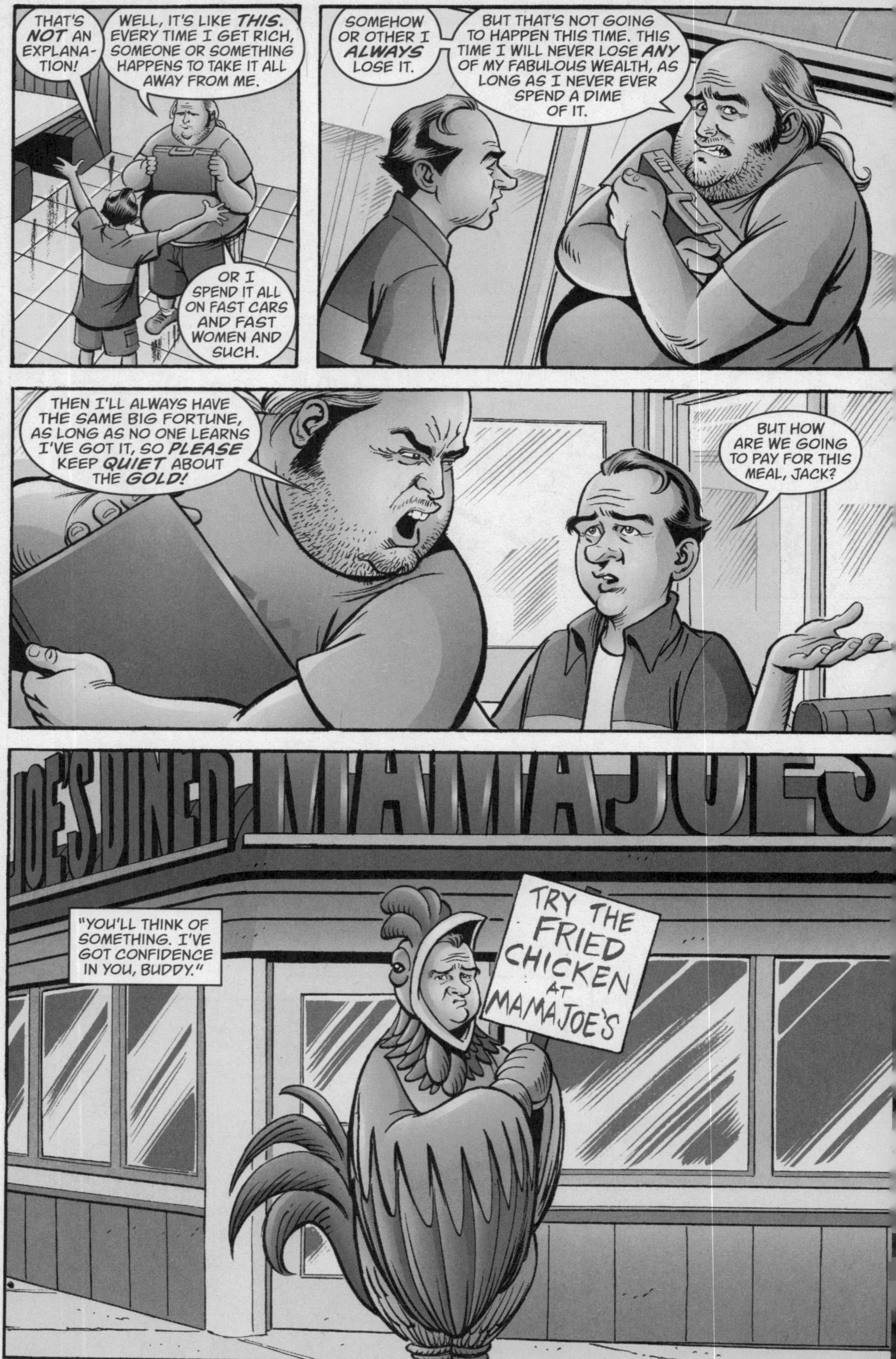
THAT'S NOT AN EXPLANATION!
WELL, IT'S LIKE THIS. EVERY TIME I GET RICH, SOMEONE OR SOMETHING HAPPENS TO TAKE IT ALL AWAY FROM ME.
OR I SPEND IT ALL ON FAST CARS AND FAST WOMEN AND SUCH.
SOMEHOW OR OTHER I ALWAYS LOSE IT.
BUT THAT'S NOT GOING TO HAPPEN THIS TIME. THIS TIME I WILL NEVER LOSE ANY OF MY FABULOUS WEALTH, AS LONG AS I NEVER EVER SPEND A DIME OF IT.
THEN I'LL ALWAYS HAVE THE SAME BIG FORTUNE, AS LONG AS NO ONE LEARNS I'VE GOT IT, SO PLEASE KEEP QUIET ABOUT THE GOLD!
BUT HOW ARE WE GOING TO PAY FOR THIS MEAL, JACK?
JOE'S DINER
MAMAJOE'S
"YOU'LL THINK OF SOMETHING. I'VE GOT CONFIDENCE IN YOU, BUDDY."
TRY THE FRIED CHICKEN AT MAMAJOE'S

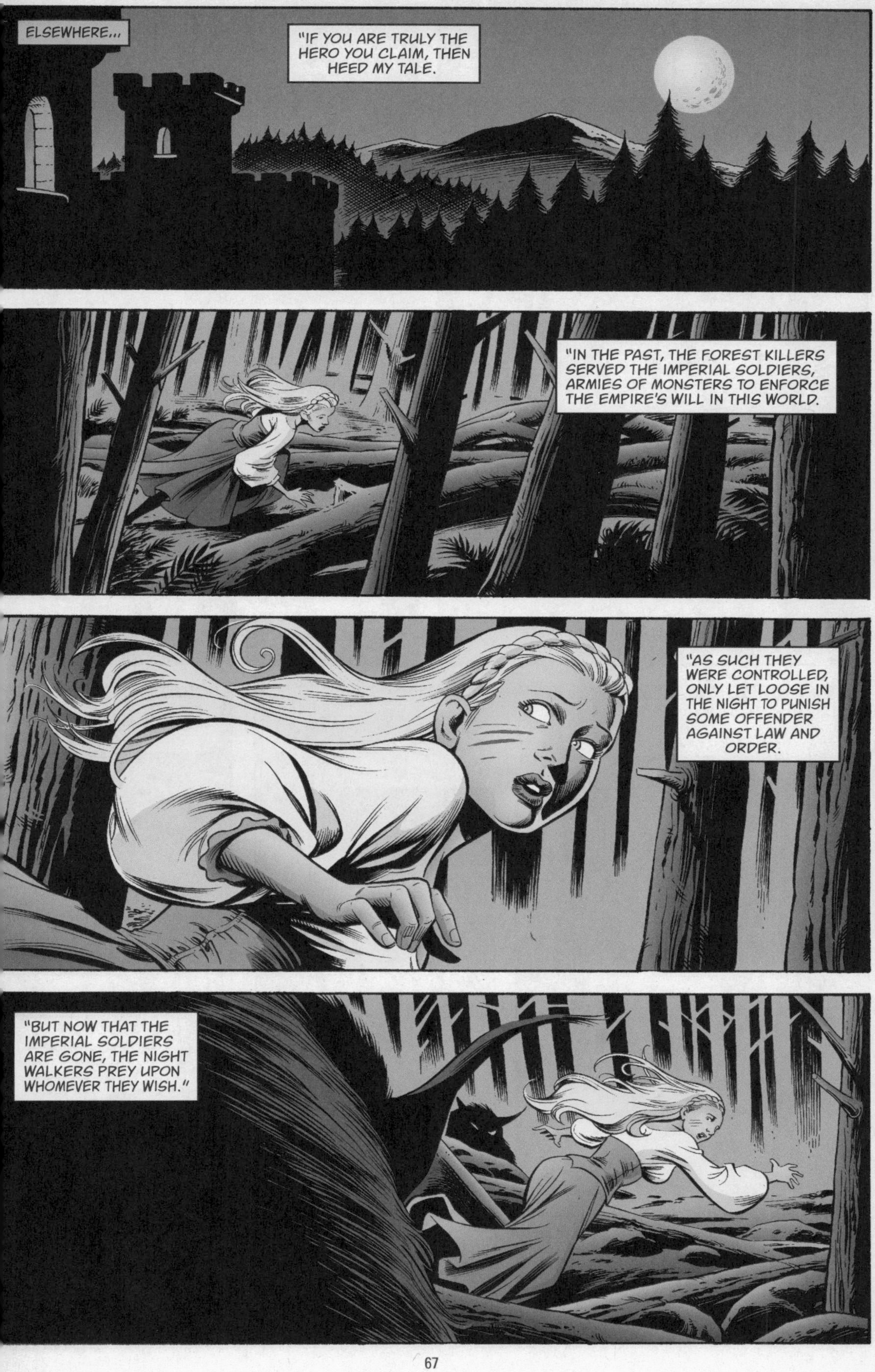
ELSEWHERE...
"IF YOU ARE TRULY THE HERO YOU CLAIM, THEN HEED MY TALE.
"IN THE PAST, THE FOREST KILLERS SERVED THE IMPERIAL SOLDIERS, ARMIES OF MONSTERS TO ENFORCE THE EMPIRE'S WILL IN THIS WORLD.
"AS SUCH THEY WERE CONTROLLED, ONLY LET LOOSE IN THE NIGHT TO PUNISH SOME OFFENDER AGAINST LAW AND ORDER.
"BUT NOW THAT THE IMPERIAL SOLDIERS ARE GONE, THE NIGHT WALKERS PREY UPON WHOMEVER THEY WISH."

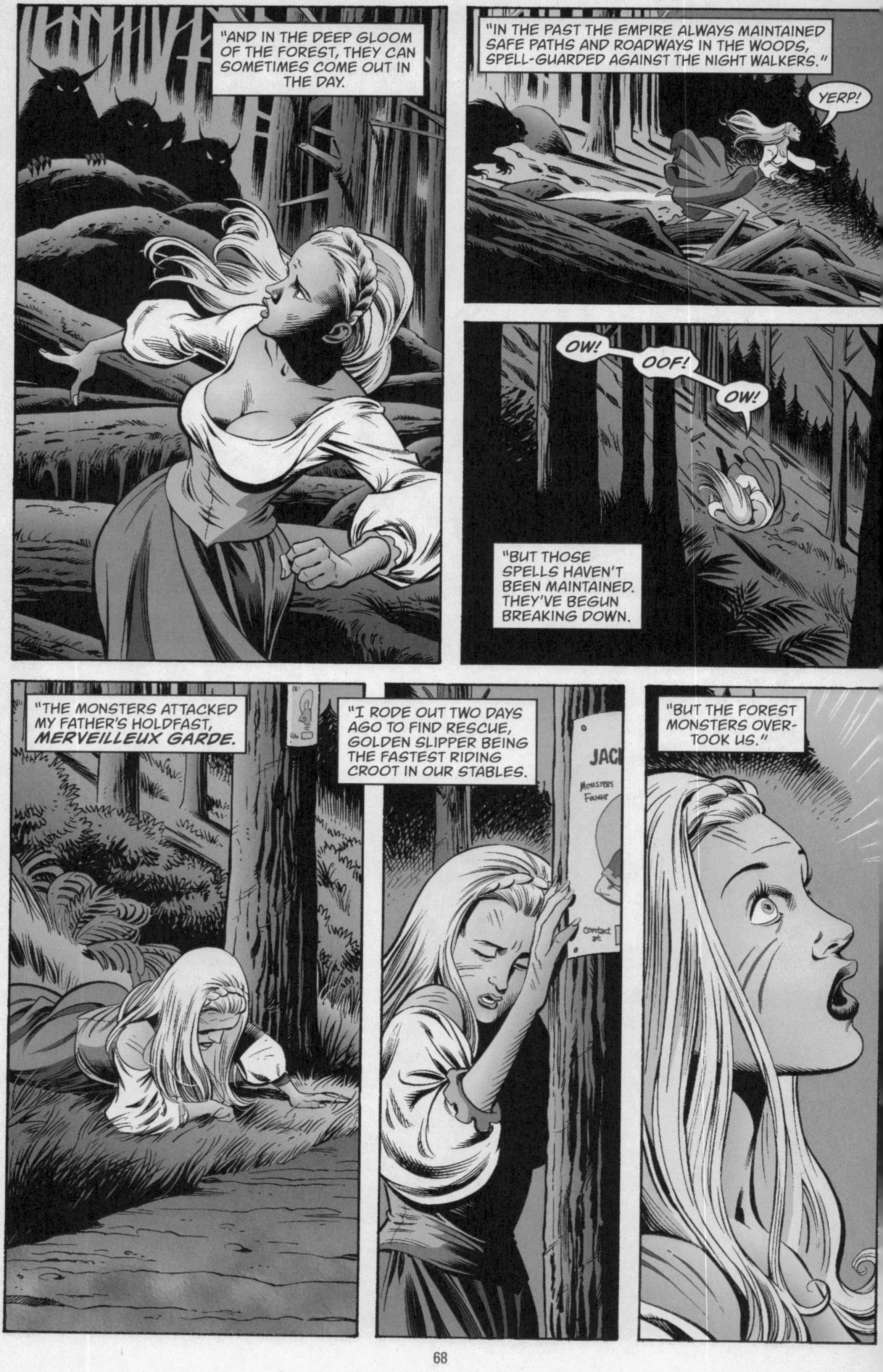
"AND IN THE DEEP GLOOM OF THE FOREST, THEY CAN SOMETIMES COME OUT IN THE DAY.
"IN THE PAST THE EMPIRE ALWAYS MAINTAINED SAFE PATHS AND ROADWAYS IN THE WOODS, SPELL-GUARDED AGAINST THE NIGHT WALKERS."
YERP!
OW!
OOF!
OW!
"BUT THOSE SPELLS HAVEN'T BEEN MAINTAINED. THEY'VE BEGUN BREAKING DOWN.
"THE MONSTERS ATTACKED MY FATHER'S HOLDFAST, MERVEILLEUX GARDE.
"I RODE OUT TWO DAYS AGO TO FIND RESCUE, GOLDEN SLIPPER BEING THE FASTEST RIDING CROOT IN OUR STABLES.
"BUT THE FOREST MONSTERS OVER-TOOK US."

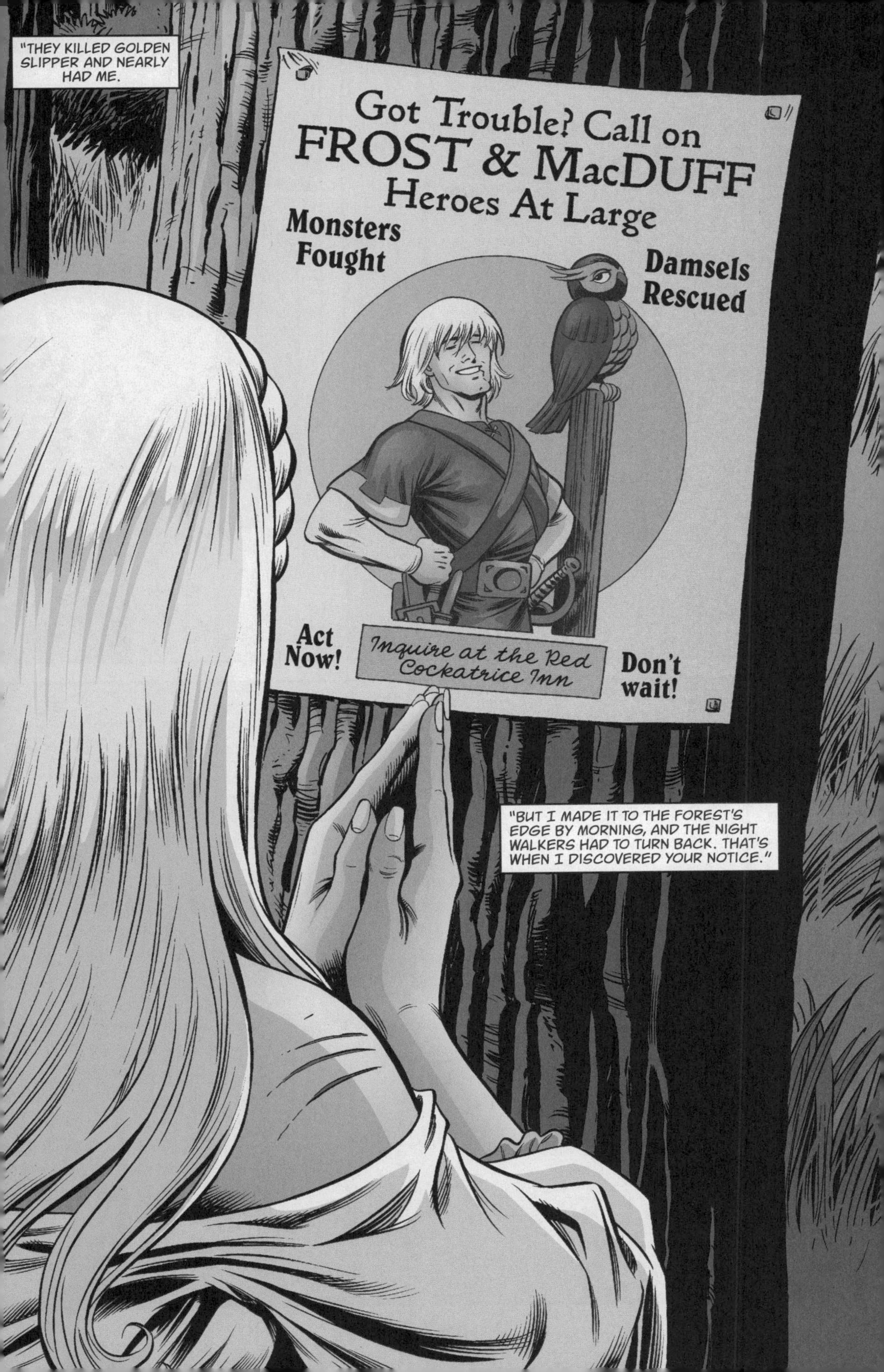
"THEY KILLED GOLDEN SLIPPER AND NEARLY HAD ME.
Got Trouble? Call on
FROST & MacDUFF
Heroes At Large
Monsters Fought
Damsels Rescued
Act Now!
Inquire at the Red Cockatrice Inn
Don't wait!
"BUT I MADE IT TO THE FOREST'S EDGE BY MORNING, AND THE NIGHT WALKERS HAD TO TURN BACK. THAT'S WHEN I DISCOVERED YOUR NOTICE."

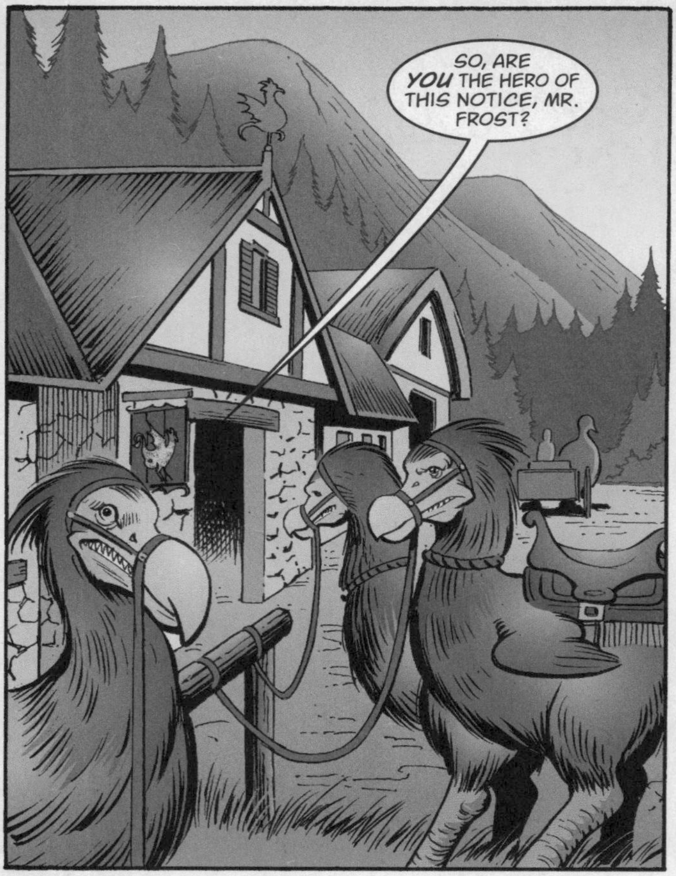
SO, ARE *YOU* THE HERO OF THIS NOTICE, MR. FROST?

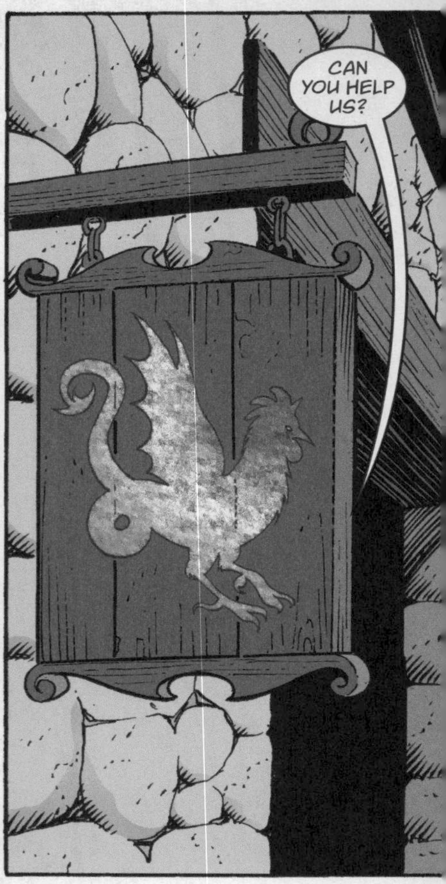
CAN YOU HELP US?

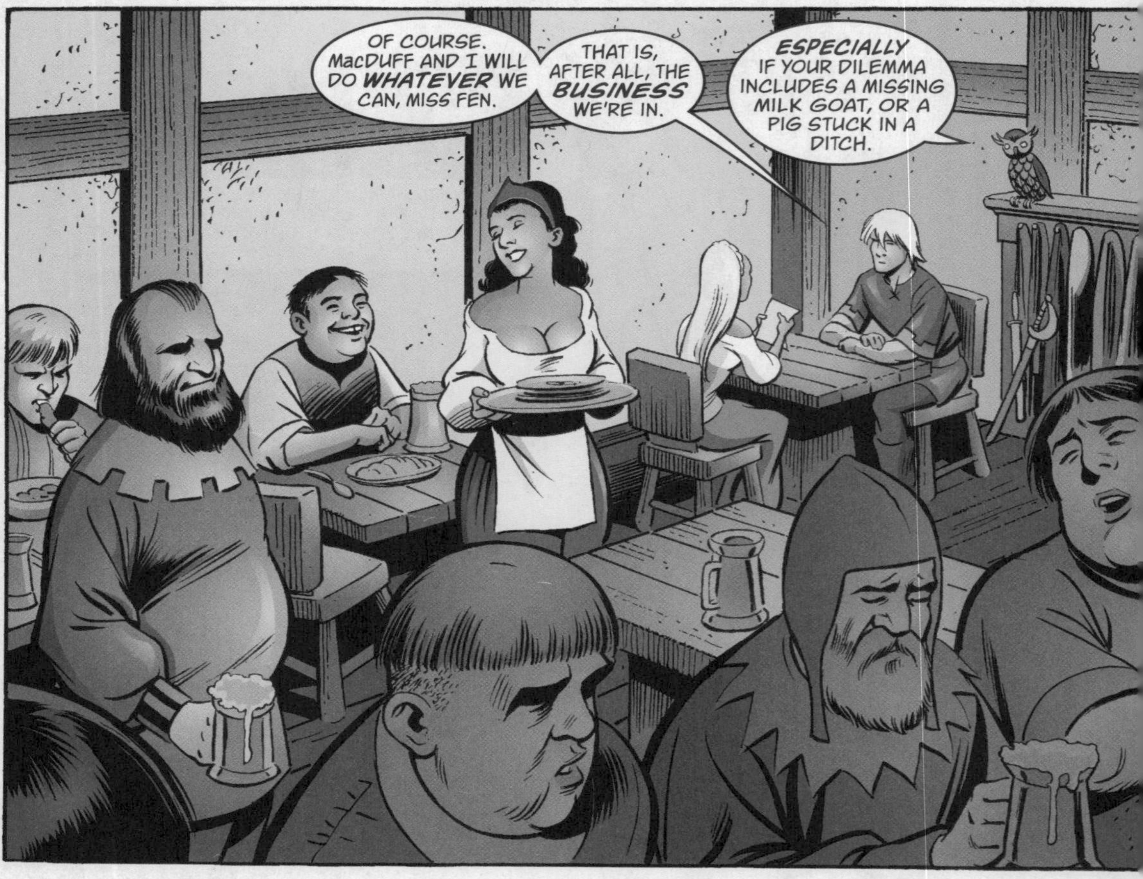
OF COURSE. MacDUFF AND I WILL DO *WHATEVER* WE CAN, MISS FEN.
THAT IS, AFTER ALL, THE *BUSINESS* WE'RE IN.
ESPECIALLY IF YOUR DILEMMA INCLUDES A MISSING MILK GOAT, OR A PIG STUCK IN A DITCH.

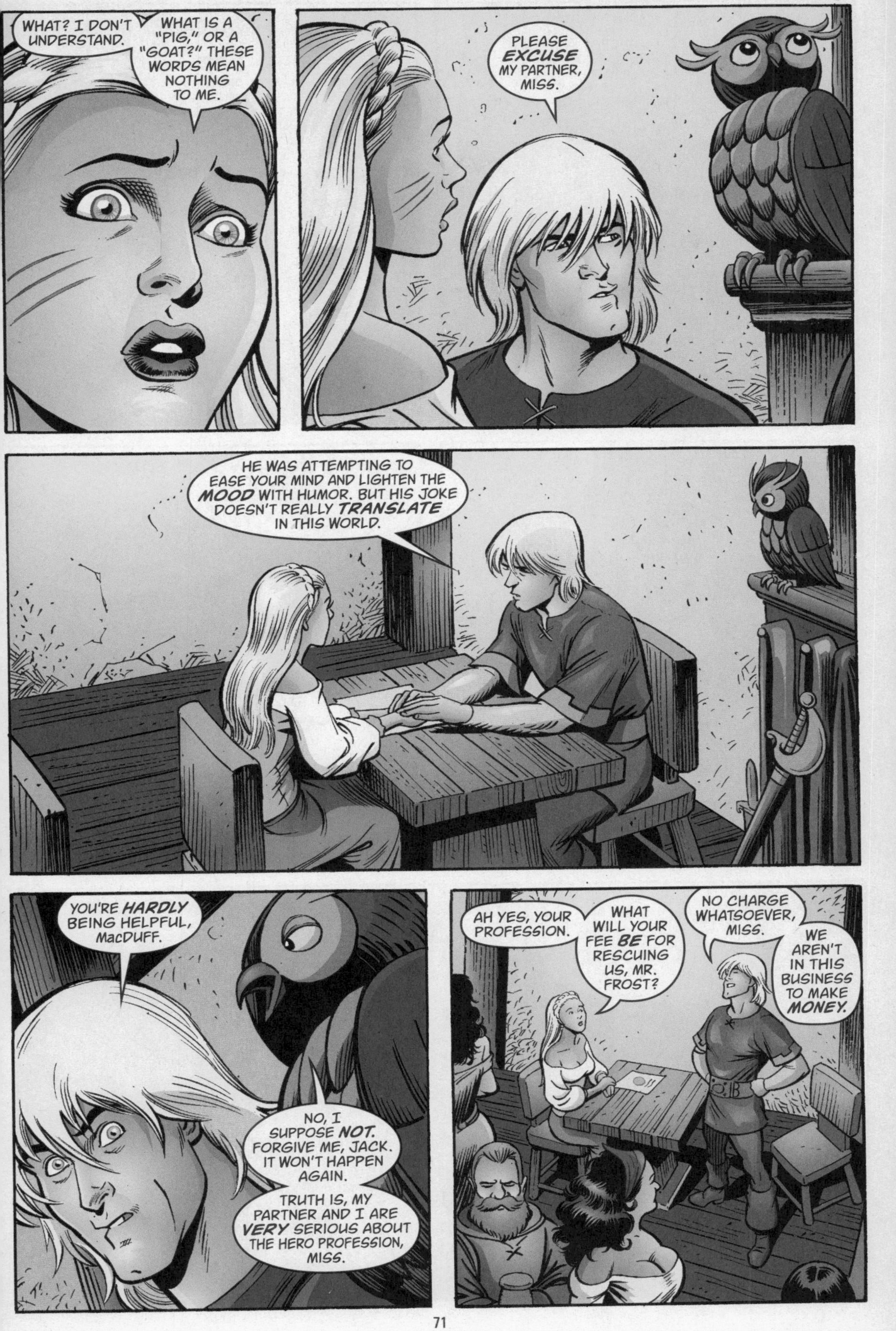
WHAT? I DON'T UNDERSTAND.
WHAT IS A "PIG," OR A "GOAT?" THESE WORDS MEAN NOTHING TO ME.
PLEASE EXCUSE MY PARTNER, MISS.
HE WAS ATTEMPTING TO EASE YOUR MIND AND LIGHTEN THE MOOD WITH HUMOR. BUT HIS JOKE DOESN'T REALLY TRANSLATE IN THIS WORLD.
YOU'RE HARDLY BEING HELPFUL, MacDUFF.
NO, I SUPPOSE NOT. FORGIVE ME, JACK. IT WON'T HAPPEN AGAIN.
TRUTH IS, MY PARTNER AND I ARE VERY SERIOUS ABOUT THE HERO PROFESSION, MISS.
AH YES, YOUR PROFESSION.
WHAT WILL YOUR FEE BE FOR RESCUING US, MR. FROST?
NO CHARGE WHATSOEVER, MISS.
WE AREN'T IN THIS BUSINESS TO MAKE MONEY.

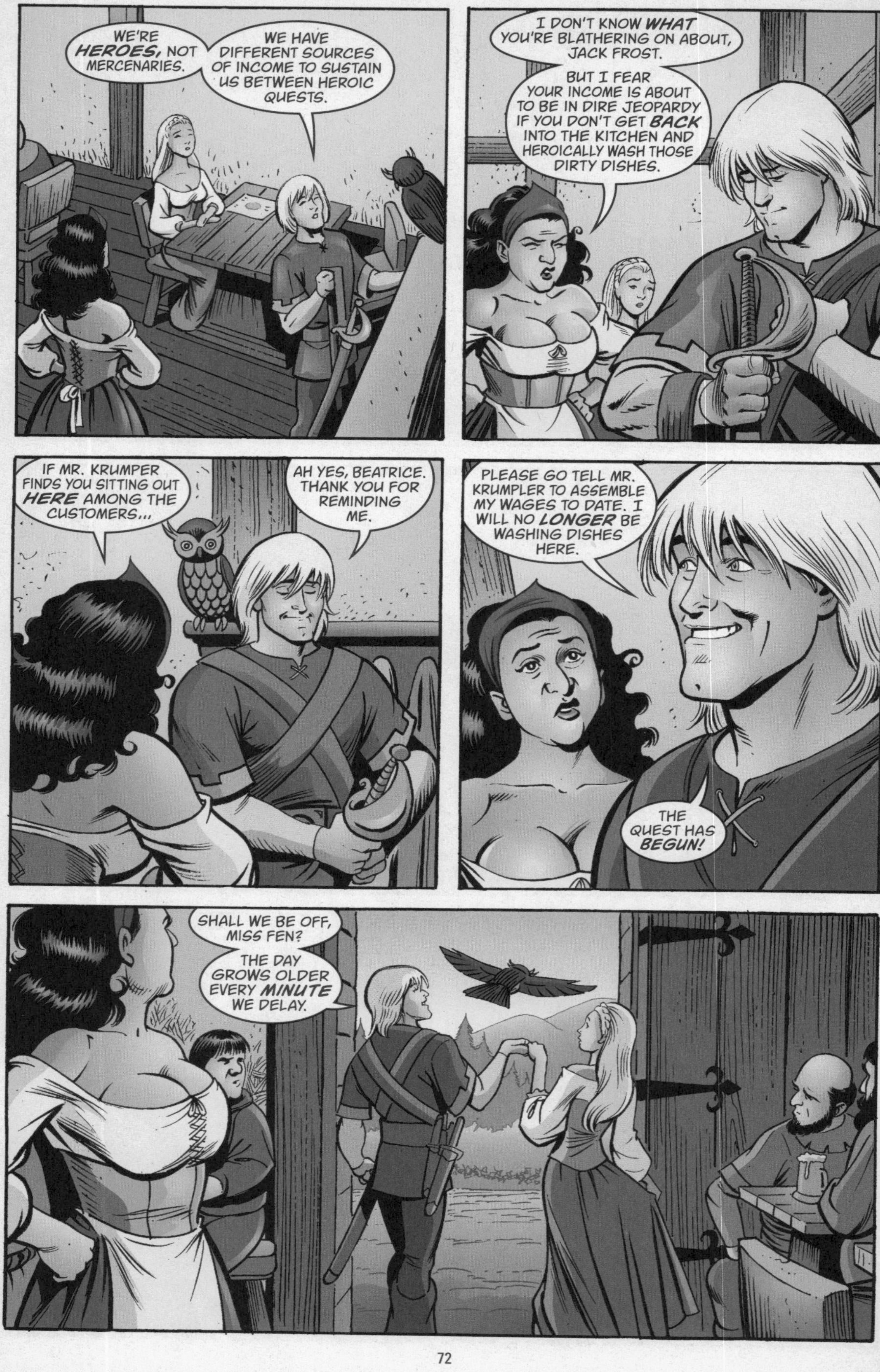
WE'RE **HEROES,** NOT MERCENARIES.
WE HAVE DIFFERENT SOURCES OF INCOME TO SUSTAIN US BETWEEN HEROIC QUESTS.
I DON'T KNOW **WHAT** YOU'RE BLATHERING ON ABOUT, JACK FROST.
BUT I FEAR YOUR INCOME IS ABOUT TO BE IN DIRE JEOPARDY IF YOU DON'T GET **BACK** INTO THE KITCHEN AND HEROICALLY WASH THOSE DIRTY DISHES.
IF MR. KRUMPER FINDS YOU SITTING OUT **HERE** AMONG THE CUSTOMERS...
AH YES, BEATRICE. THANK YOU FOR REMINDING ME.
PLEASE GO TELL MR. KRUMPLER TO ASSEMBLE MY WAGES TO DATE. I WILL NO **LONGER** BE WASHING DISHES HERE.
THE QUEST HAS **BEGUN!**
SHALL WE BE OFF, MISS FEN?
THE DAY GROWS OLDER EVERY **MINUTE** WE DELAY.

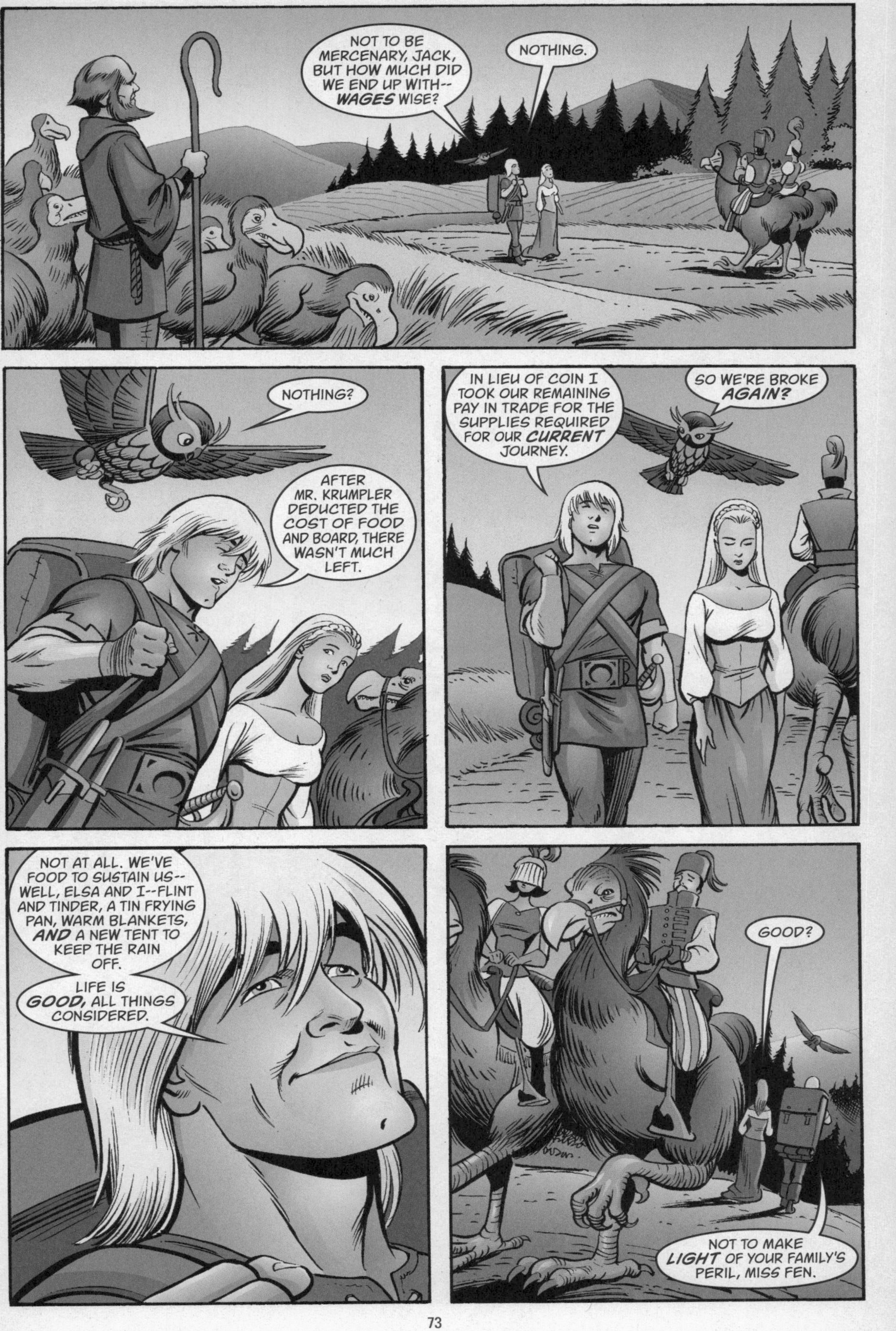
NOT TO BE MERCENARY, JACK, BUT HOW MUCH DID WE END UP WITH-- WAGES WISE?
NOTHING.
NOTHING?
AFTER MR. KRUMPLER DEDUCTED THE COST OF FOOD AND BOARD, THERE WASN'T MUCH LEFT.
IN LIEU OF COIN I TOOK OUR REMAINING PAY IN TRADE FOR THE SUPPLIES REQUIRED FOR OUR CURRENT JOURNEY.
SO WE'RE BROKE AGAIN?
NOT AT ALL. WE'VE FOOD TO SUSTAIN US--WELL, ELSA AND I--FLINT AND TINDER, A TIN FRYING PAN, WARM BLANKETS, AND A NEW TENT TO KEEP THE RAIN OFF.
LIFE IS GOOD, ALL THINGS CONSIDERED.
GOOD?
NOT TO MAKE LIGHT OF YOUR FAMILY'S PERIL, MISS FEN.

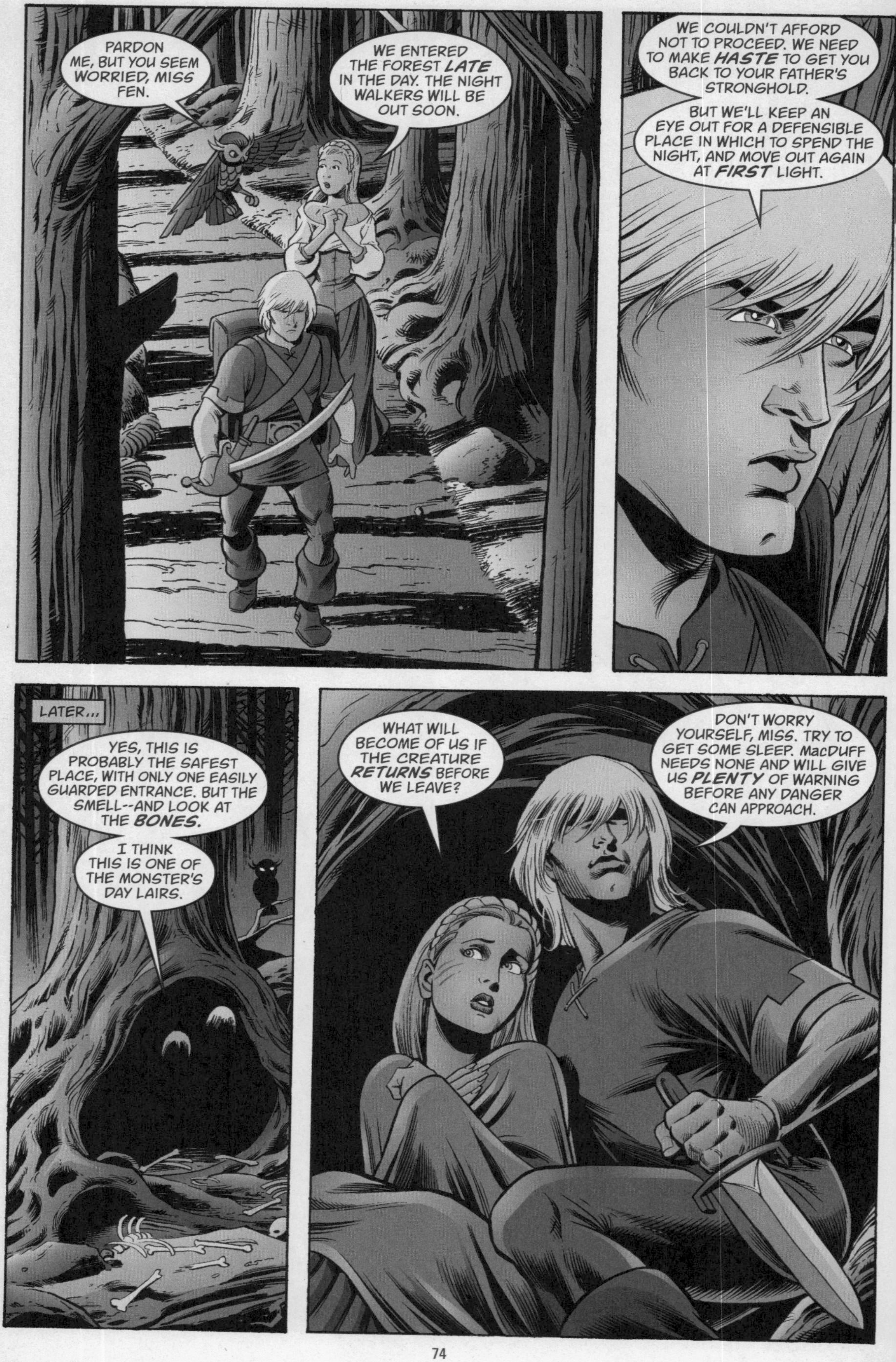

PARDON ME, BUT YOU SEEM WORRIED, MISS FEN.
WE ENTERED THE FOREST LATE IN THE DAY. THE NIGHT WALKERS WILL BE OUT SOON.
WE COULDN'T AFFORD NOT TO PROCEED. WE NEED TO MAKE HASTE TO GET YOU BACK TO YOUR FATHER'S STRONGHOLD.
BUT WE'LL KEEP AN EYE OUT FOR A DEFENSIBLE PLACE IN WHICH TO SPEND THE NIGHT, AND MOVE OUT AGAIN AT FIRST LIGHT.
LATER...
YES, THIS IS PROBABLY THE SAFEST PLACE, WITH ONLY ONE EASILY GUARDED ENTRANCE. BUT THE SMELL--AND LOOK AT THE BONES.
I THINK THIS IS ONE OF THE MONSTER'S DAY LAIRS.
WHAT WILL BECOME OF US IF THE CREATURE RETURNS BEFORE WE LEAVE?
DON'T WORRY YOURSELF, MISS. TRY TO GET SOME SLEEP. MacDUFF NEEDS NONE AND WILL GIVE US PLENTY OF WARNING BEFORE ANY DANGER CAN APPROACH.

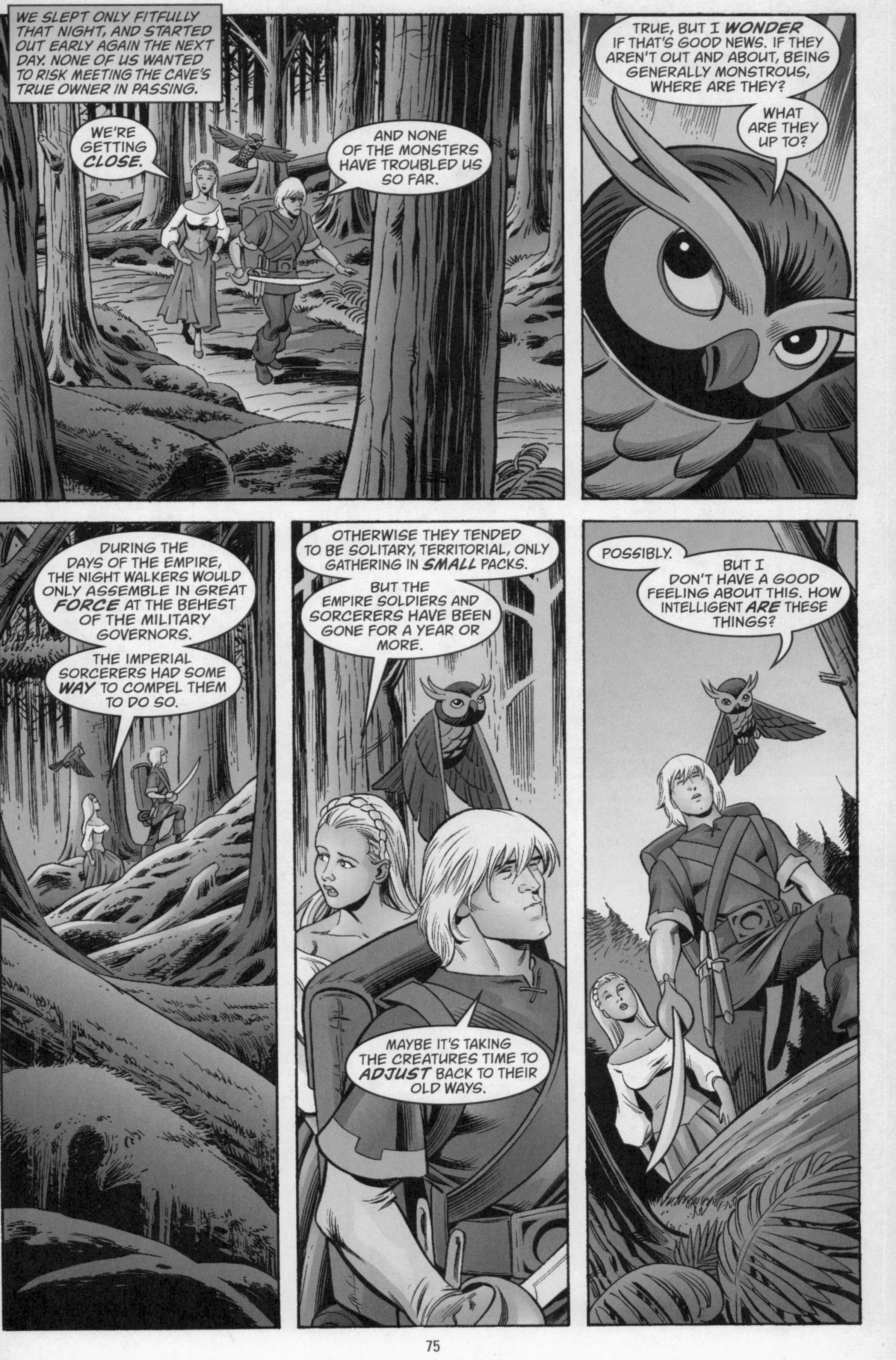
WE SLEPT ONLY FITFULLY THAT NIGHT, AND STARTED OUT EARLY AGAIN THE NEXT DAY. NONE OF US WANTED TO RISK MEETING THE CAVE'S TRUE OWNER IN PASSING.
WE'RE GETTING CLOSE.
AND NONE OF THE MONSTERS HAVE TROUBLED US SO FAR.
TRUE, BUT I WONDER IF THAT'S GOOD NEWS. IF THEY AREN'T OUT AND ABOUT, BEING GENERALLY MONSTROUS, WHERE ARE THEY?
WHAT ARE THEY UP TO?
DURING THE DAYS OF THE EMPIRE, THE NIGHT WALKERS WOULD ONLY ASSEMBLE IN GREAT FORCE AT THE BEHEST OF THE MILITARY GOVERNORS.
THE IMPERIAL SORCERERS HAD SOME WAY TO COMPEL THEM TO DO SO.
OTHERWISE THEY TENDED TO BE SOLITARY, TERRITORIAL, ONLY GATHERING IN SMALL PACKS.
BUT THE EMPIRE SOLDIERS AND SORCERERS HAVE BEEN GONE FOR A YEAR OR MORE.
MAYBE IT'S TAKING THE CREATURES TIME TO ADJUST BACK TO THEIR OLD WAYS.
POSSIBLY.
BUT I DON'T HAVE A GOOD FEELING ABOUT THIS. HOW INTELLIGENT ARE THESE THINGS?

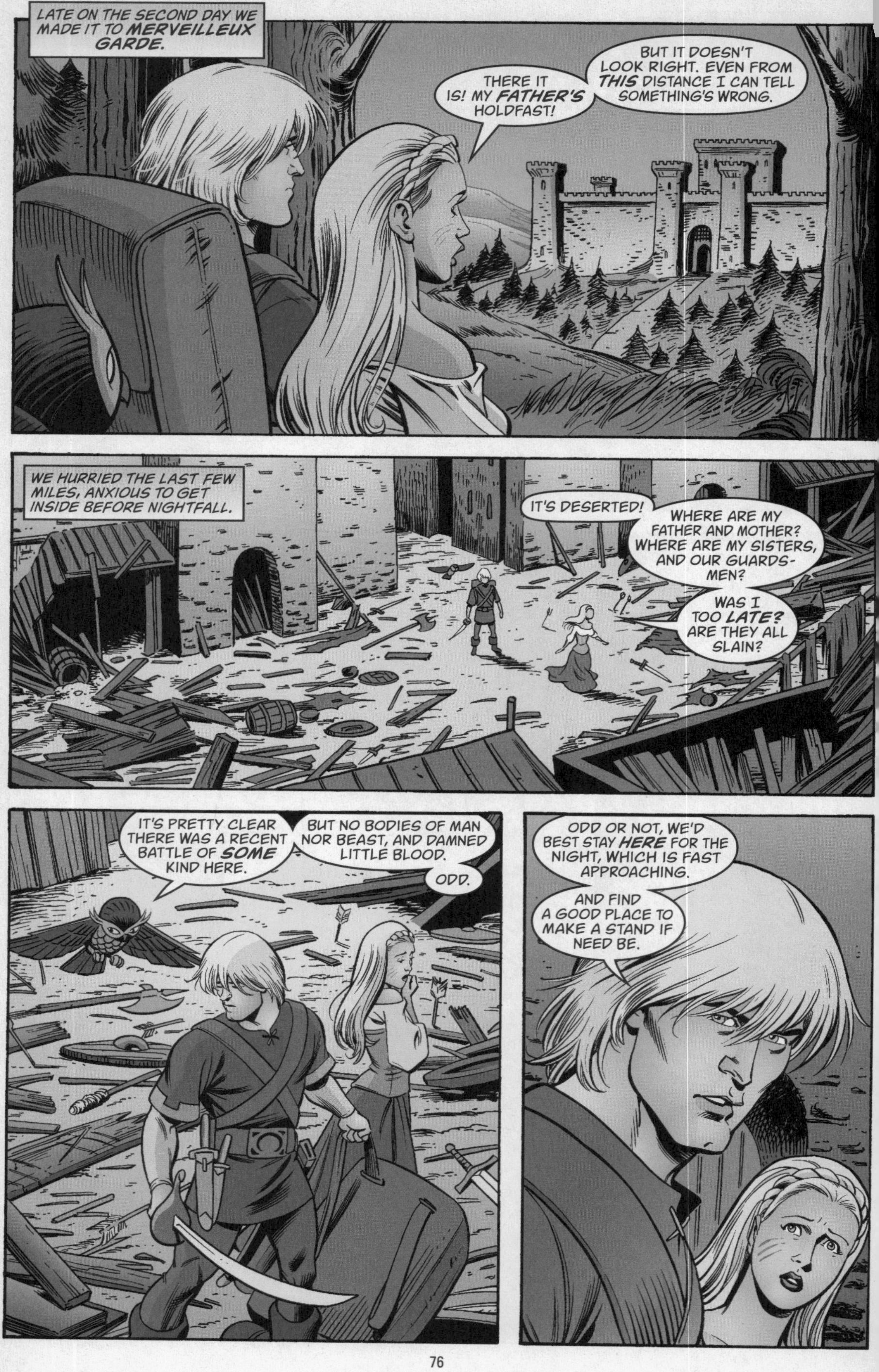
LATE ON THE SECOND DAY WE MADE IT TO MERVEILLEUX GARDE.
THERE IT IS! MY FATHER'S HOLDFAST!
BUT IT DOESN'T LOOK RIGHT. EVEN FROM THIS DISTANCE I CAN TELL SOMETHING'S WRONG.
WE HURRIED THE LAST FEW MILES, ANXIOUS TO GET INSIDE BEFORE NIGHTFALL.
IT'S DESERTED!
WHERE ARE MY FATHER AND MOTHER? WHERE ARE MY SISTERS, AND OUR GUARDSMEN?
WAS I TOO LATE? ARE THEY ALL SLAIN?
IT'S PRETTY CLEAR THERE WAS A RECENT BATTLE OF SOME KIND HERE.
BUT NO BODIES OF MAN NOR BEAST, AND DAMNED LITTLE BLOOD.
ODD.
ODD OR NOT, WE'D BEST STAY HERE FOR THE NIGHT, WHICH IS FAST APPROACHING.
AND FIND A GOOD PLACE TO MAKE A STAND IF NEED BE.

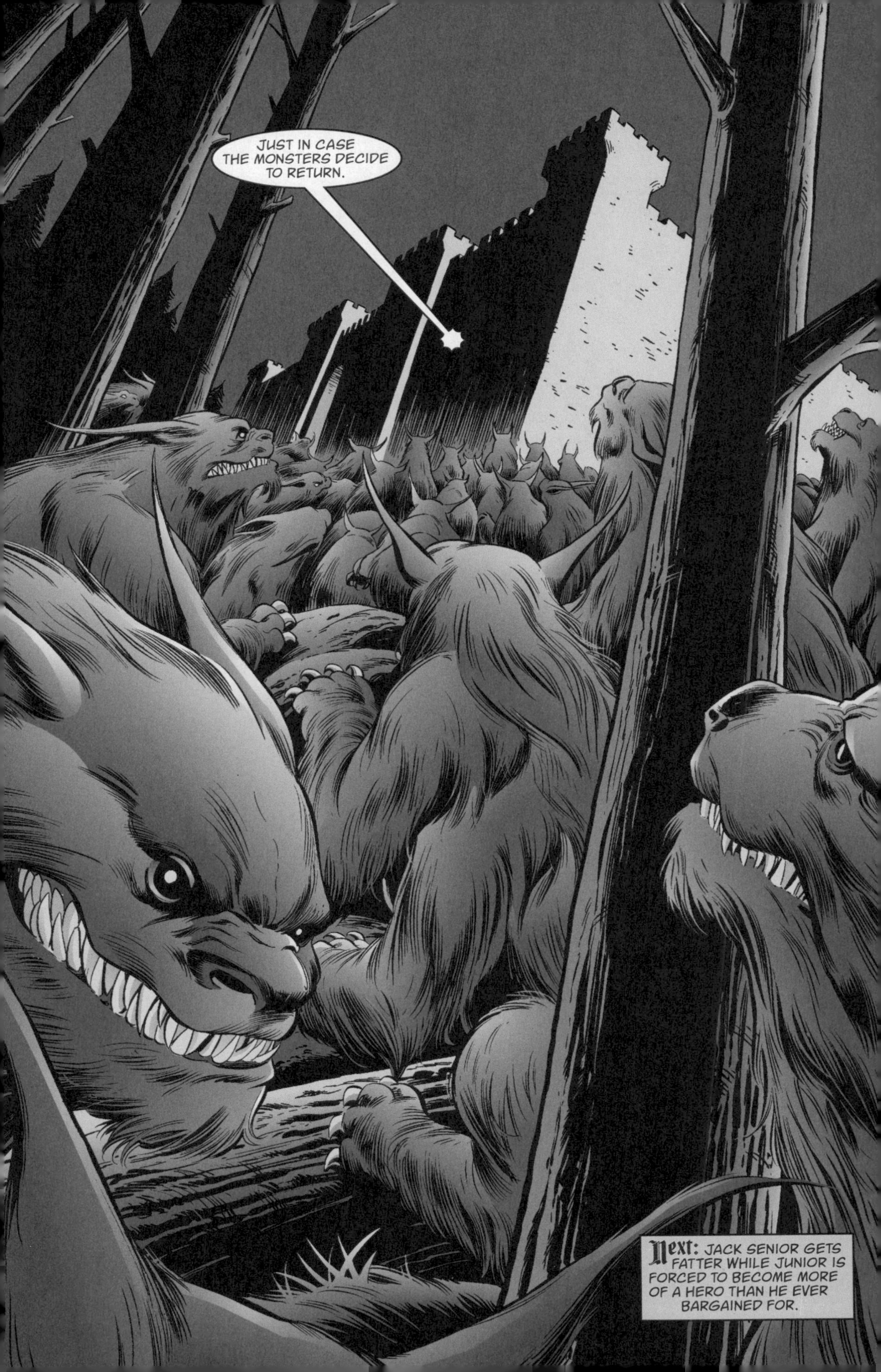
JUST IN CASE THE MONSTERS DECIDE TO RETURN.
Next: JACK SENIOR GETS FATTER WHILE JUNIOR IS FORCED TO BECOME MORE OF A HERO THAN HE EVER BARGAINED FOR.

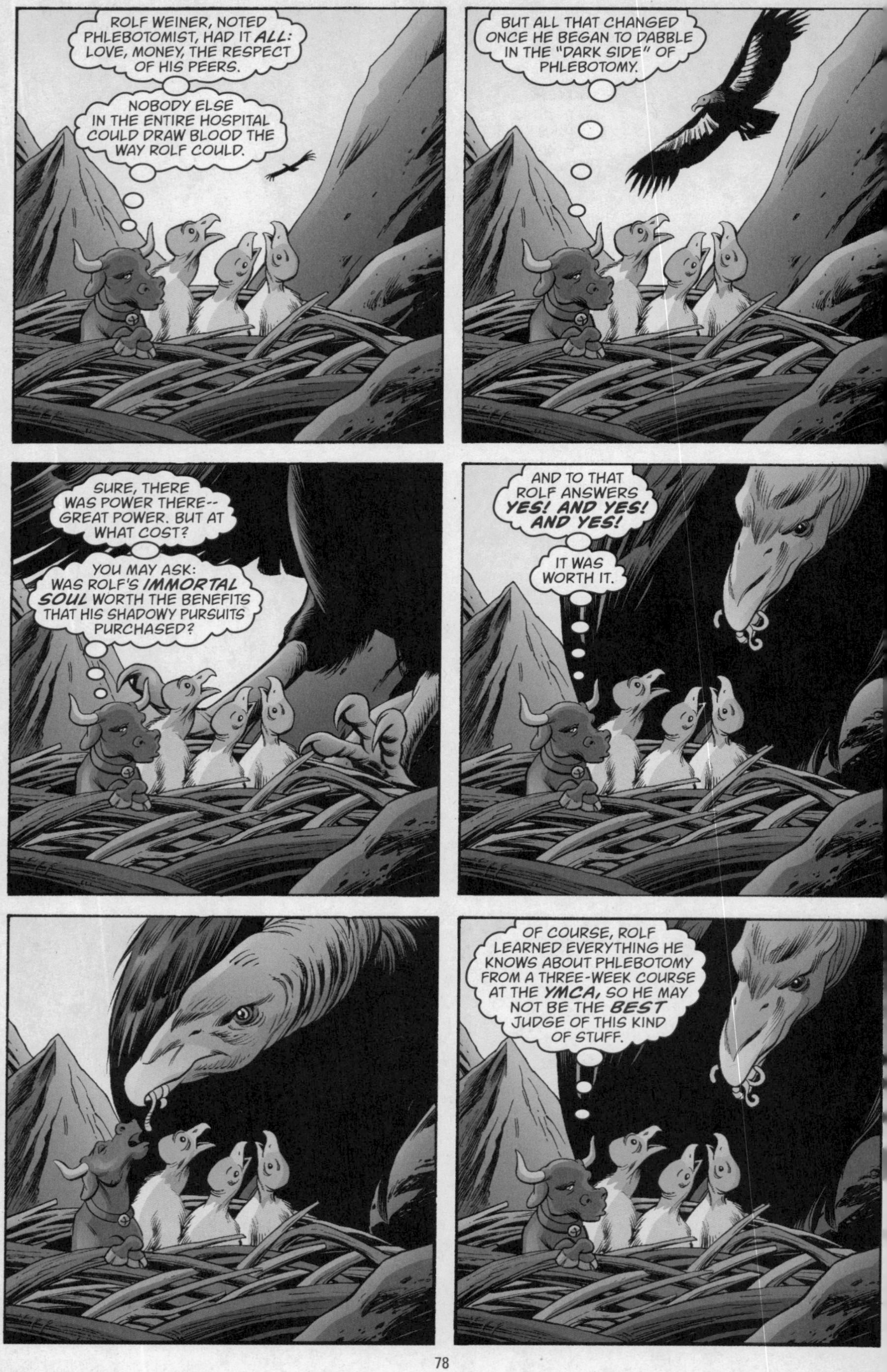
ROLF WEINER, NOTED PHLEBOTOMIST, HAD IT *ALL:* LOVE, MONEY, THE RESPECT OF HIS PEERS.
NOBODY ELSE IN THE ENTIRE HOSPITAL COULD DRAW BLOOD THE WAY ROLF COULD.
BUT ALL THAT CHANGED ONCE HE BEGAN TO DABBLE IN THE "*DARK SIDE*" OF PHLEBOTOMY.
SURE, THERE WAS POWER THERE-- GREAT POWER. BUT AT WHAT COST?
YOU MAY ASK: WAS ROLF'S *IMMORTAL SOUL* WORTH THE BENEFITS THAT HIS SHADOWY PURSUITS PURCHASED?
AND TO THAT ROLF ANSWERS *YES! AND YES! AND YES!*
IT WAS WORTH IT.
OF COURSE, ROLF LEARNED EVERYTHING HE KNOWS ABOUT PHLEBOTOMY FROM A THREE-WEEK COURSE AT THE *YMCA,* SO HE MAY NOT BE THE *BEST* JUDGE OF THIS KIND OF STUFF.

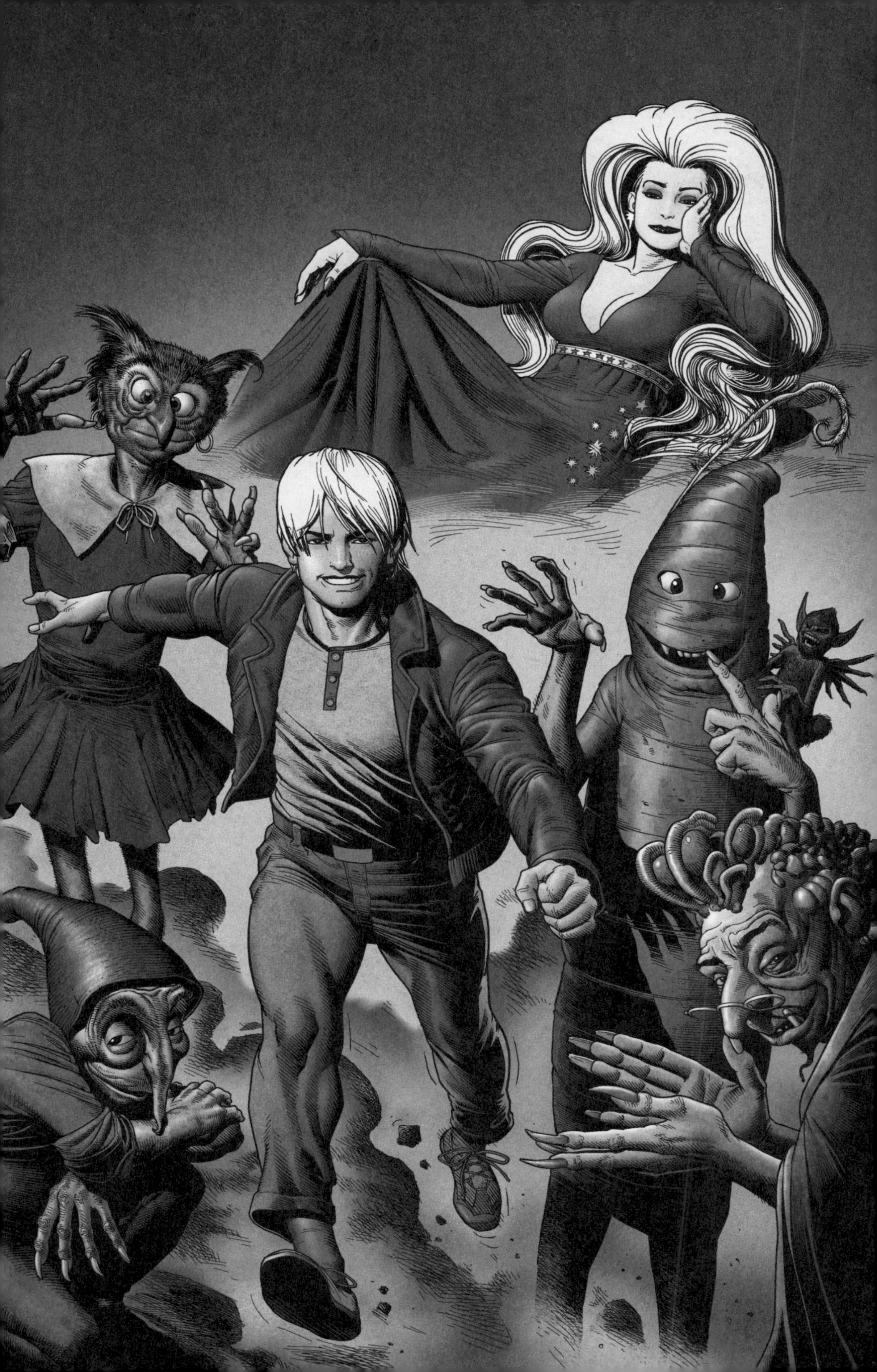

"THAT'S JUST A FACT OF LIFE.
MONSTERS NEED TO BE CONTROLLED, OR KILLED."

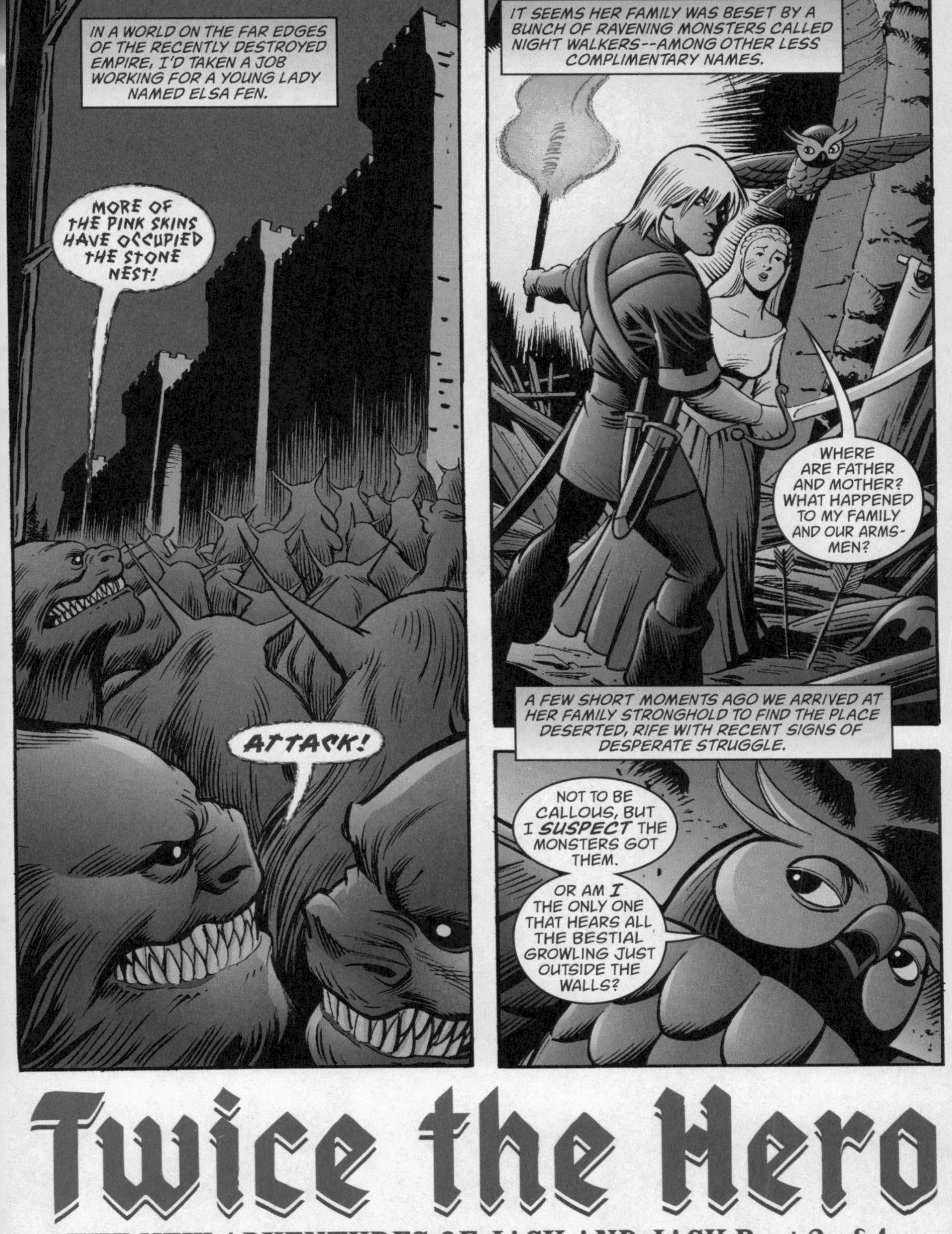
IN A WORLD ON THE FAR EDGES OF THE RECENTLY DESTROYED EMPIRE, I'D TAKEN A JOB WORKING FOR A YOUNG LADY NAMED ELSA FEN.
MORE OF THE PINK SKINS HAVE OCCUPIED THE STONE NEST!
ATTACK!
IT SEEMS HER FAMILY WAS BESET BY A BUNCH OF RAVENING MONSTERS CALLED NIGHT WALKERS--AMONG OTHER LESS COMPLIMENTARY NAMES.
WHERE ARE FATHER AND MOTHER? WHAT HAPPENED TO MY FAMILY AND OUR ARMS-MEN?
A FEW SHORT MOMENTS AGO WE ARRIVED AT HER FAMILY STRONGHOLD TO FIND THE PLACE DESERTED, RIFE WITH RECENT SIGNS OF DESPERATE STRUGGLE.
NOT TO BE CALLOUS, BUT I SUSPECT THE MONSTERS GOT THEM.
OR AM I THE ONLY ONE THAT HEARS ALL THE BESTIAL GROWLING JUST OUTSIDE THE WALLS?

Twice the Hero

THE NEW ADVENTURES OF JACK AND JACK Part 3 of 4

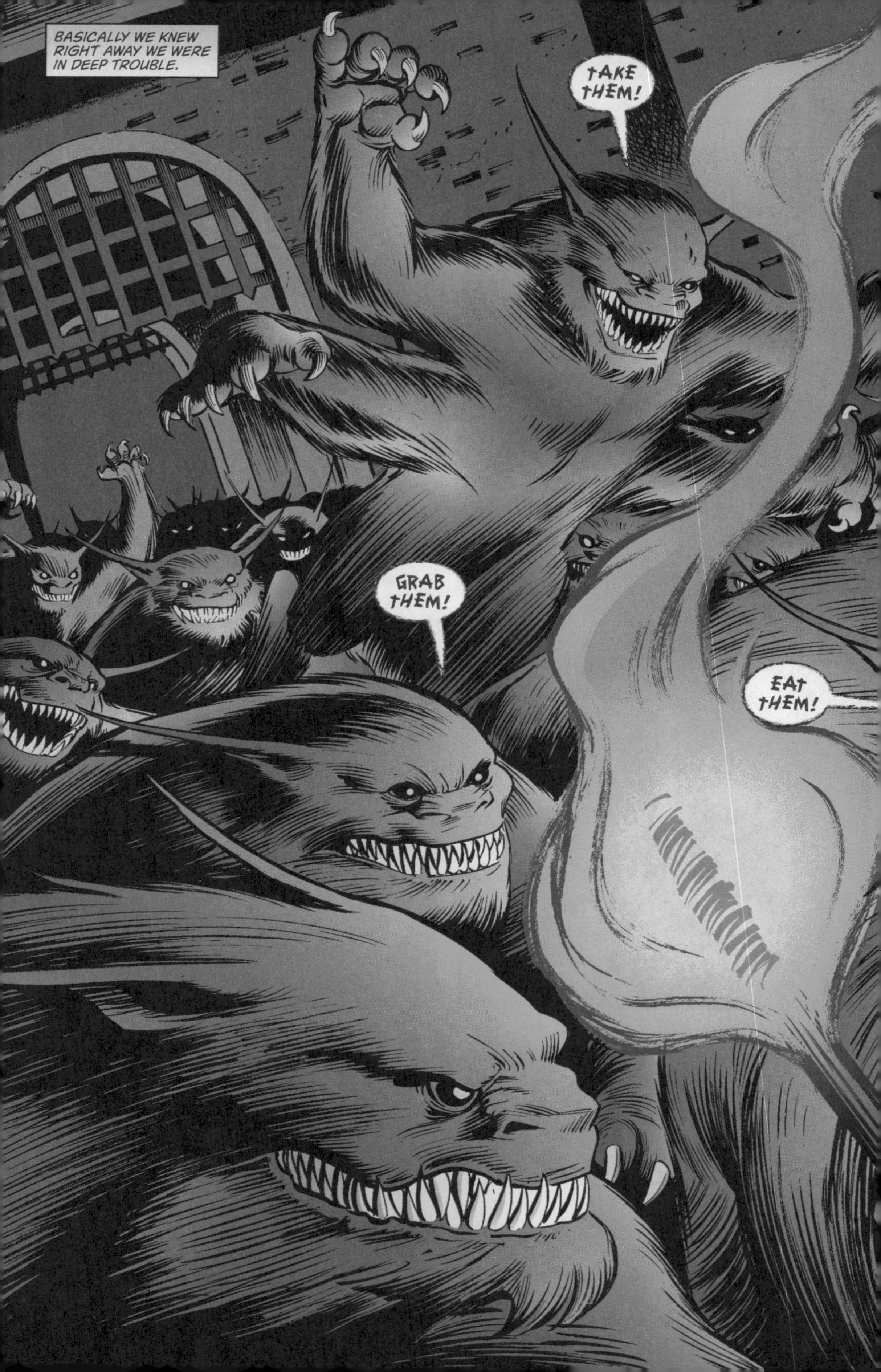
BASICALLY WE KNEW RIGHT AWAY WE WERE IN DEEP TROUBLE.
TAKE THEM!
GRAB THEM!
EAT THEM!

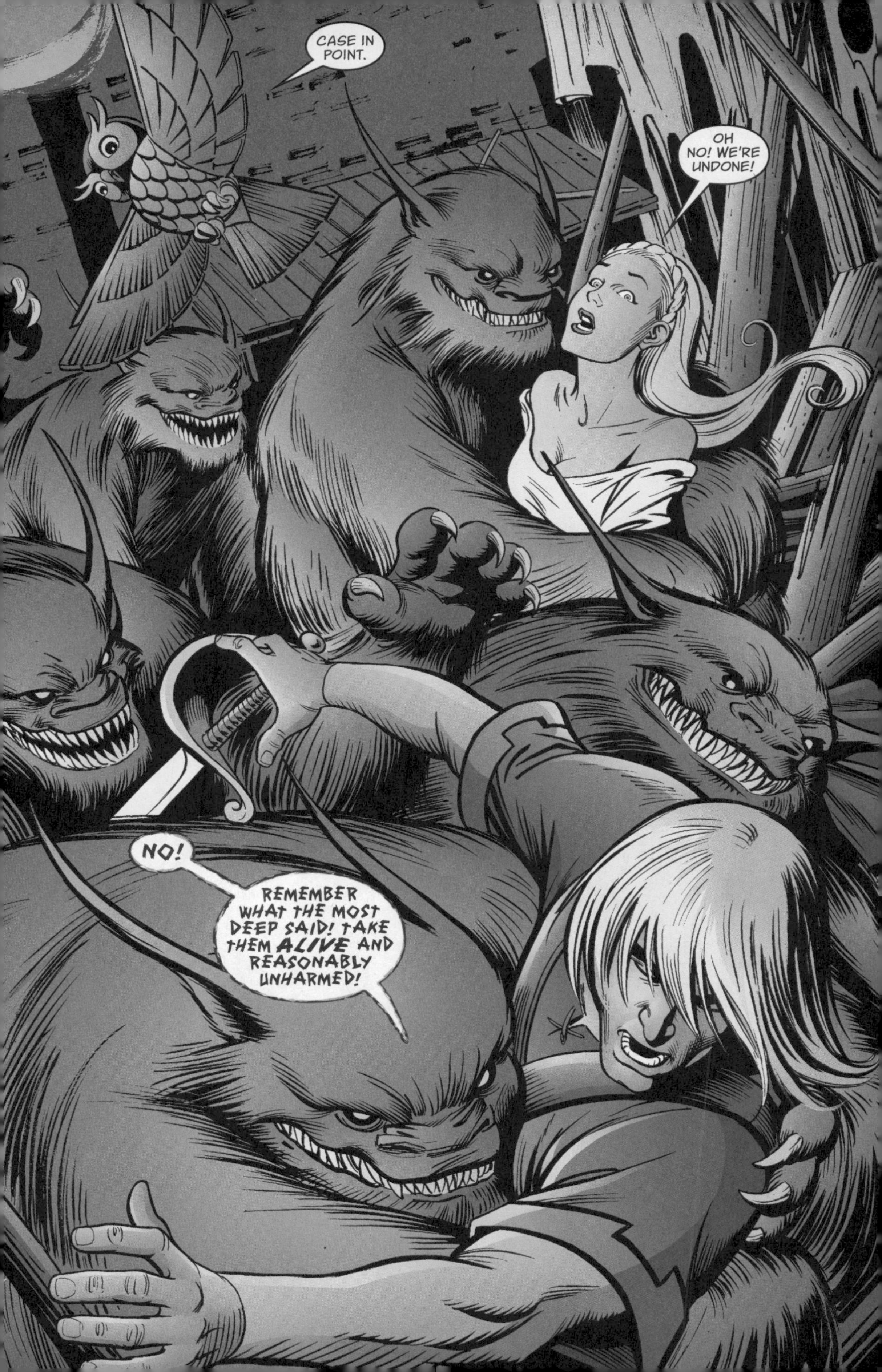
CASE IN POINT.
OH NO! WE'RE UNDONE!
NO!
REMEMBER WHAT THE MOST DEEP SAID! TAKE THEM ALIVE AND REASONABLY UNHARMED!

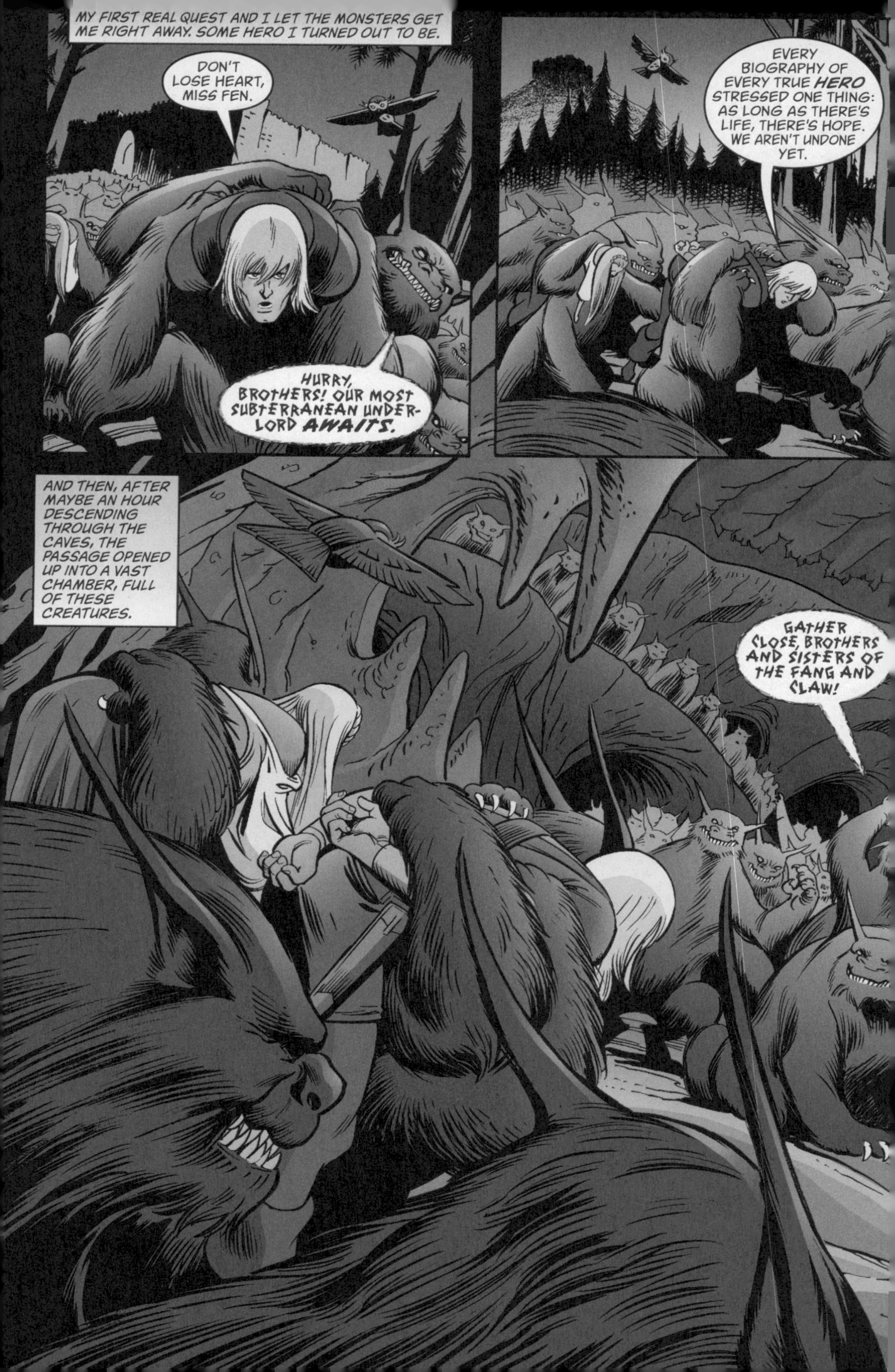
MY FIRST REAL QUEST AND I LET THE MONSTERS GET ME RIGHT AWAY. SOME HERO I TURNED OUT TO BE.
DON'T LOSE HEART, MISS FEN.
HURRY, BROTHERS! OUR MOST SUBTERRANEAN UNDER-LORD AWAITS.
EVERY BIOGRAPHY OF EVERY TRUE HERO STRESSED ONE THING: AS LONG AS THERE'S LIFE, THERE'S HOPE. WE AREN'T UNDONE YET.
AND THEN, AFTER MAYBE AN HOUR DESCENDING THROUGH THE CAVES, THE PASSAGE OPENED UP INTO A VAST CHAMBER, FULL OF THESE CREATURES.
GATHER CLOSE, BROTHERS AND SISTERS OF THE FANG AND CLAW!

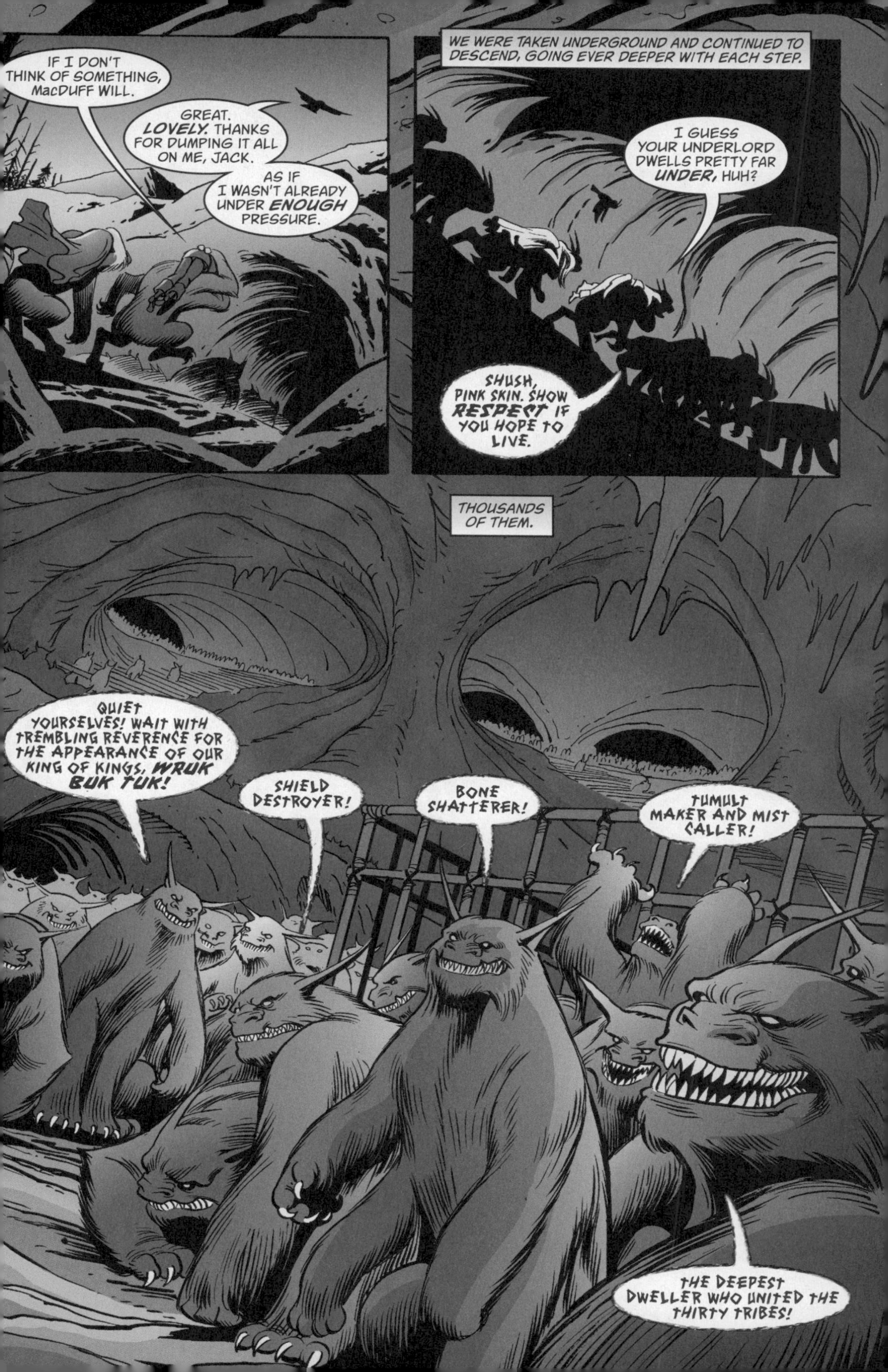
IF I DON'T THINK OF SOMETHING, MacDUFF WILL.
GREAT. LOVELY. THANKS FOR DUMPING IT ALL ON ME, JACK.
AS IF I WASN'T ALREADY UNDER ENOUGH PRESSURE.
WE WERE TAKEN UNDERGROUND AND CONTINUED TO DESCEND, GOING EVER DEEPER WITH EACH STEP.
I GUESS YOUR UNDERLORD DWELLS PRETTY FAR UNDER, HUH?
SHUSH, PINK SKIN. SHOW RESPECT IF YOU HOPE TO LIVE.
THOUSANDS OF THEM.
QUIET YOURSELVES! WAIT WITH TREMBLING REVERENCE FOR THE APPEARANCE OF OUR KING OF KINGS, WRUK BUK TUK!
SHIELD DESTROYER!
BONE SHATTERER!
TUMULT MAKER AND MIST CALLER!
THE DEEPEST DWELLER WHO UNITED THE THIRTY TRIBES!

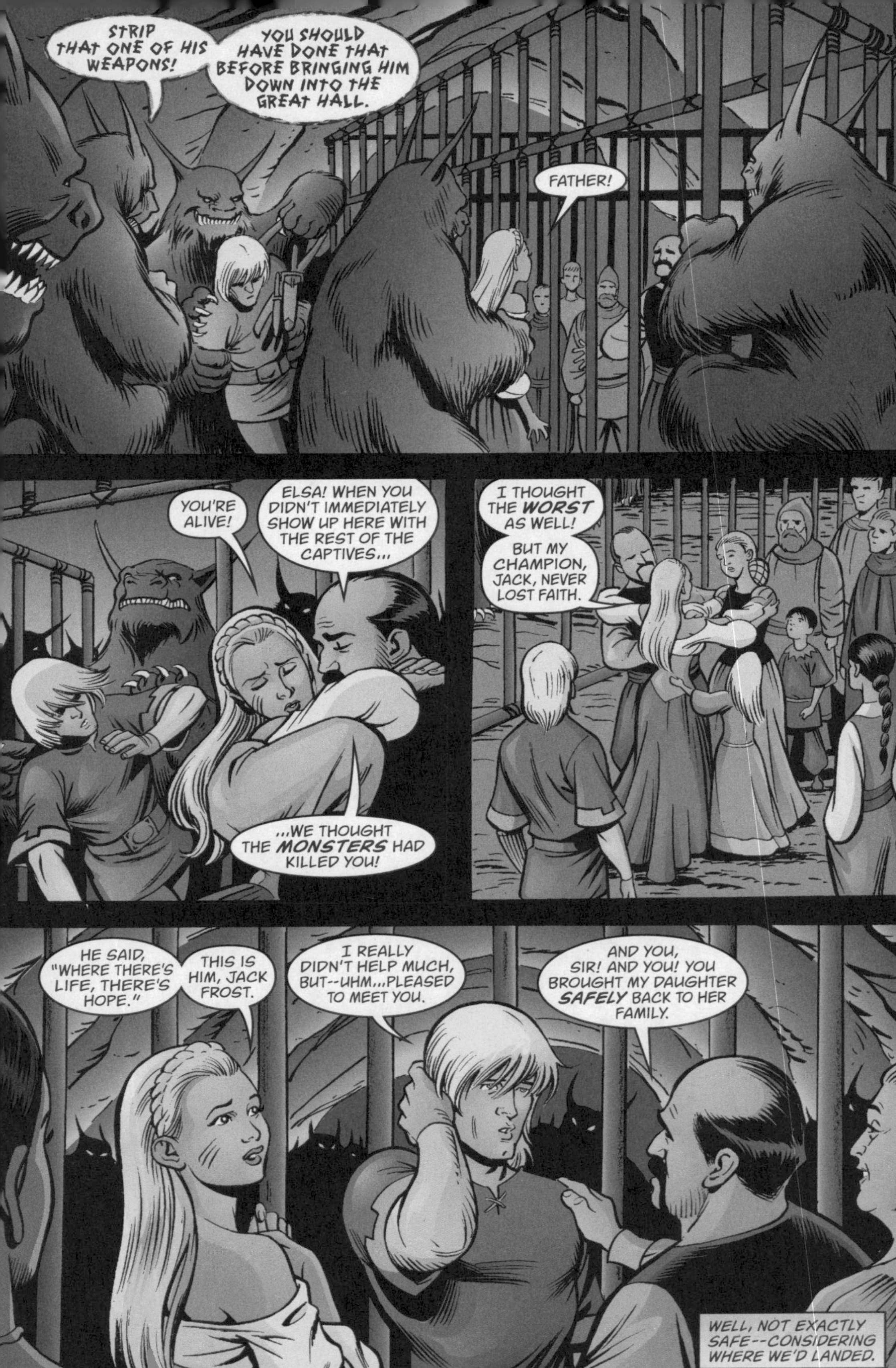
STRIP THAT ONE OF HIS WEAPONS!
YOU SHOULD HAVE DONE THAT BEFORE BRINGING HIM DOWN INTO THE GREAT HALL.
FATHER!
YOU'RE ALIVE!
ELSA! WHEN YOU DIDN'T IMMEDIATELY SHOW UP HERE WITH THE REST OF THE CAPTIVES...
...WE THOUGHT THE MONSTERS HAD KILLED YOU!
I THOUGHT THE WORST AS WELL!
BUT MY CHAMPION, JACK, NEVER LOST FAITH.
HE SAID, "WHERE THERE'S LIFE, THERE'S HOPE."
THIS IS HIM, JACK FROST.
I REALLY DIDN'T HELP MUCH, BUT--UHM...PLEASED TO MEET YOU.
AND YOU, SIR! AND YOU! YOU BROUGHT MY DAUGHTER SAFELY BACK TO HER FAMILY.
WELL, NOT EXACTLY SAFE--CONSIDERING WHERE WE'D LANDED.

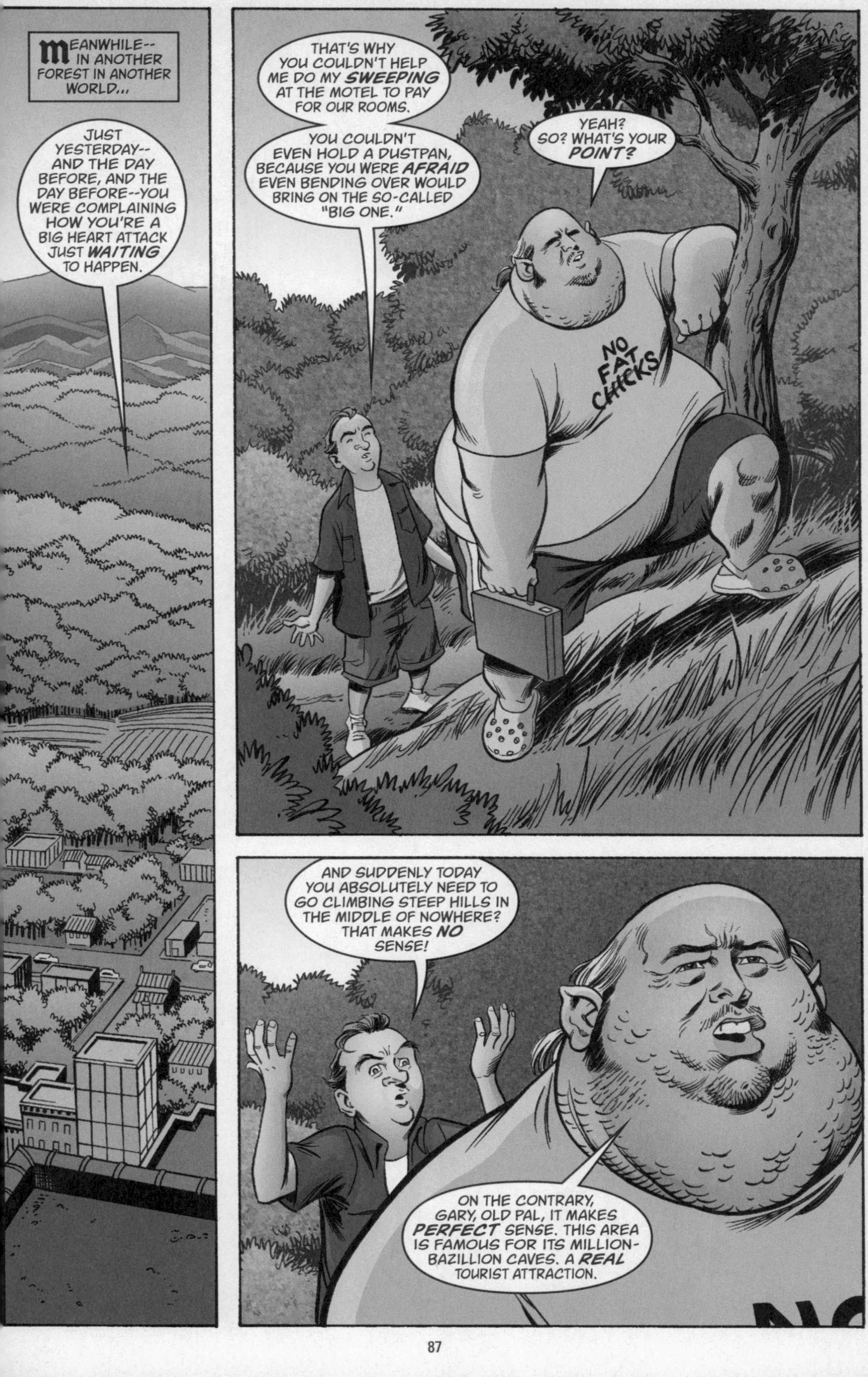
MEANWHILE-- IN ANOTHER FOREST IN ANOTHER WORLD...
JUST YESTERDAY-- AND THE DAY BEFORE, AND THE DAY BEFORE--YOU WERE COMPLAINING HOW YOU'RE A BIG HEART ATTACK JUST WAITING TO HAPPEN.
THAT'S WHY YOU COULDN'T HELP ME DO MY SWEEPING AT THE MOTEL TO PAY FOR OUR ROOMS.
YOU COULDN'T EVEN HOLD A DUSTPAN, BECAUSE YOU WERE AFRAID EVEN BENDING OVER WOULD BRING ON THE SO-CALLED "BIG ONE."
YEAH? SO? WHAT'S YOUR POINT?
NO FAT CHICKS
AND SUDDENLY TODAY YOU ABSOLUTELY NEED TO GO CLIMBING STEEP HILLS IN THE MIDDLE OF NOWHERE? THAT MAKES NO SENSE!
ON THE CONTRARY, GARY, OLD PAL, IT MAKES PERFECT SENSE. THIS AREA IS FAMOUS FOR ITS MILLION-BAZILLION CAVES. A REAL TOURIST ATTRACTION.

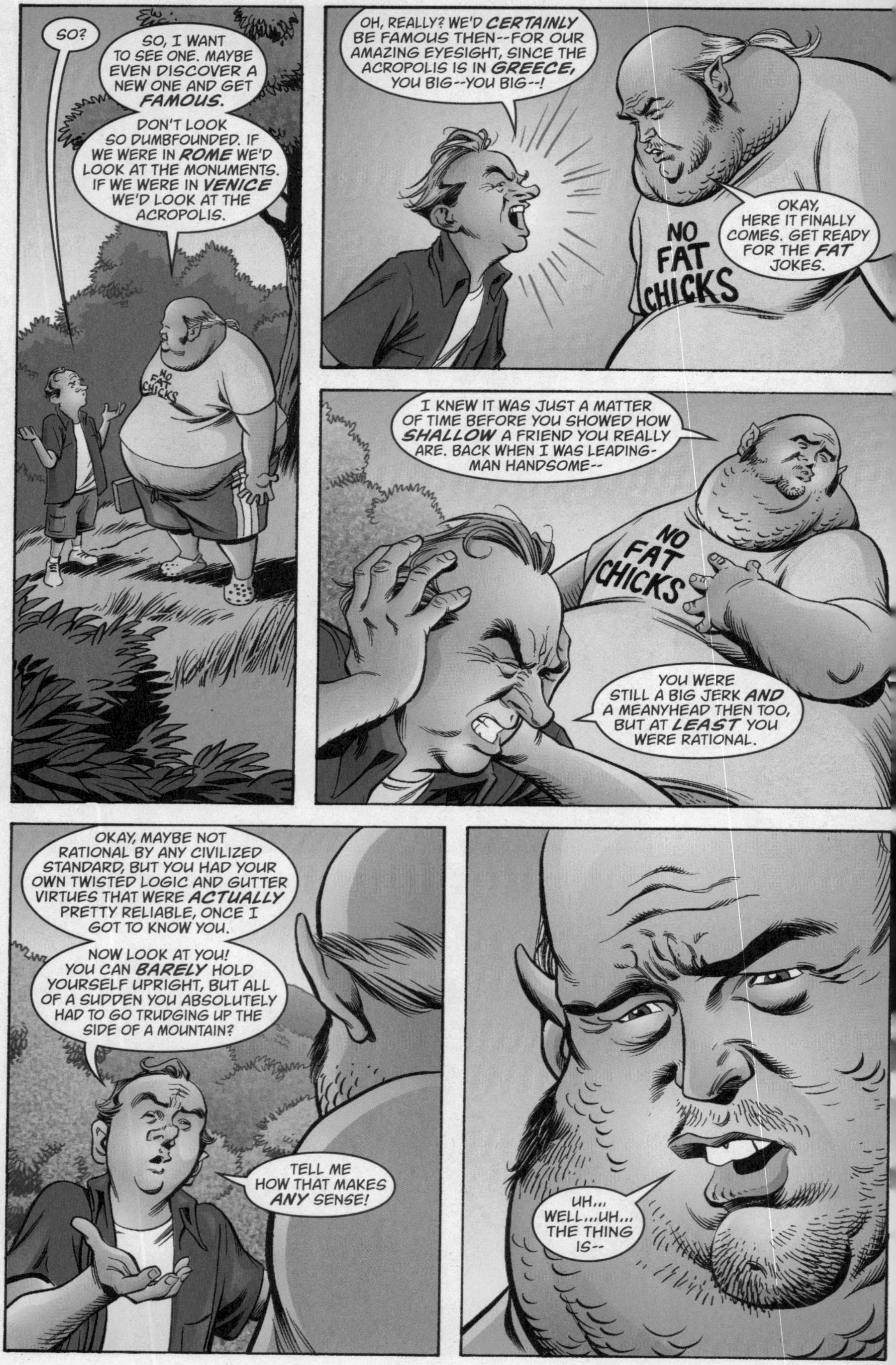
SO?
SO, I WANT TO SEE ONE. MAYBE EVEN DISCOVER A NEW ONE AND GET FAMOUS.
DON'T LOOK SO DUMBFOUNDED. IF WE WERE IN ROME WE'D LOOK AT THE MONUMENTS. IF WE WERE IN VENICE WE'D LOOK AT THE ACROPOLIS.
NO FAT CHICKS
OH, REALLY? WE'D CERTAINLY BE FAMOUS THEN--FOR OUR AMAZING EYESIGHT, SINCE THE ACROPOLIS IS IN GREECE, YOU BIG--YOU BIG--!
OKAY, HERE IT FINALLY COMES. GET READY FOR THE FAT JOKES.
NO FAT CHICKS
I KNEW IT WAS JUST A MATTER OF TIME BEFORE YOU SHOWED HOW SHALLOW A FRIEND YOU REALLY ARE. BACK WHEN I WAS LEADING-MAN HANDSOME--
NO FAT CHICKS
YOU WERE STILL A BIG JERK AND A MEANYHEAD THEN TOO, BUT AT LEAST YOU WERE RATIONAL.
OKAY, MAYBE NOT RATIONAL BY ANY CIVILIZED STANDARD, BUT YOU HAD YOUR OWN TWISTED LOGIC AND GUTTER VIRTUES THAT WERE ACTUALLY PRETTY RELIABLE, ONCE I GOT TO KNOW YOU.
NOW LOOK AT YOU! YOU CAN BARELY HOLD YOURSELF UPRIGHT, BUT ALL OF A SUDDEN YOU ABSOLUTELY HAD TO GO TRUDGING UP THE SIDE OF A MOUNTAIN?
TELL ME HOW THAT MAKES ANY SENSE!
UH... WELL...UH... THE THING IS--

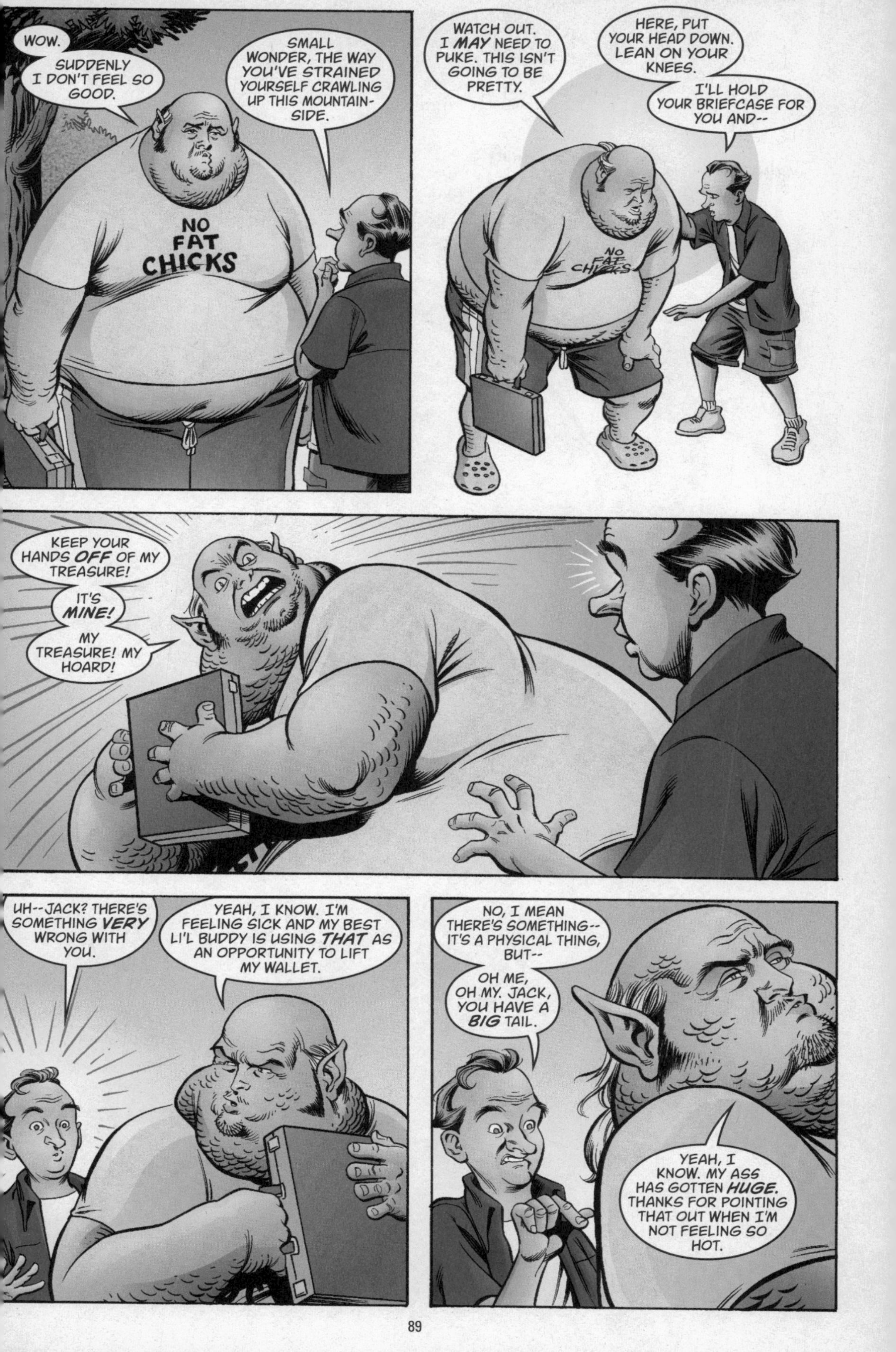
WOW.
SUDDENLY I DON'T FEEL SO GOOD.
SMALL WONDER, THE WAY YOU'VE STRAINED YOURSELF CRAWLING UP THIS MOUNTAIN-SIDE.
NO FAT CHICKS
WATCH OUT. I MAY NEED TO PUKE. THIS ISN'T GOING TO BE PRETTY.
HERE, PUT YOUR HEAD DOWN. LEAN ON YOUR KNEES.
I'LL HOLD YOUR BRIEFCASE FOR YOU AND--
NO FAT CHICKS
KEEP YOUR HANDS OFF OF MY TREASURE!
IT'S MINE!
MY TREASURE! MY HOARD!
UH--JACK? THERE'S SOMETHING VERY WRONG WITH YOU.
YEAH, I KNOW. I'M FEELING SICK AND MY BEST LI'L BUDDY IS USING THAT AS AN OPPORTUNITY TO LIFT MY WALLET.
NO, I MEAN THERE'S SOMETHING-- IT'S A PHYSICAL THING, BUT--
OH ME, OH MY. JACK, YOU HAVE A BIG TAIL.
YEAH, I KNOW. MY ASS HAS GOTTEN HUGE. THANKS FOR POINTING THAT OUT WHEN I'M NOT FEELING SO HOT.

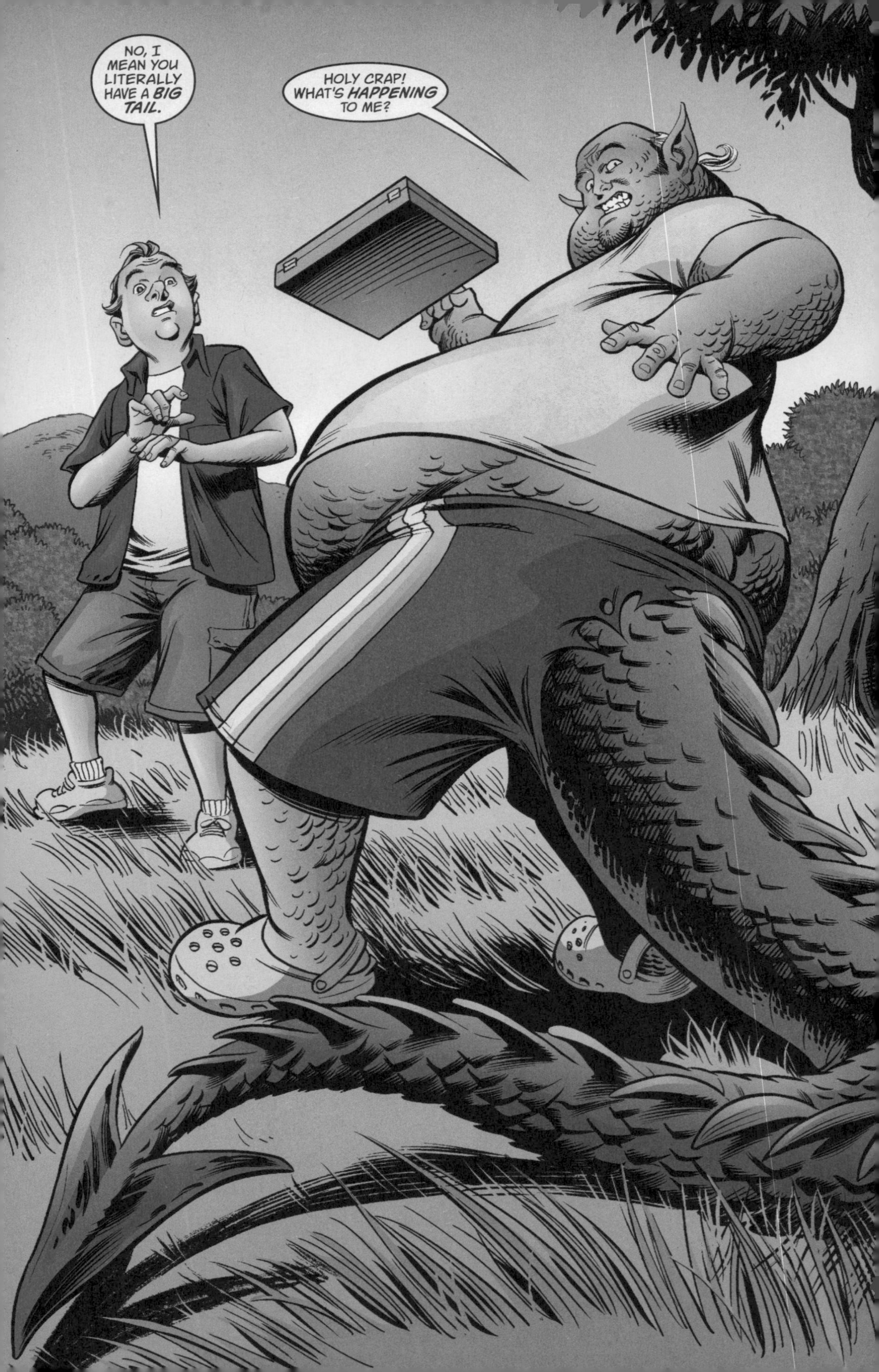
NO, I MEAN YOU LITERALLY HAVE A BIG TAIL.
HOLY CRAP! WHAT'S HAPPENING TO ME?

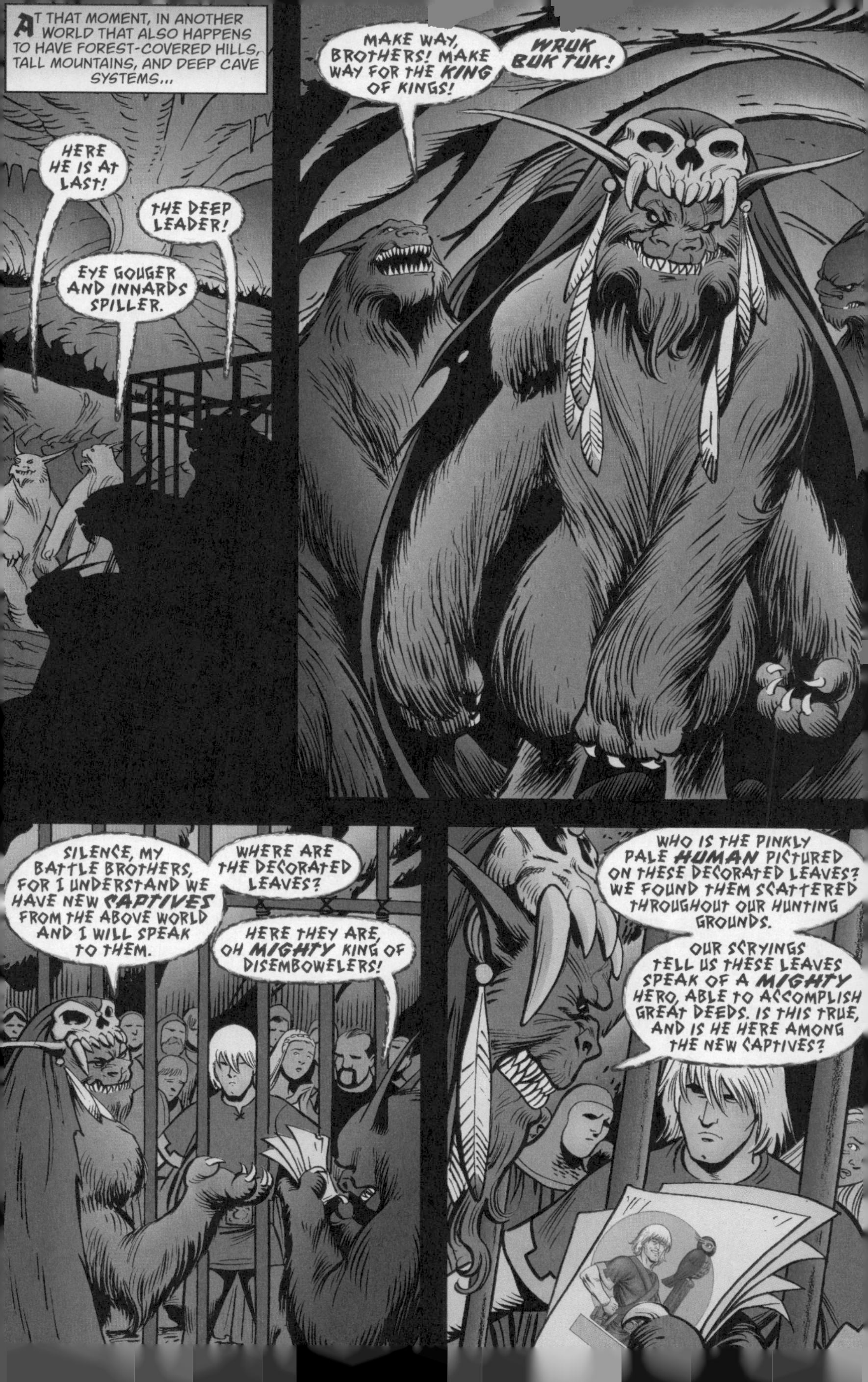

AT THAT MOMENT, IN ANOTHER WORLD THAT ALSO HAPPENS TO HAVE FOREST-COVERED HILLS, TALL MOUNTAINS, AND DEEP CAVE SYSTEMS...
HERE HE IS AT LAST!
THE DEEP LEADER!
EYE GOUGER AND INNARDS SPILLER.
MAKE WAY, BROTHERS! MAKE WAY FOR THE KING OF KINGS!
WRUK BUK TUK!
SILENCE, MY BATTLE BROTHERS, FOR I UNDERSTAND WE HAVE NEW CAPTIVES FROM THE ABOVE WORLD AND I WILL SPEAK TO THEM.
WHERE ARE THE DECORATED LEAVES?
HERE THEY ARE, OH MIGHTY KING OF DISEMBOWELERS!
WHO IS THE PINKLY PALE HUMAN PICTURED ON THESE DECORATED LEAVES? WE FOUND THEM SCATTERED THROUGHOUT OUR HUNTING GROUNDS.
OUR SCRYINGS TELL US THESE LEAVES SPEAK OF A MIGHTY HERO, ABLE TO ACCOMPLISH GREAT DEEDS. IS THIS TRUE, AND IS HE HERE AMONG THE NEW CAPTIVES?

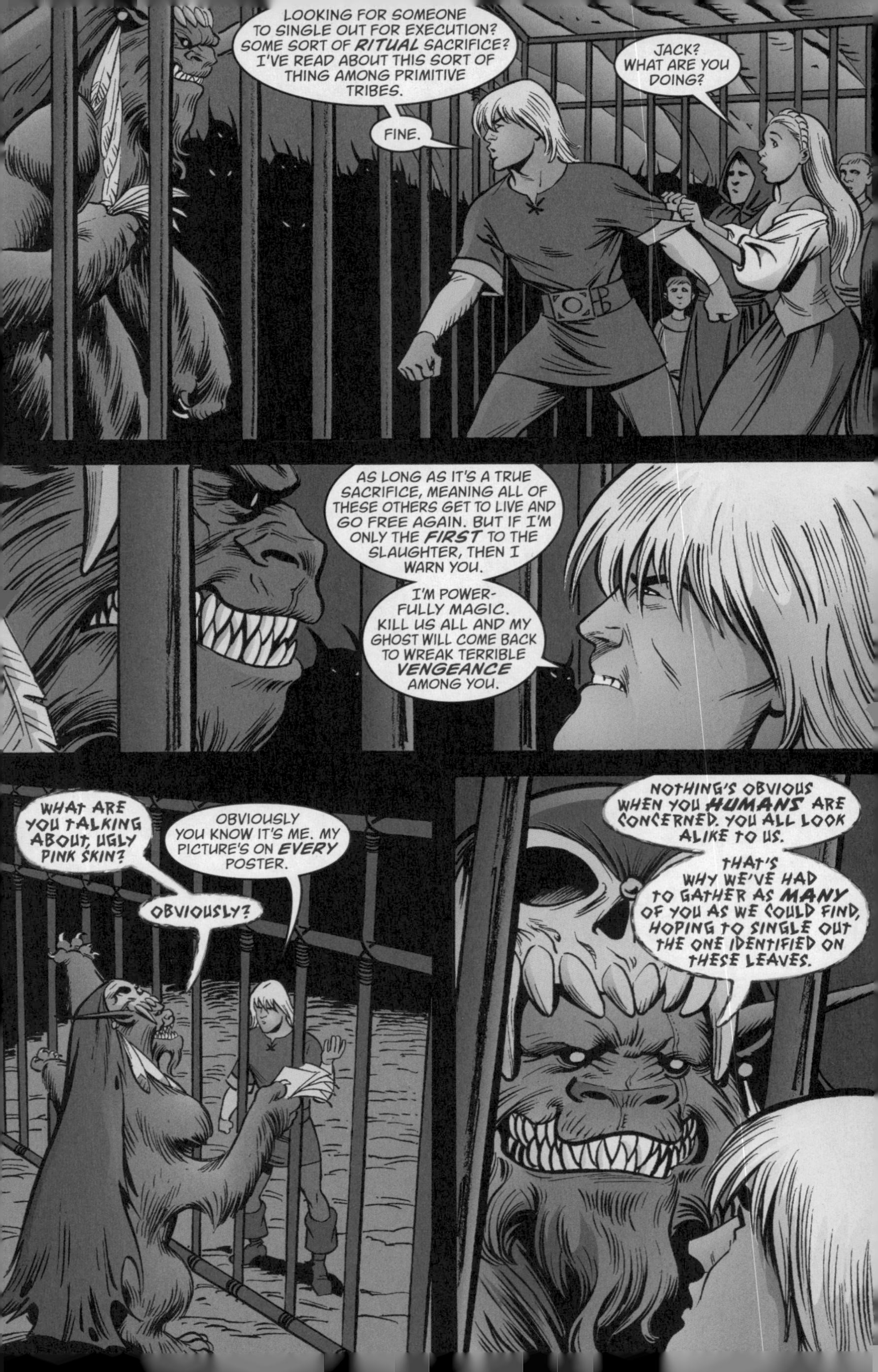
LOOKING FOR SOMEONE TO SINGLE OUT FOR EXECUTION? SOME SORT OF RITUAL SACRIFICE? I'VE READ ABOUT THIS SORT OF THING AMONG PRIMITIVE TRIBES.
JACK? WHAT ARE YOU DOING?
FINE.
AS LONG AS IT'S A TRUE SACRIFICE, MEANING ALL OF THESE OTHERS GET TO LIVE AND GO FREE AGAIN. BUT IF I'M ONLY THE FIRST TO THE SLAUGHTER, THEN I WARN YOU.
I'M POWER-FULLY MAGIC. KILL US ALL AND MY GHOST WILL COME BACK TO WREAK TERRIBLE VENGEANCE AMONG YOU.
WHAT ARE YOU TALKING ABOUT, UGLY PINK SKIN?
OBVIOUSLY YOU KNOW IT'S ME. MY PICTURE'S ON EVERY POSTER.
OBVIOUSLY?
NOTHING'S OBVIOUS WHEN YOU HUMANS ARE CONCERNED. YOU ALL LOOK ALIKE TO US.
THAT'S WHY WE'VE HAD TO GATHER AS MANY OF YOU AS WE COULD FIND, HOPING TO SINGLE OUT THE ONE IDENTIFIED ON THESE LEAVES.

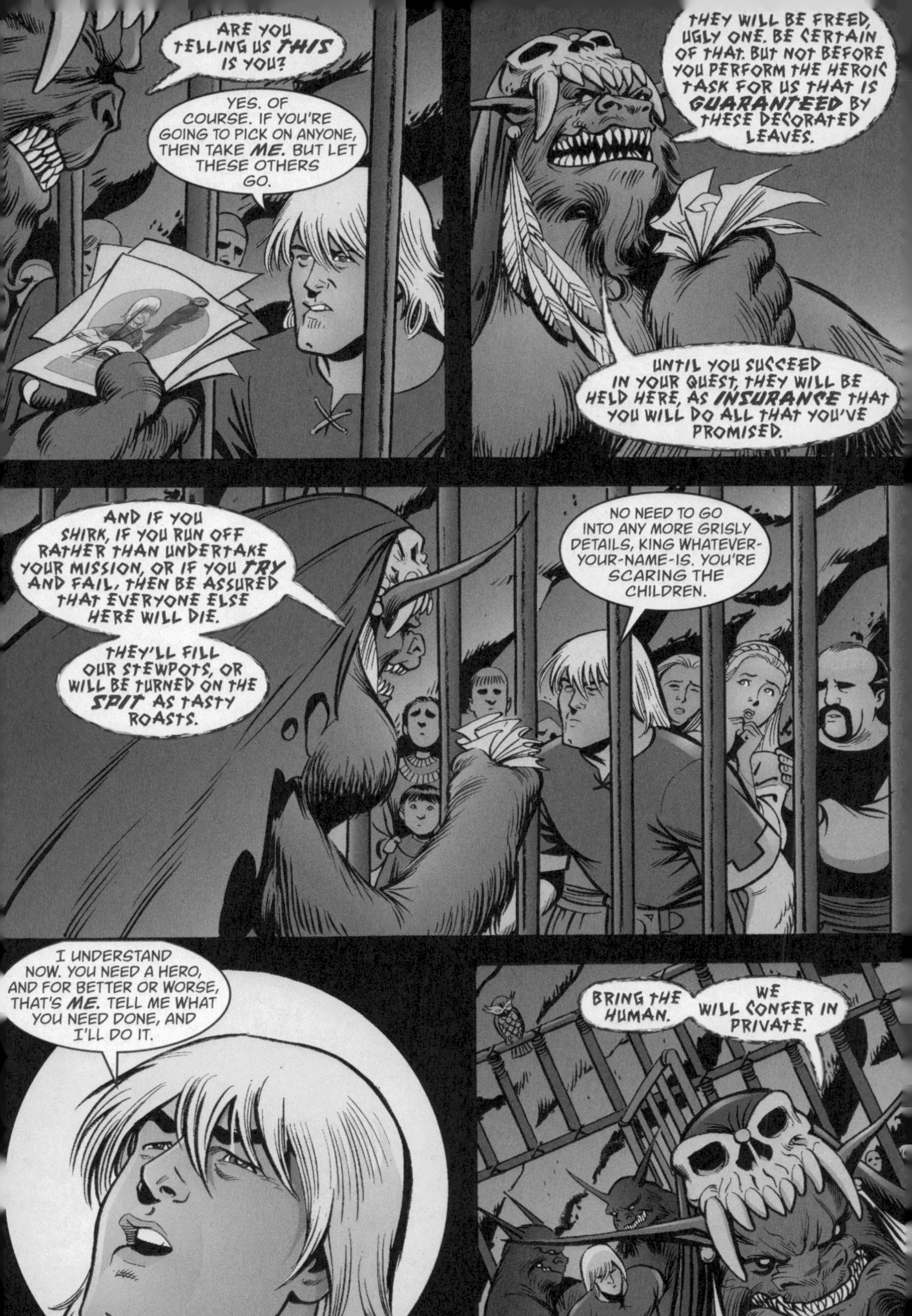
ARE YOU TELLING US THIS IS YOU?
YES. OF COURSE. IF YOU'RE GOING TO PICK ON ANYONE, THEN TAKE ME. BUT LET THESE OTHERS GO.
THEY WILL BE FREED, UGLY ONE. BE CERTAIN OF THAT. BUT NOT BEFORE YOU PERFORM THE HEROIC TASK FOR US THAT IS GUARANTEED BY THESE DECORATED LEAVES.
UNTIL YOU SUCCEED IN YOUR QUEST, THEY WILL BE HELD HERE, AS INSURANCE THAT YOU WILL DO ALL THAT YOU'VE PROMISED.
AND IF YOU SHIRK, IF YOU RUN OFF RATHER THAN UNDERTAKE YOUR MISSION, OR IF YOU TRY AND FAIL, THEN BE ASSURED THAT EVERYONE ELSE HERE WILL DIE.
THEY'LL FILL OUR STEWPOTS, OR WILL BE TURNED ON THE SPIT AS TASTY ROASTS.
NO NEED TO GO INTO ANY MORE GRISLY DETAILS, KING WHATEVER-YOUR-NAME-IS. YOU'RE SCARING THE CHILDREN.
I UNDERSTAND NOW. YOU NEED A HERO, AND FOR BETTER OR WORSE, THAT'S ME. TELL ME WHAT YOU NEED DONE, AND I'LL DO IT.
BRING THE HUMAN.
WE WILL CONFER IN PRIVATE.

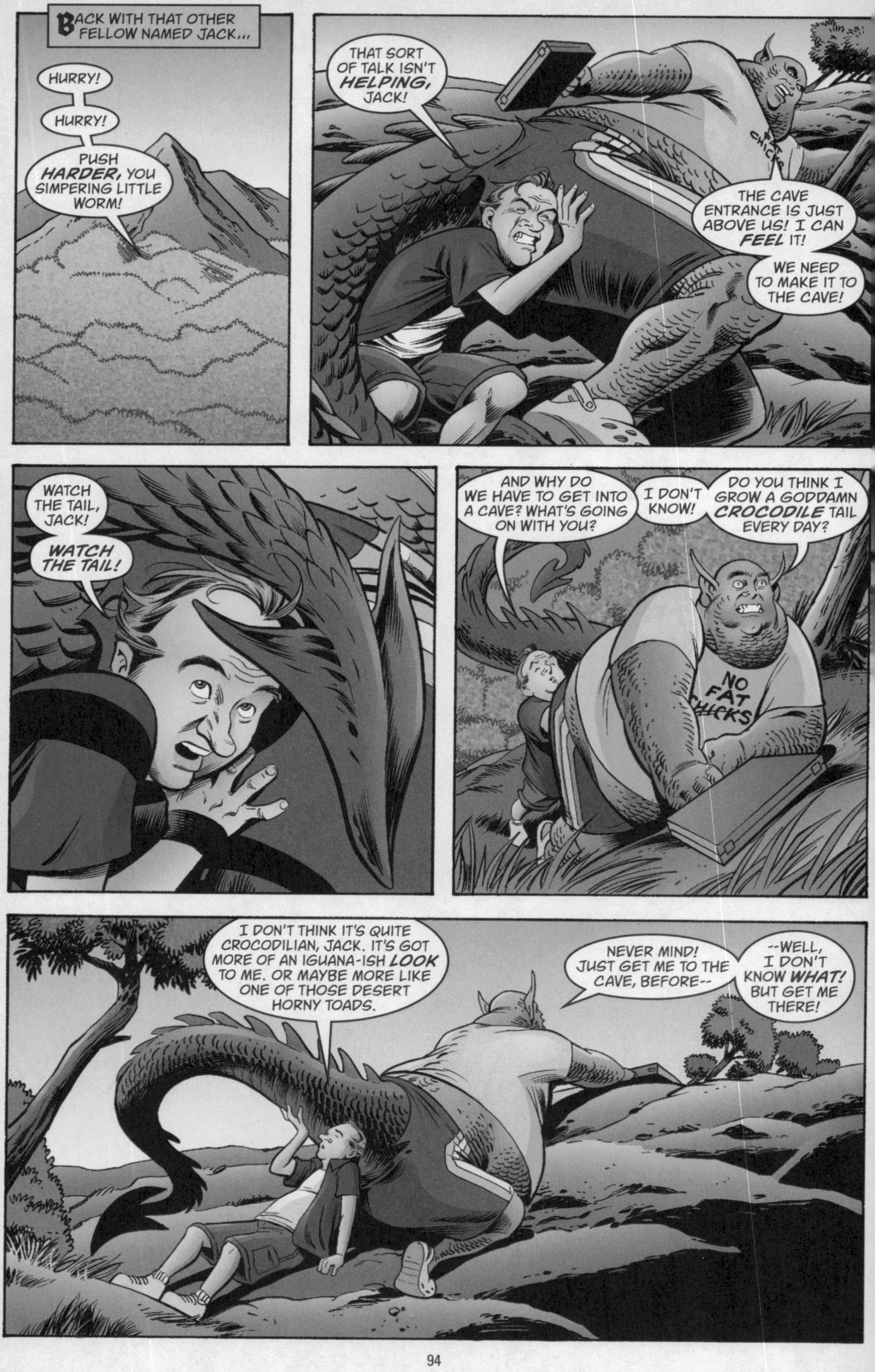
BACK WITH THAT OTHER FELLOW NAMED JACK...
HURRY!
HURRY!
PUSH HARDER, YOU SIMPERING LITTLE WORM!
THAT SORT OF TALK ISN'T HELPING, JACK!
THE CAVE ENTRANCE IS JUST ABOVE US! I CAN FEEL IT!
WE NEED TO MAKE IT TO THE CAVE!
WATCH THE TAIL, JACK!
WATCH THE TAIL!
AND WHY DO WE HAVE TO GET INTO A CAVE? WHAT'S GOING ON WITH YOU?
I DON'T KNOW!
DO YOU THINK I GROW A GODDAMN CROCODILE TAIL EVERY DAY?
NO FAT CHICKS
I DON'T THINK IT'S QUITE CROCODILIAN, JACK. IT'S GOT MORE OF AN IGUANA-ISH LOOK TO ME. OR MAYBE MORE LIKE ONE OF THOSE DESERT HORNY TOADS.
NEVER MIND! JUST GET ME TO THE CAVE, BEFORE--
--WELL, I DON'T KNOW WHAT! BUT GET ME THERE!

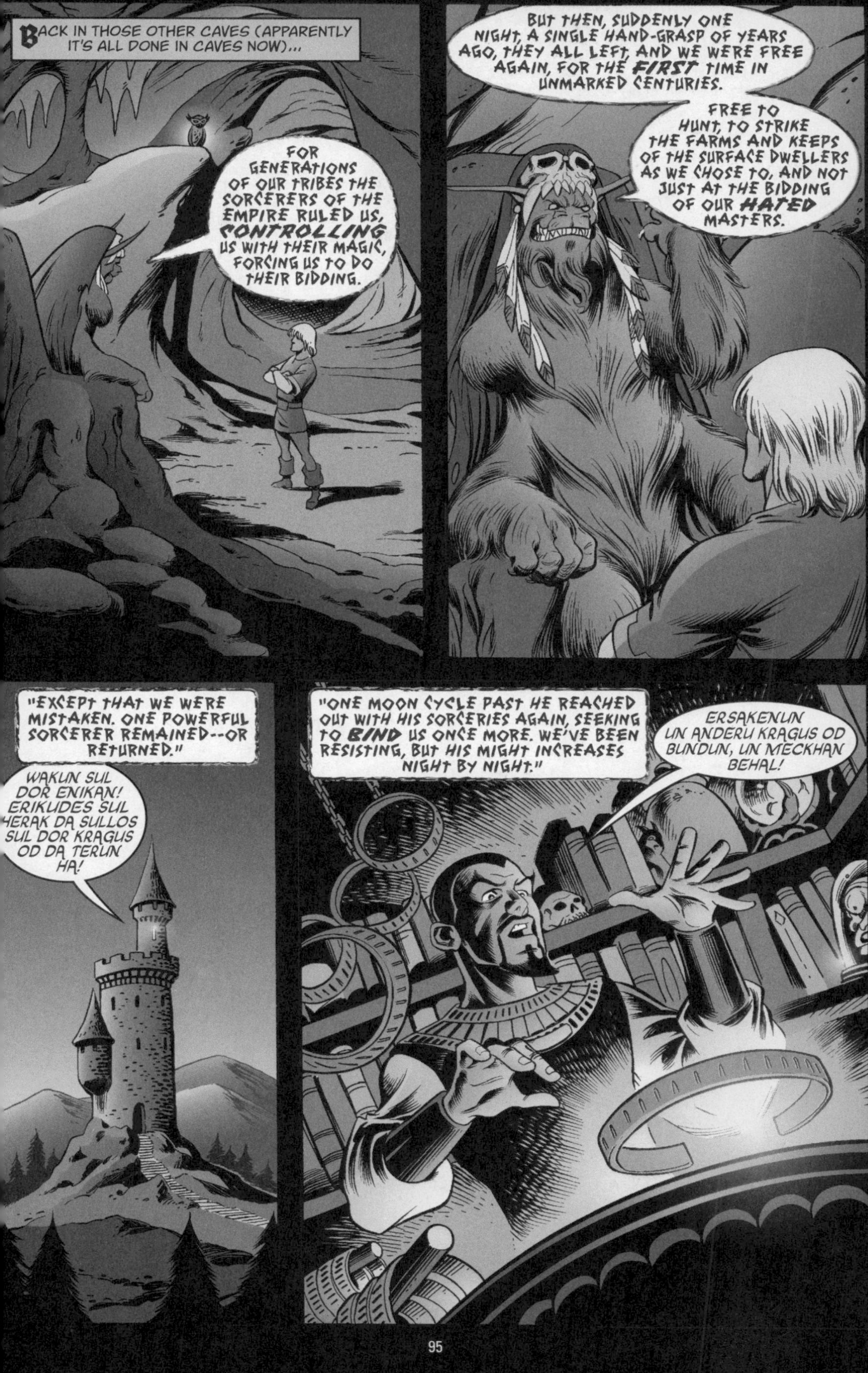

BACK IN THOSE OTHER CAVES (APPARENTLY IT'S ALL DONE IN CAVES NOW)...
FOR GENERATIONS OF OUR TRIBES THE SORCERERS OF THE EMPIRE RULED US, CONTROLLING US WITH THEIR MAGIC, FORCING US TO DO THEIR BIDDING.
BUT THEN, SUDDENLY ONE NIGHT, A SINGLE HAND-GRASP OF YEARS AGO, THEY ALL LEFT, AND WE WERE FREE AGAIN, FOR THE FIRST TIME IN UNMARKED CENTURIES.
FREE TO HUNT, TO STRIKE THE FARMS AND KEEPS OF THE SURFACE DWELLERS AS WE CHOSE TO, AND NOT JUST AT THE BIDDING OF OUR HATED MASTERS.
"EXCEPT THAT WE WERE MISTAKEN. ONE POWERFUL SORCERER REMAINED--OR RETURNED."
WAKUN SUL DOR ENIKAN! ERIKUDES SUL HERAK DA SULLOS SUL DOR KRAGUS OD DA TERUN HA!
"ONE MOON CYCLE PAST HE REACHED OUT WITH HIS SORCERIES AGAIN, SEEKING TO BIND US ONCE MORE. WE'VE BEEN RESISTING, BUT HIS MIGHT INCREASES NIGHT BY NIGHT."
ERSAKENUN UN ANDERU KRAGUS OD BUNDUN, UN MECKHAN BEHAL!

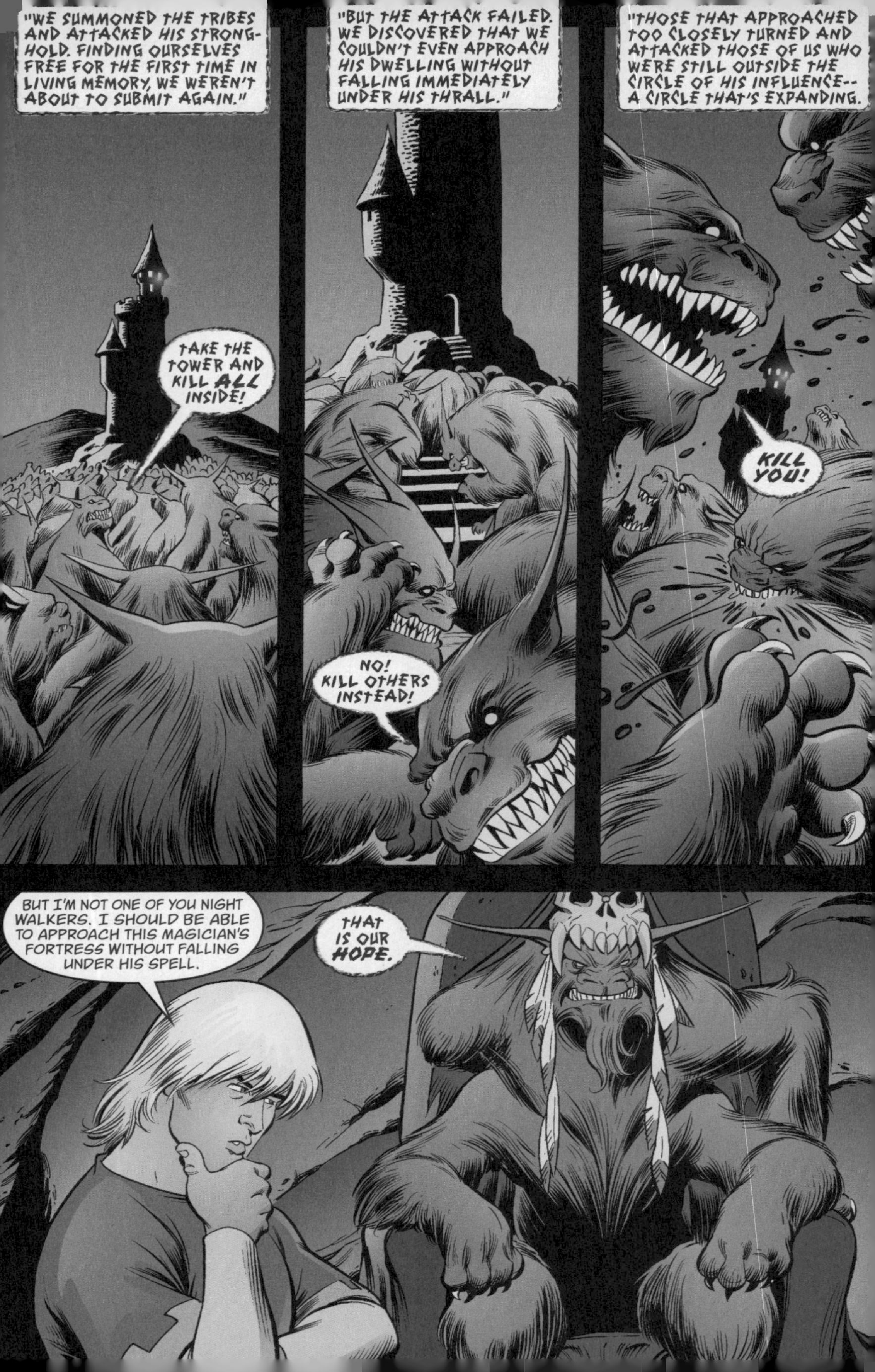
"WE SUMMONED THE TRIBES AND ATTACKED HIS STRONG-HOLD. FINDING OURSELVES FREE FOR THE FIRST TIME IN LIVING MEMORY, WE WEREN'T ABOUT TO SUBMIT AGAIN."
TAKE THE TOWER AND KILL ALL INSIDE!
"BUT THE ATTACK FAILED. WE DISCOVERED THAT WE COULDN'T EVEN APPROACH HIS DWELLING WITHOUT FALLING IMMEDIATELY UNDER HIS THRALL."
NO! KILL OTHERS INSTEAD!
"THOSE THAT APPROACHED TOO CLOSELY TURNED AND ATTACKED THOSE OF US WHO WERE STILL OUTSIDE THE CIRCLE OF HIS INFLUENCE-- A CIRCLE THAT'S EXPANDING."
KILL YOU!
BUT I'M NOT ONE OF YOU NIGHT WALKERS. I SHOULD BE ABLE TO APPROACH THIS MAGICIAN'S FORTRESS WITHOUT FALLING UNDER HIS SPELL.
THAT IS OUR HOPE.

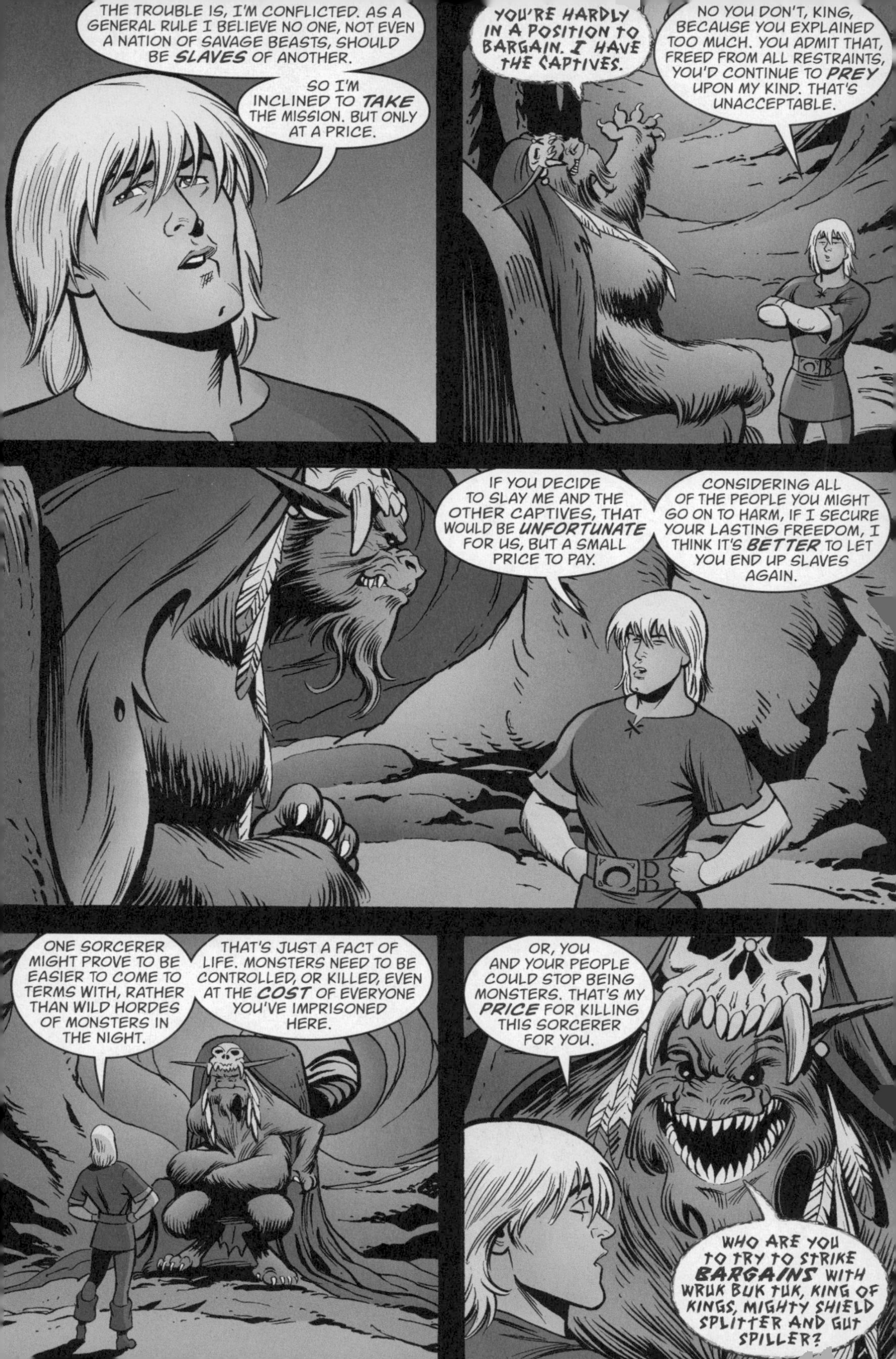
THE TROUBLE IS, I'M CONFLICTED. AS A GENERAL RULE I BELIEVE NO ONE, NOT EVEN A NATION OF SAVAGE BEASTS, SHOULD BE SLAVES OF ANOTHER.
SO I'M INCLINED TO TAKE THE MISSION. BUT ONLY AT A PRICE.
YOU'RE HARDLY IN A POSITION TO BARGAIN. I HAVE THE CAPTIVES.
NO YOU DON'T, KING, BECAUSE YOU EXPLAINED TOO MUCH. YOU ADMIT THAT, FREED FROM ALL RESTRAINTS, YOU'D CONTINUE TO PREY UPON MY KIND. THAT'S UNACCEPTABLE.
IF YOU DECIDE TO SLAY ME AND THE OTHER CAPTIVES, THAT WOULD BE UNFORTUNATE FOR US, BUT A SMALL PRICE TO PAY.
CONSIDERING ALL OF THE PEOPLE YOU MIGHT GO ON TO HARM, IF I SECURE YOUR LASTING FREEDOM, I THINK IT'S BETTER TO LET YOU END UP SLAVES AGAIN.
ONE SORCERER MIGHT PROVE TO BE EASIER TO COME TO TERMS WITH, RATHER THAN WILD HORDES OF MONSTERS IN THE NIGHT.
THAT'S JUST A FACT OF LIFE. MONSTERS NEED TO BE CONTROLLED, OR KILLED, EVEN AT THE COST OF EVERYONE YOU'VE IMPRISONED HERE.
OR, YOU AND YOUR PEOPLE COULD STOP BEING MONSTERS. THAT'S MY PRICE FOR KILLING THIS SORCERER FOR YOU.
WHO ARE YOU TO TRY TO STRIKE BARGAINS WITH WRUK BUK TUK, KING OF KINGS, MIGHTY SHIELD SPLITTER AND GUT SPILLER?

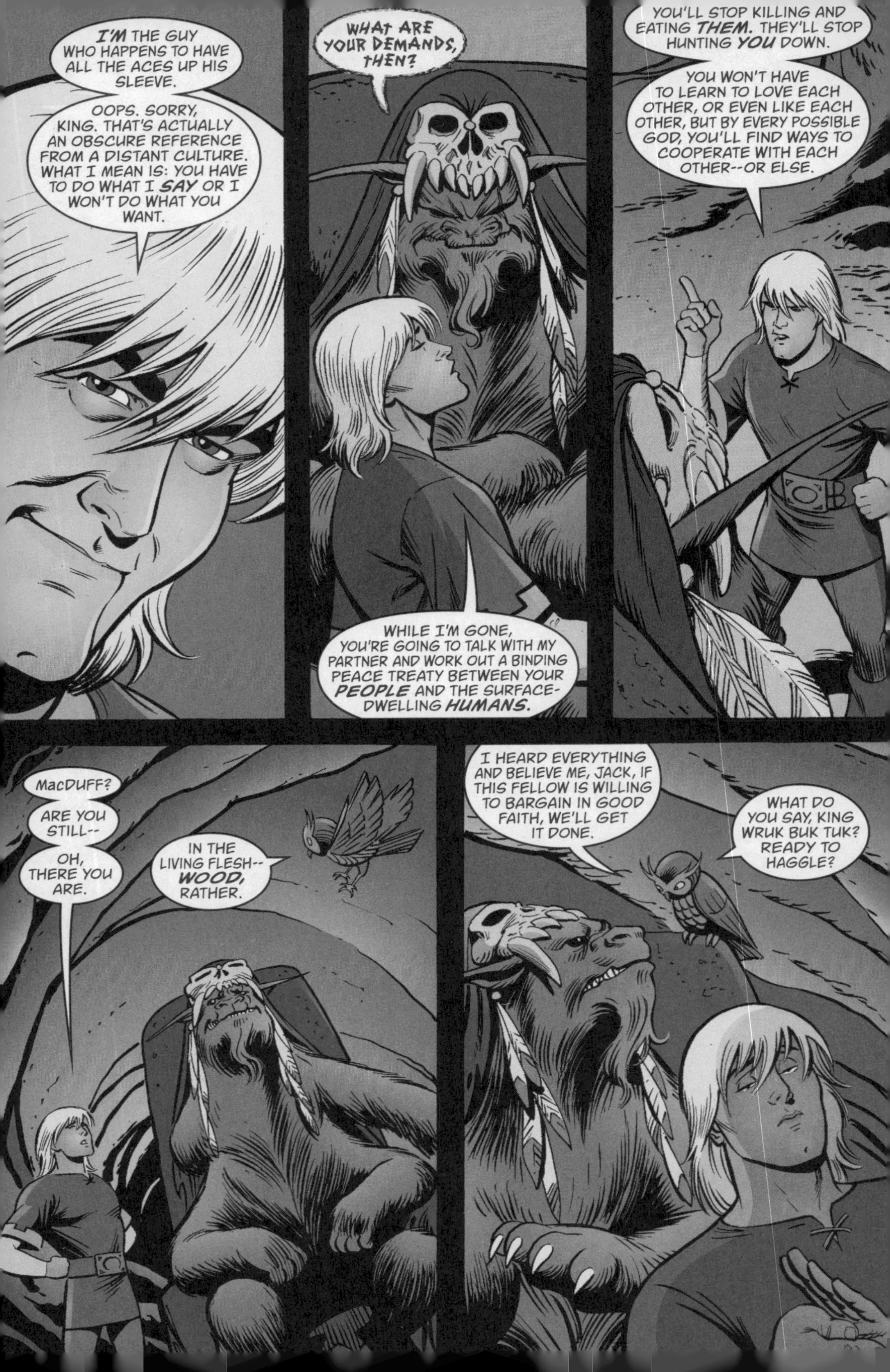

I'M THE GUY WHO HAPPENS TO HAVE ALL THE ACES UP HIS SLEEVE.
OOPS. SORRY, KING. THAT'S ACTUALLY AN OBSCURE REFERENCE FROM A DISTANT CULTURE. WHAT I MEAN IS: YOU HAVE TO DO WHAT I SAY OR I WON'T DO WHAT YOU WANT.
WHAT ARE YOUR DEMANDS, THEN?
WHILE I'M GONE, YOU'RE GOING TO TALK WITH MY PARTNER AND WORK OUT A BINDING PEACE TREATY BETWEEN YOUR PEOPLE AND THE SURFACE-DWELLING HUMANS.
YOU'LL STOP KILLING AND EATING THEM. THEY'LL STOP HUNTING YOU DOWN.
YOU WON'T HAVE TO LEARN TO LOVE EACH OTHER, OR EVEN LIKE EACH OTHER, BUT BY EVERY POSSIBLE GOD, YOU'LL FIND WAYS TO COOPERATE WITH EACH OTHER--OR ELSE.
MacDUFF?
ARE YOU STILL--
OH, THERE YOU ARE.
IN THE LIVING FLESH--WOOD, RATHER.
I HEARD EVERYTHING AND BELIEVE ME, JACK, IF THIS FELLOW IS WILLING TO BARGAIN IN GOOD FAITH, WE'LL GET IT DONE.
WHAT DO YOU SAY, KING WRUK BUK TUK? READY TO HAGGLE?

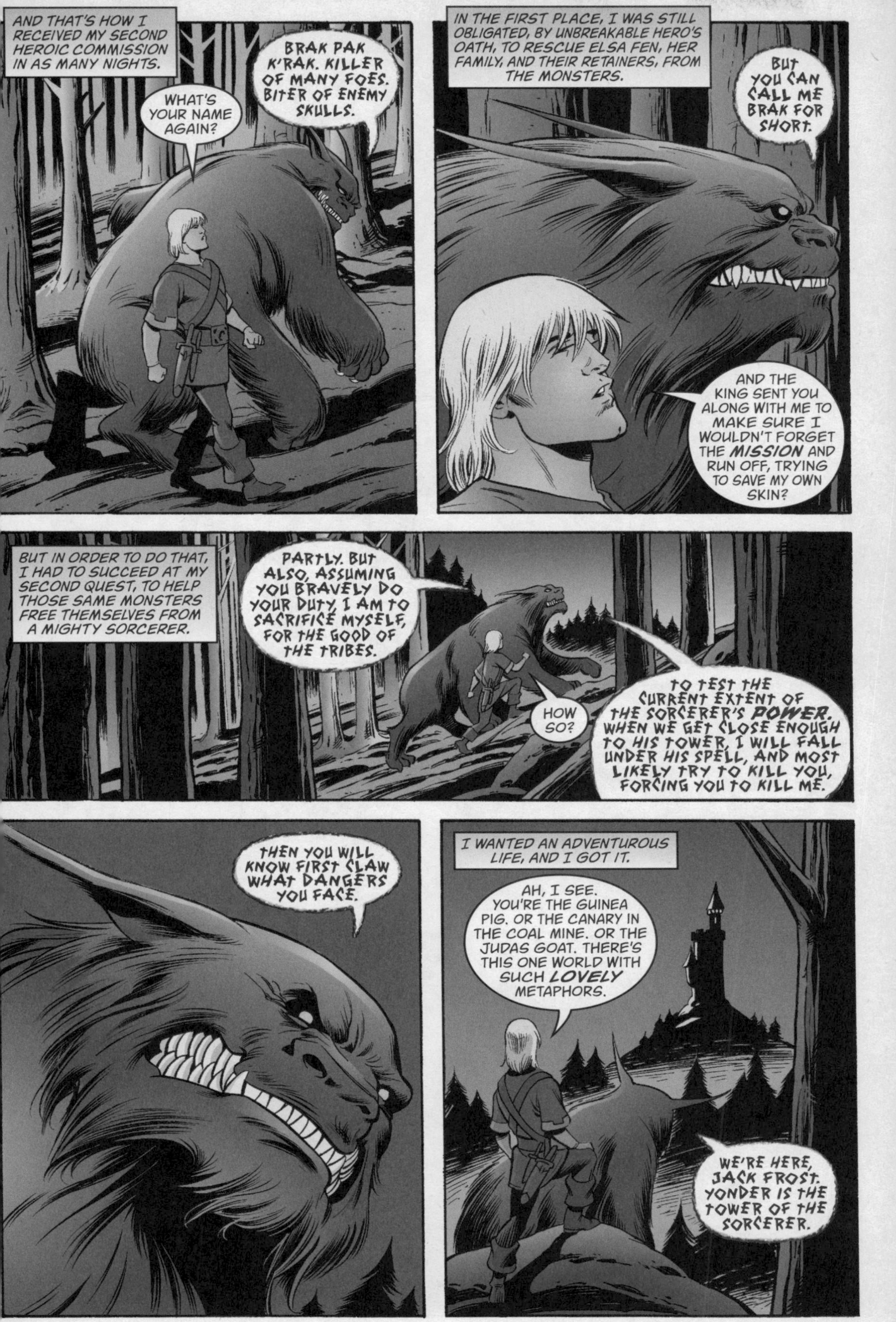

AND THAT'S HOW I RECEIVED MY SECOND HEROIC COMMISSION IN AS MANY NIGHTS.
WHAT'S YOUR NAME AGAIN?
BRAK PAK K'RAK. KILLER OF MANY FOES. BITER OF ENEMY SKULLS.
IN THE FIRST PLACE, I WAS STILL OBLIGATED, BY UNBREAKABLE HERO'S OATH, TO RESCUE ELSA FEN, HER FAMILY, AND THEIR RETAINERS, FROM THE MONSTERS.
BUT YOU CAN CALL ME BRAK FOR SHORT.
AND THE KING SENT YOU ALONG WITH ME TO MAKE SURE I WOULDN'T FORGET THE **MISSION** AND RUN OFF, TRYING TO SAVE MY OWN SKIN?
BUT IN ORDER TO DO THAT, I HAD TO SUCCEED AT MY SECOND QUEST, TO HELP THOSE SAME MONSTERS FREE THEMSELVES FROM A MIGHTY SORCERER.
PARTLY. BUT ALSO, ASSUMING YOU BRAVELY DO YOUR DUTY, I AM TO SACRIFICE MYSELF, FOR THE GOOD OF THE TRIBES.
HOW SO?
TO TEST THE CURRENT EXTENT OF THE SORCERER'S **POWER.** WHEN WE GET CLOSE ENOUGH TO HIS TOWER, I WILL FALL UNDER HIS SPELL, AND MOST LIKELY TRY TO KILL YOU, FORCING YOU TO KILL ME.
THEN YOU WILL KNOW FIRST CLAW WHAT DANGERS YOU FACE.
I WANTED AN ADVENTUROUS LIFE, AND I GOT IT.
AH, I SEE. YOU'RE THE GUINEA PIG. OR THE CANARY IN THE COAL MINE. OR THE JUDAS GOAT. THERE'S THIS ONE WORLD WITH SUCH **LOVELY** METAPHORS.
WE'RE HERE, JACK FROST. YONDER IS THE TOWER OF THE SORCERER.

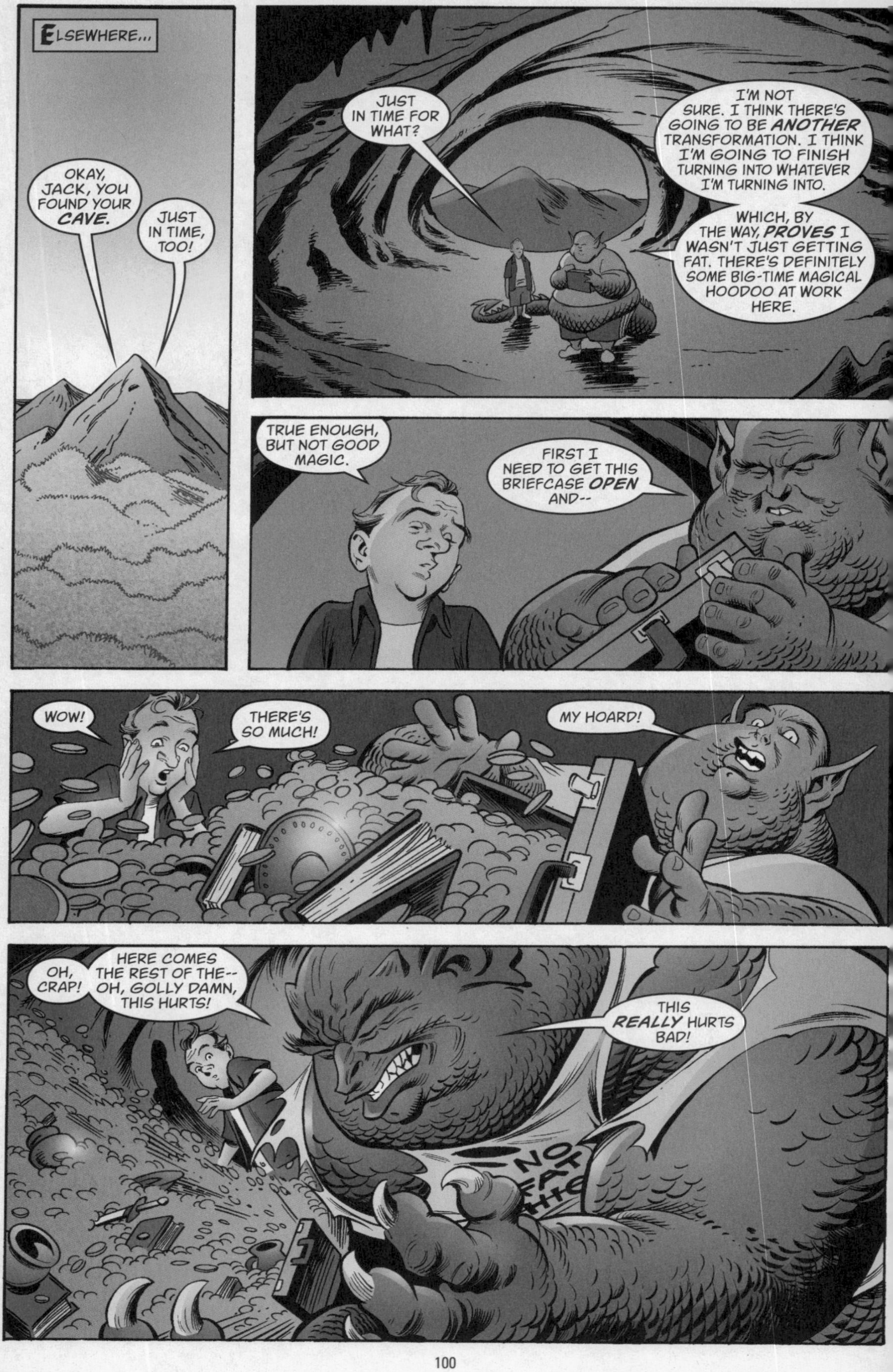
ELSEWHERE...
OKAY, JACK, YOU FOUND YOUR CAVE.
JUST IN TIME, TOO!
JUST IN TIME FOR WHAT?
I'M NOT SURE. I THINK THERE'S GOING TO BE ANOTHER TRANSFORMATION. I THINK I'M GOING TO FINISH TURNING INTO WHATEVER I'M TURNING INTO.
WHICH, BY THE WAY, PROVES I WASN'T JUST GETTING FAT. THERE'S DEFINITELY SOME BIG-TIME MAGICAL HOODOO AT WORK HERE.
TRUE ENOUGH, BUT NOT GOOD MAGIC.
FIRST I NEED TO GET THIS BRIEFCASE OPEN AND--
WOW!
THERE'S SO MUCH!
MY HOARD!
OH, CRAP!
HERE COMES THE REST OF THE-- OH, GOLLY DAMN, THIS HURTS!
THIS REALLY HURTS BAD!

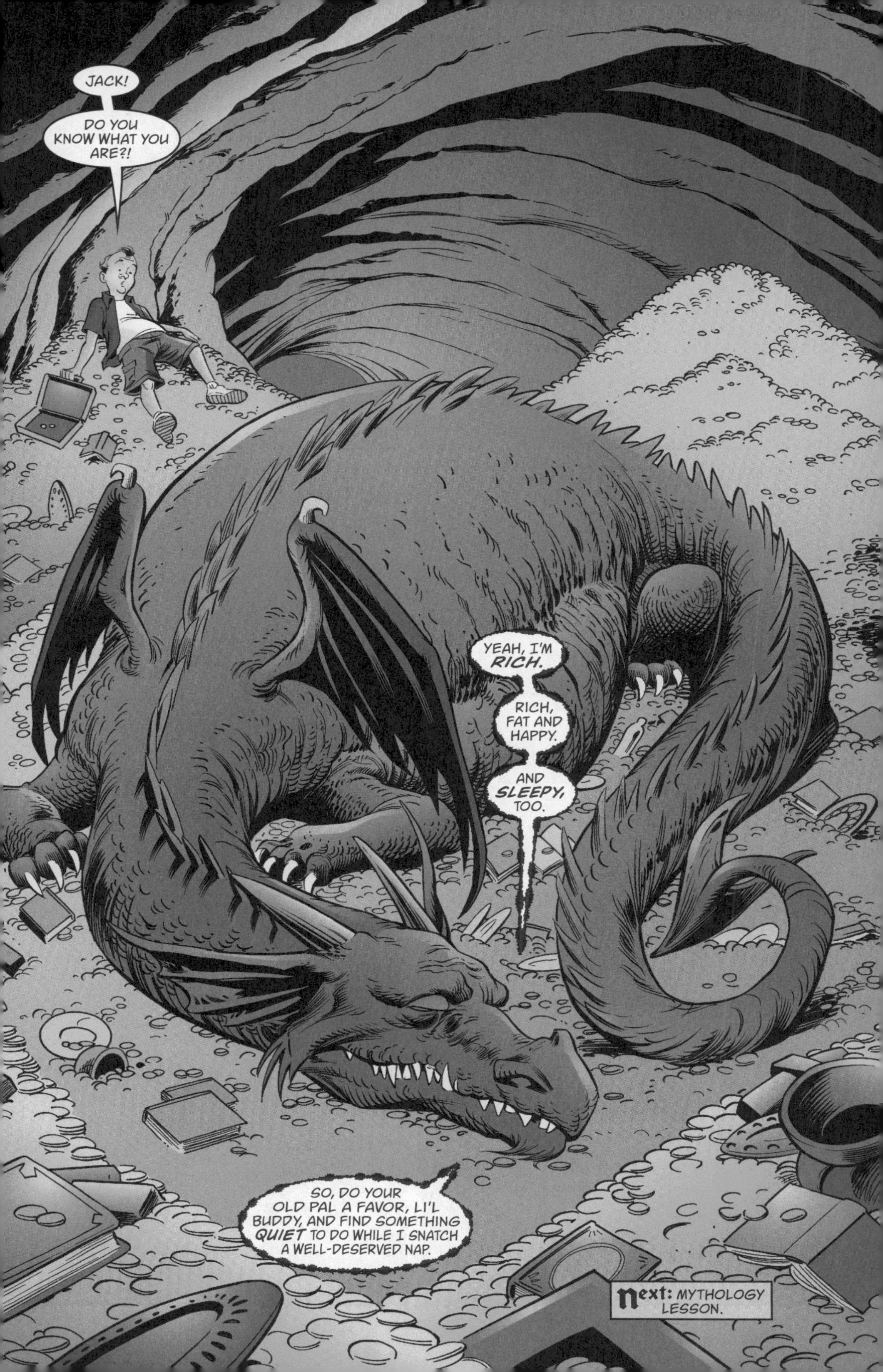
JACK!
DO YOU KNOW WHAT YOU ARE?!
YEAH, I'M RICH.
RICH, FAT AND HAPPY.
AND SLEEPY, TOO.
SO, DO YOUR OLD PAL A FAVOR, LI'L BUDDY, AND FIND SOMETHING QUIET TO DO WHILE I SNATCH A WELL-DESERVED NAP.
next: MYTHOLOGY LESSON.

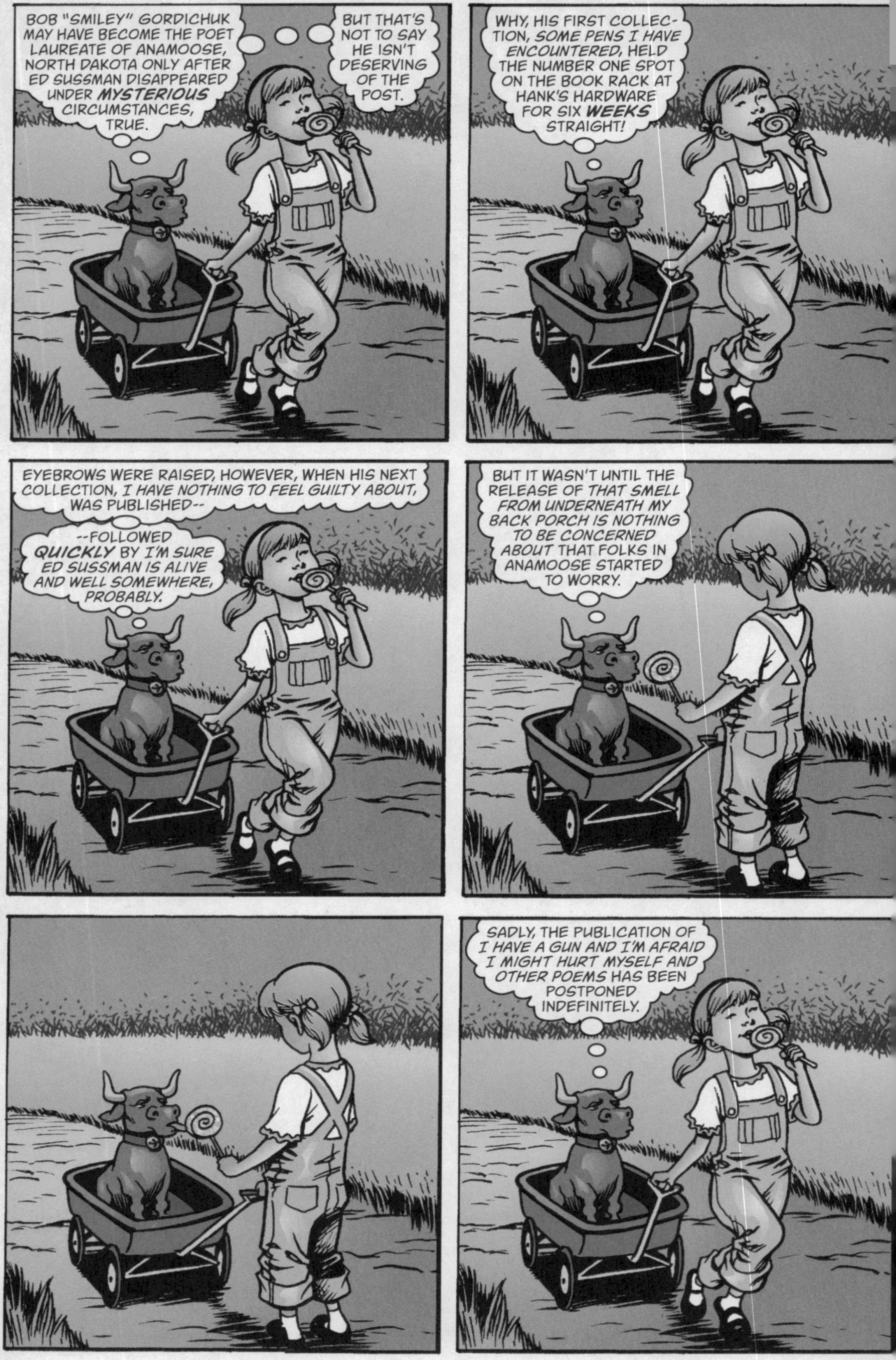
BOB "SMILEY" GORDICHUK MAY HAVE BECOME THE POET LAUREATE OF ANAMOOSE, NORTH DAKOTA ONLY AFTER ED SUSSMAN DISAPPEARED UNDER *MYSTERIOUS* CIRCUMSTANCES, TRUE.
BUT THAT'S NOT TO SAY HE ISN'T DESERVING OF THE POST.
WHY, HIS FIRST COLLECTION, *SOME PENS I HAVE ENCOUNTERED*, HELD THE NUMBER ONE SPOT ON THE BOOK RACK AT HANK'S HARDWARE FOR SIX *WEEKS* STRAIGHT!
EYEBROWS WERE RAISED, HOWEVER, WHEN HIS NEXT COLLECTION, *I HAVE NOTHING TO FEEL GUILTY ABOUT*, WAS PUBLISHED--
--FOLLOWED *QUICKLY* BY *I'M SURE ED SUSSMAN IS ALIVE AND WELL SOMEWHERE, PROBABLY.*
BUT IT WASN'T UNTIL THE RELEASE OF *THAT SMELL FROM UNDERNEATH MY BACK PORCH IS NOTHING TO BE CONCERNED ABOUT* THAT FOLKS IN ANAMOOSE STARTED TO WORRY.
SADLY, THE PUBLICATION OF *I HAVE A GUN AND I'M AFRAID I MIGHT HURT MYSELF AND OTHER POEMS* HAS BEEN POSTPONED INDEFINITELY.

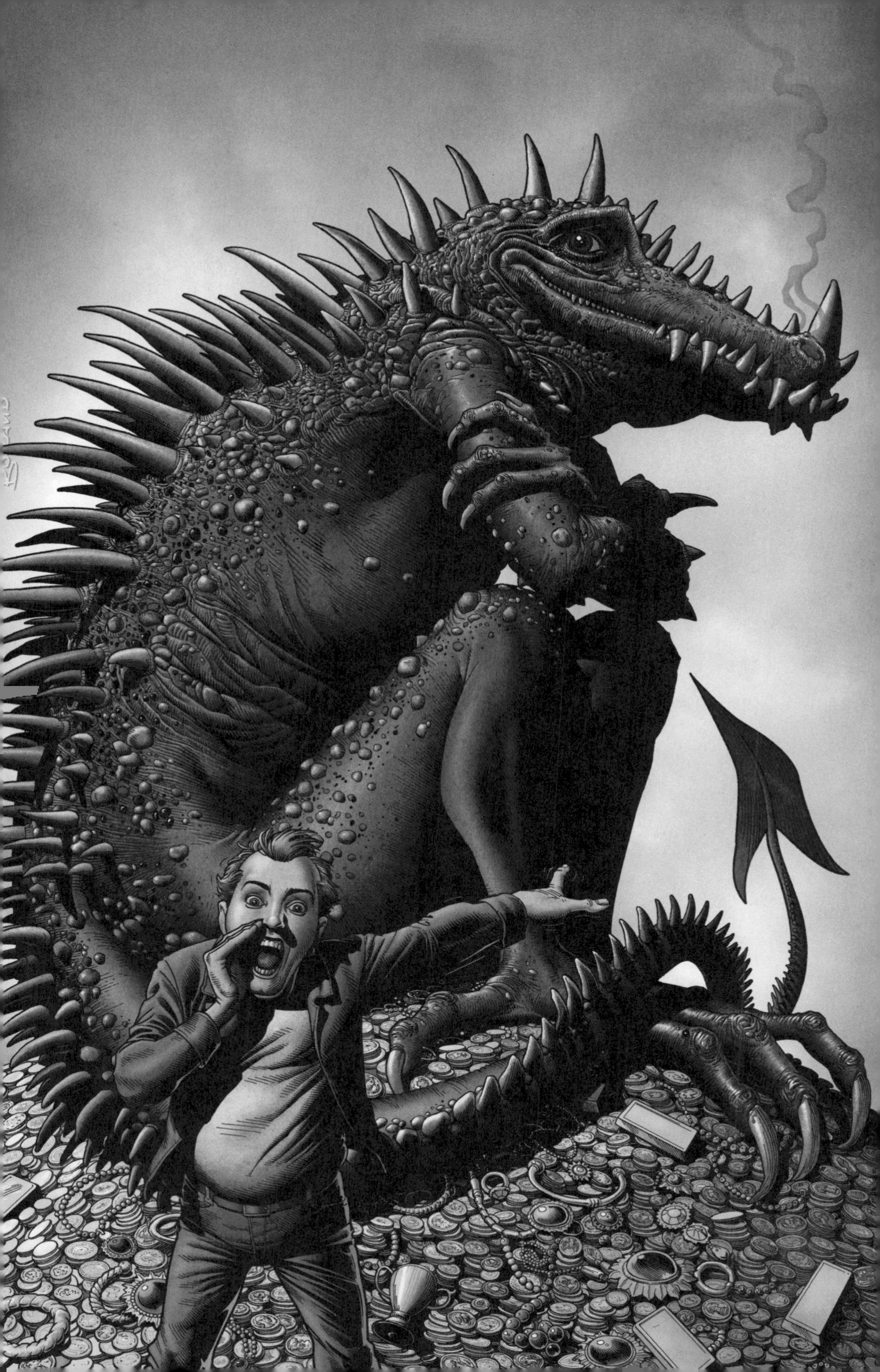

"YOU, SIR, ARE **CLEARLY** A DICK."

YOO HOO!
OVER HERE!
RIGHT ON TIME, MR. DRIVER MAN.
IS SHE GENTLE?
AS A LADYBUG. GOT MY CASH?
EVERY DING DANG DOLLAR, SIR! DID YOU REMEMBER THE *REST* OF MY DELIVERY?
OH YEAH, IN THE CAB. ONE SUPER-SIZED SNAPPY MEAL, DELUXE FEAST O' FISH SANDWICH, WITH DOUBLE FRIES.

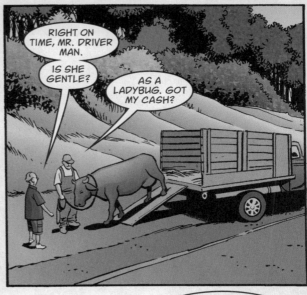

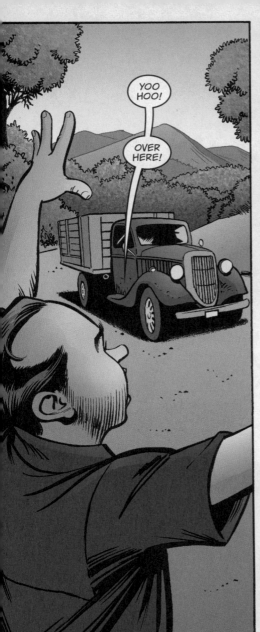

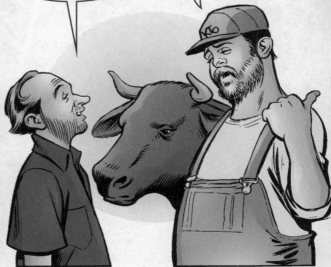

Jack Dragon

THE NEW ADVENTURES OF JACK AND JACK Part 4 of 4

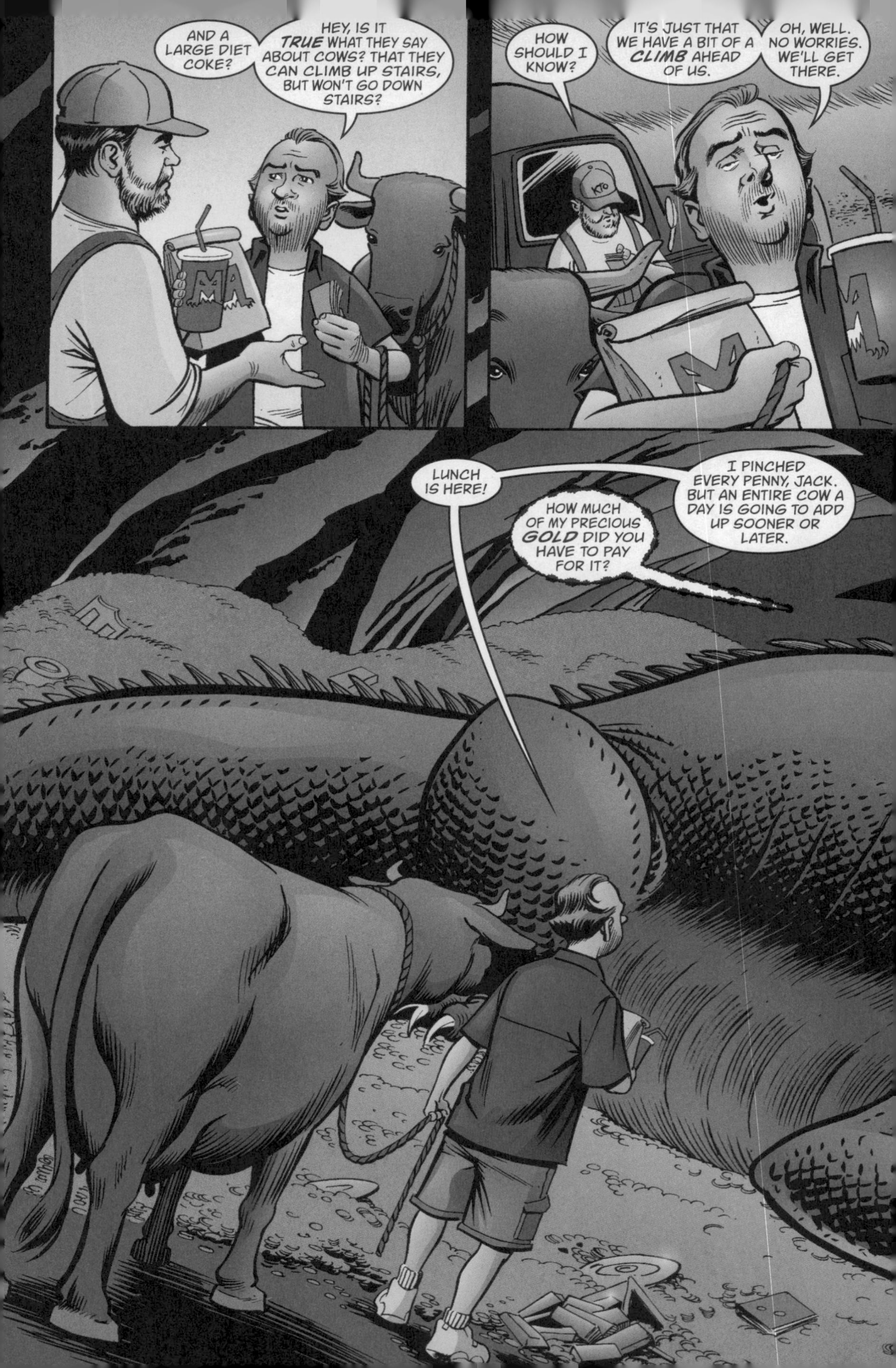
AND A LARGE DIET COKE?
HEY, IS IT TRUE WHAT THEY SAY ABOUT COWS? THAT THEY CAN CLIMB UP STAIRS, BUT WON'T GO DOWN STAIRS?
HOW SHOULD I KNOW?
IT'S JUST THAT WE HAVE A BIT OF A CLIMB AHEAD OF US.
OH, WELL. NO WORRIES. WE'LL GET THERE.
LUNCH IS HERE!
HOW MUCH OF MY PRECIOUS GOLD DID YOU HAVE TO PAY FOR IT?
I PINCHED EVERY PENNY, JACK. BUT AN ENTIRE COW A DAY IS GOING TO ADD UP SOONER OR LATER.

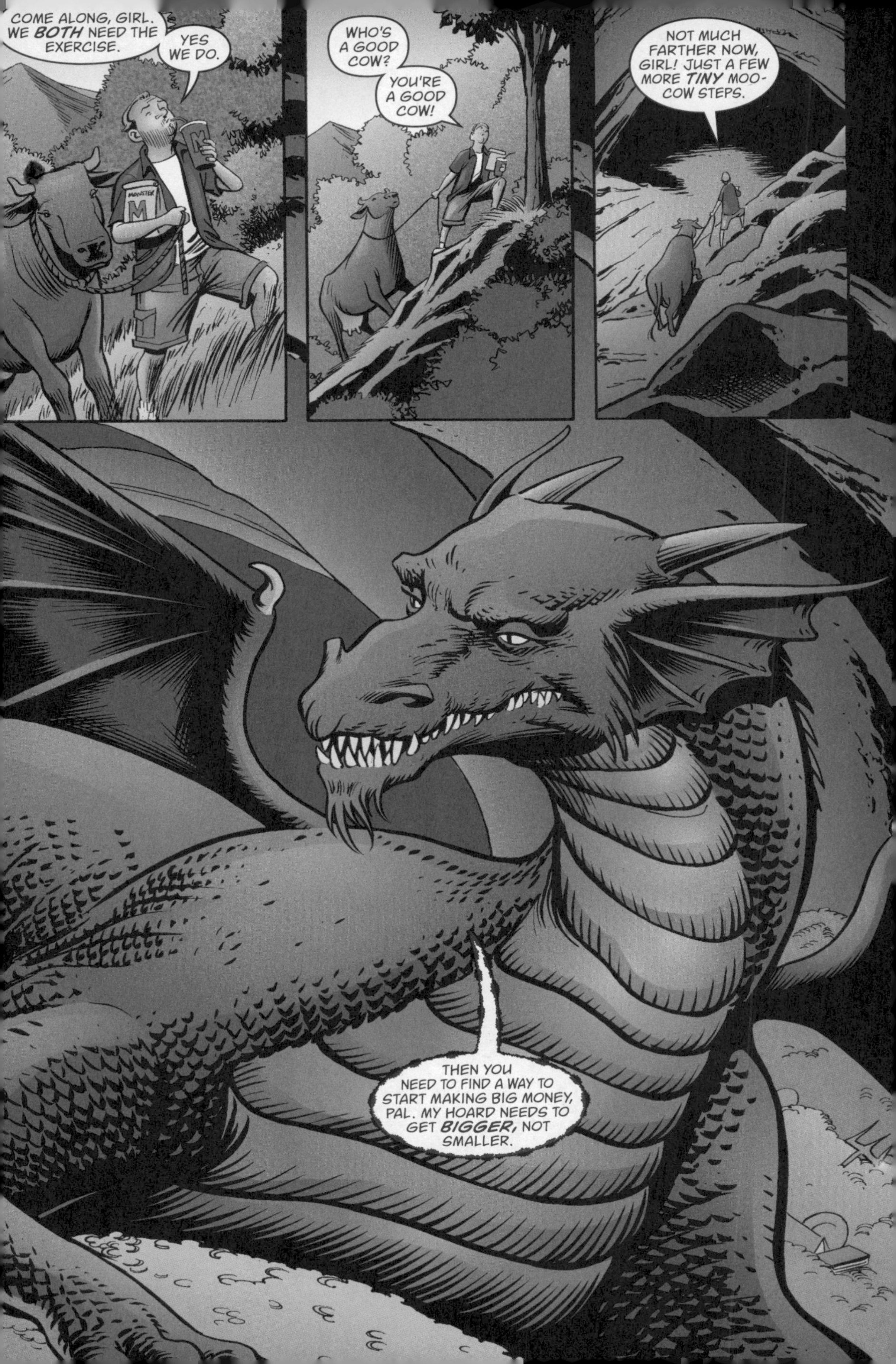

COME ALONG, GIRL. WE BOTH NEED THE EXERCISE.
YES WE DO.
WHO'S A GOOD COW?
YOU'RE A GOOD COW!
NOT MUCH FARTHER NOW, GIRL! JUST A FEW MORE TINY MOO-COW STEPS.
THEN YOU NEED TO FIND A WAY TO START MAKING BIG MONEY, PAL. MY HOARD NEEDS TO GET BIGGER, NOT SMALLER.

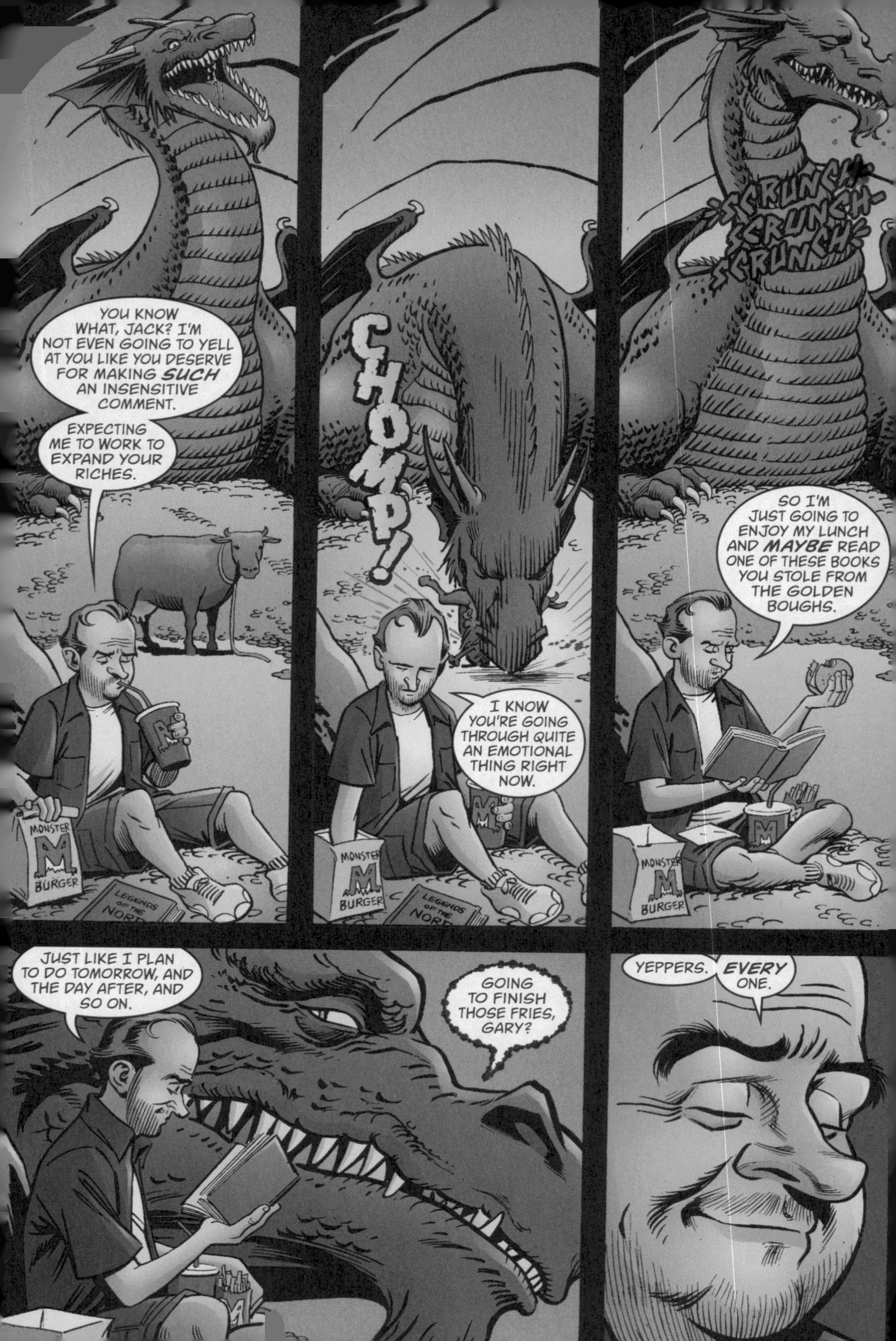
YOU KNOW WHAT, JACK? I'M NOT EVEN GOING TO YELL AT YOU LIKE YOU DESERVE FOR MAKING SUCH AN INSENSITIVE COMMENT.
EXPECTING ME TO WORK TO EXPAND YOUR RICHES.
MONSTER M BURGER
LEGENDS OF THE NORD
CHOMP!
I KNOW YOU'RE GOING THROUGH QUITE AN EMOTIONAL THING RIGHT NOW.
MONSTER M BURGER
LEGENDS OF THE NORD
SCRUNCH-SCRUNCH-SCRUNCH
SO I'M JUST GOING TO ENJOY MY LUNCH AND MAYBE READ ONE OF THESE BOOKS YOU STOLE FROM THE GOLDEN BOUGHS.
MONSTER M BURGER
JUST LIKE I PLAN TO DO TOMORROW, AND THE DAY AFTER, AND SO ON.
GOING TO FINISH THOSE FRIES, GARY?
YEPPERS.
EVERY ONE.

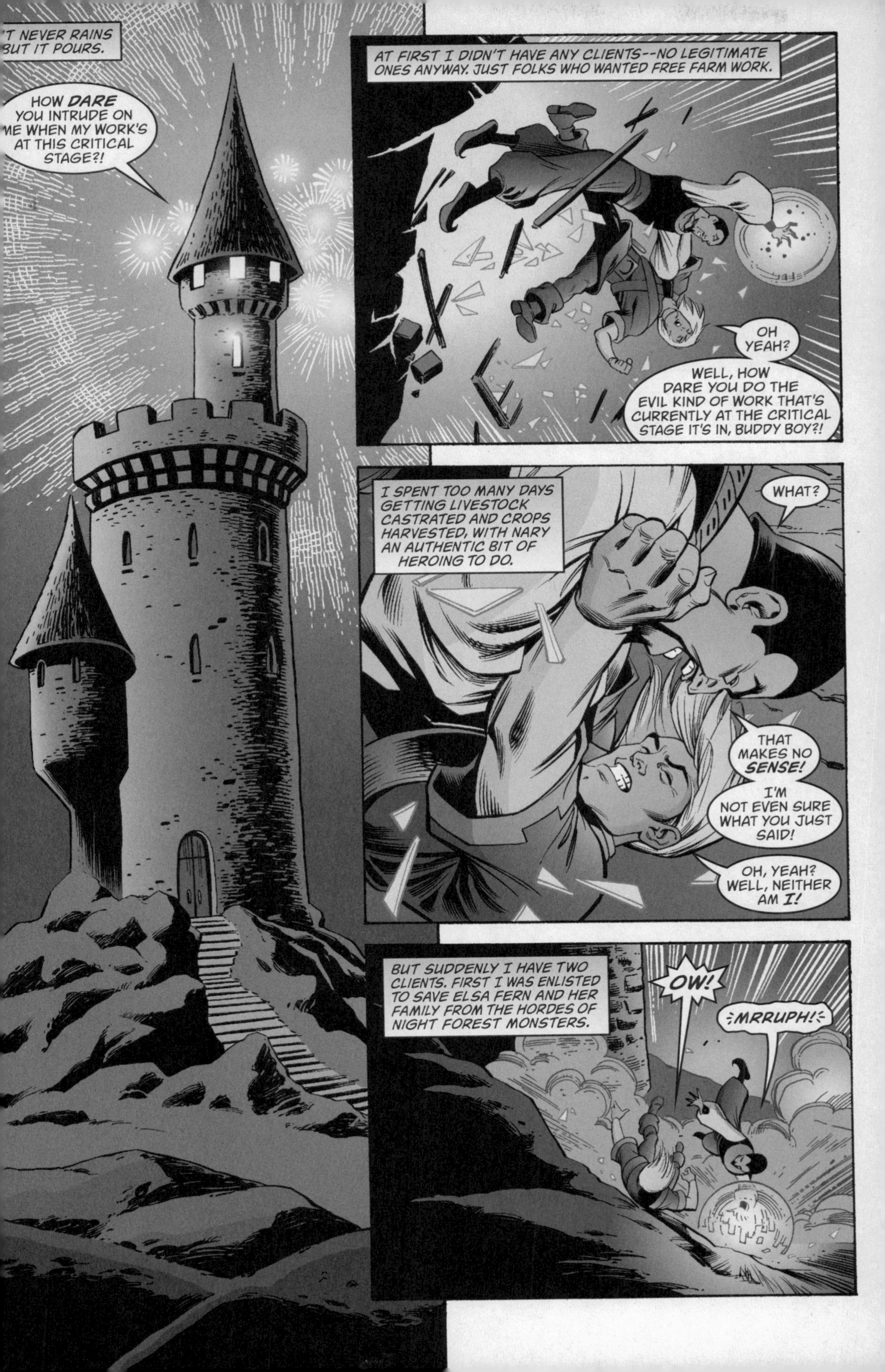

'T NEVER RAINS BUT IT POURS.
HOW DARE YOU INTRUDE ON ME WHEN MY WORK'S AT THIS CRITICAL STAGE?!
AT FIRST I DIDN'T HAVE ANY CLIENTS--NO LEGITIMATE ONES ANYWAY. JUST FOLKS WHO WANTED FREE FARM WORK.
OH YEAH?
WELL, HOW DARE YOU DO THE EVIL KIND OF WORK THAT'S CURRENTLY AT THE CRITICAL STAGE IT'S IN, BUDDY BOY?!
I SPENT TOO MANY DAYS GETTING LIVESTOCK CASTRATED AND CROPS HARVESTED, WITH NARY AN AUTHENTIC BIT OF HEROING TO DO.
WHAT?
THAT MAKES NO SENSE!
I'M NOT EVEN SURE WHAT YOU JUST SAID!
OH, YEAH? WELL, NEITHER AM I!
BUT SUDDENLY I HAVE TWO CLIENTS. FIRST I WAS ENLISTED TO SAVE ELSA FERN AND HER FAMILY FROM THE HORDES OF NIGHT FOREST MONSTERS.
OW!
MRRUPH!

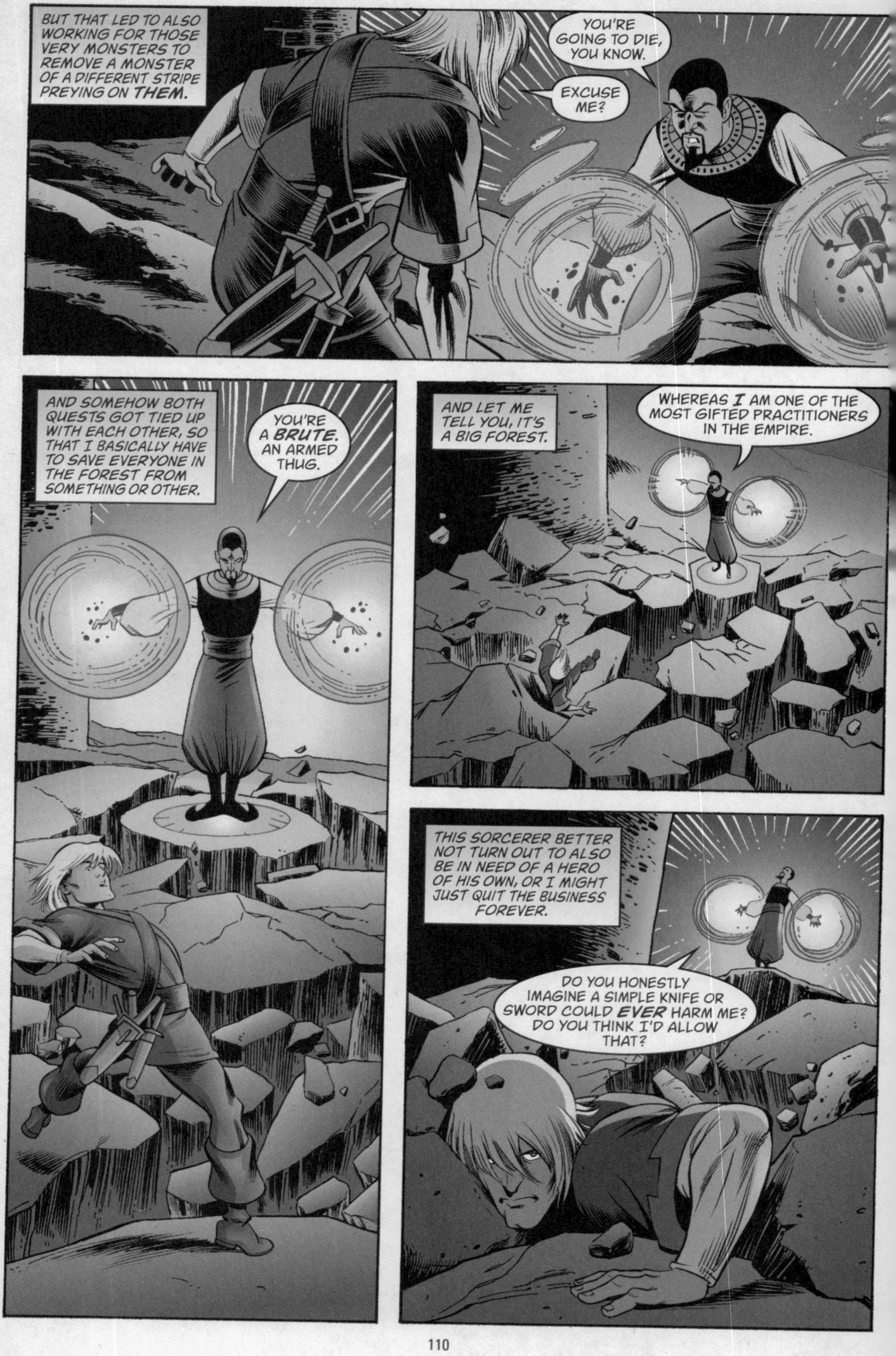

BUT THAT LED TO ALSO WORKING FOR THOSE VERY MONSTERS TO REMOVE A MONSTER OF A DIFFERENT STRIPE PREYING ON THEM.
YOU'RE GOING TO DIE, YOU KNOW.
EXCUSE ME?
AND SOMEHOW BOTH QUESTS GOT TIED UP WITH EACH OTHER, SO THAT I BASICALLY HAVE TO SAVE EVERYONE IN THE FOREST FROM SOMETHING OR OTHER.
YOU'RE A BRUTE. AN ARMED THUG.
AND LET ME TELL YOU, IT'S A BIG FOREST.
WHEREAS I AM ONE OF THE MOST GIFTED PRACTITIONERS IN THE EMPIRE.
THIS SORCERER BETTER NOT TURN OUT TO ALSO BE IN NEED OF A HERO OF HIS OWN, OR I MIGHT JUST QUIT THE BUSINESS FOREVER.
DO YOU HONESTLY IMAGINE A SIMPLE KNIFE OR SWORD COULD EVER HARM ME? DO YOU THINK I'D ALLOW THAT?

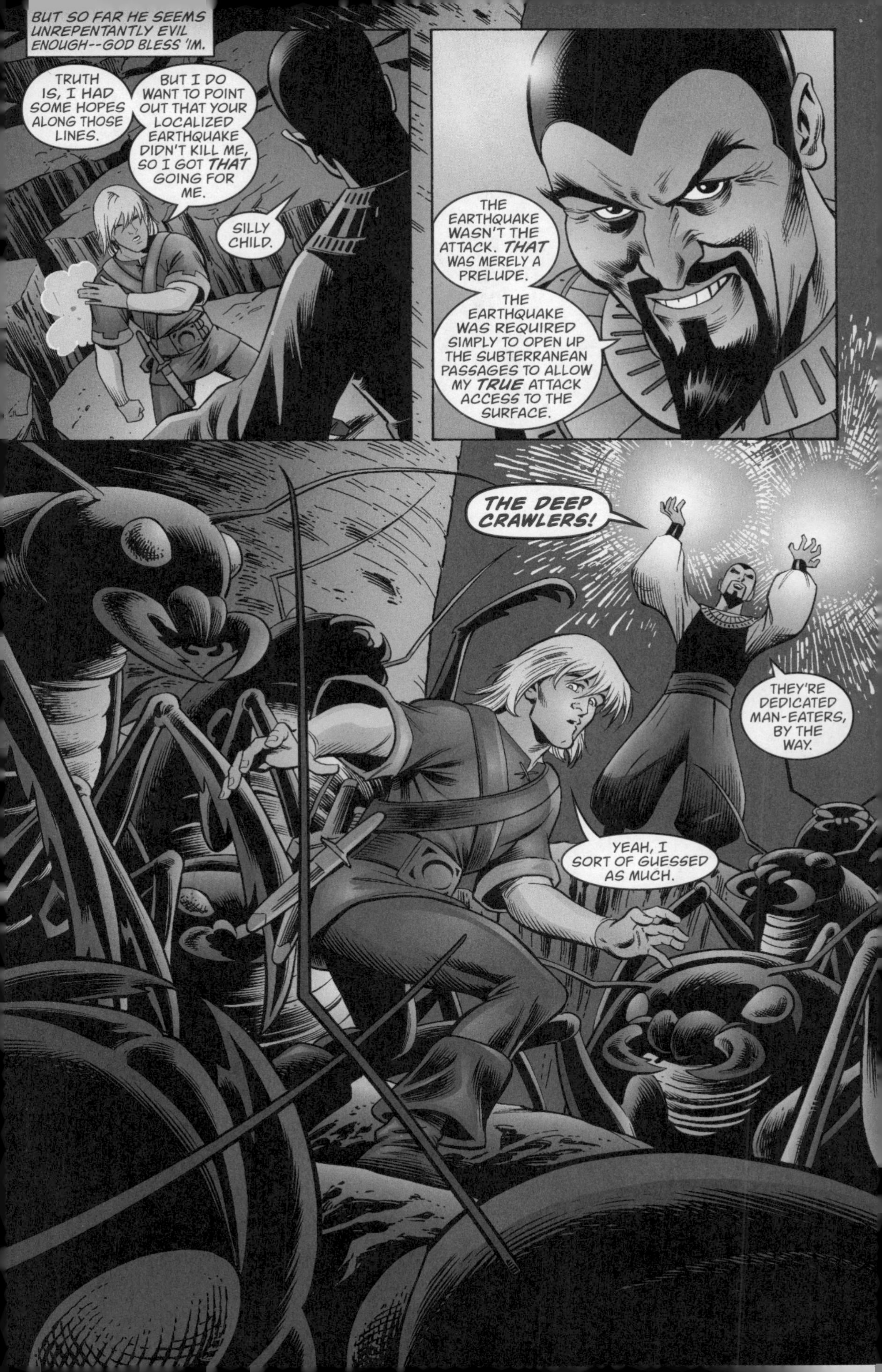
BUT SO FAR HE SEEMS UNREPENTANTLY EVIL ENOUGH--GOD BLESS 'IM.
TRUTH IS, I HAD SOME HOPES ALONG THOSE LINES.
BUT I DO WANT TO POINT OUT THAT YOUR LOCALIZED EARTHQUAKE DIDN'T KILL ME, SO I GOT THAT GOING FOR ME.
SILLY CHILD.
THE EARTHQUAKE WASN'T THE ATTACK. THAT WAS MERELY A PRELUDE.
THE EARTHQUAKE WAS REQUIRED SIMPLY TO OPEN UP THE SUBTERRANEAN PASSAGES TO ALLOW MY TRUE ATTACK ACCESS TO THE SURFACE.
THE DEEP CRAWLERS!
THEY'RE DEDICATED MAN-EATERS, BY THE WAY.
YEAH, I SORT OF GUESSED AS MUCH.

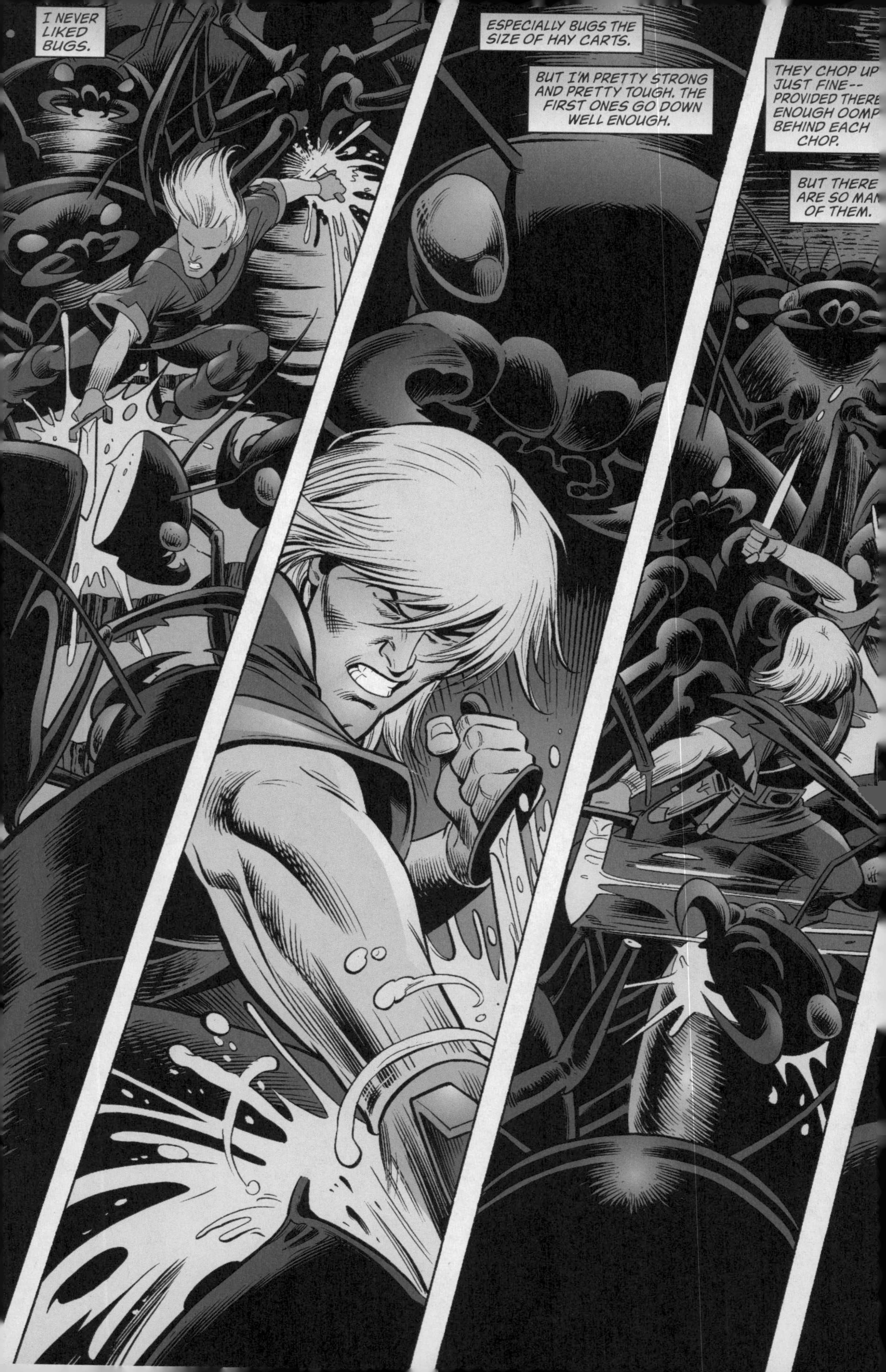

I NEVER LIKED BUGS.
ESPECIALLY BUGS THE SIZE OF HAY CARTS.
BUT I'M PRETTY STRONG AND PRETTY TOUGH. THE FIRST ONES GO DOWN WELL ENOUGH.
THEY CHOP UP JUST FINE-- PROVIDED THERE ENOUGH OOMP BEHIND EACH CHOP.
BUT THERE ARE SO MAN OF THEM.

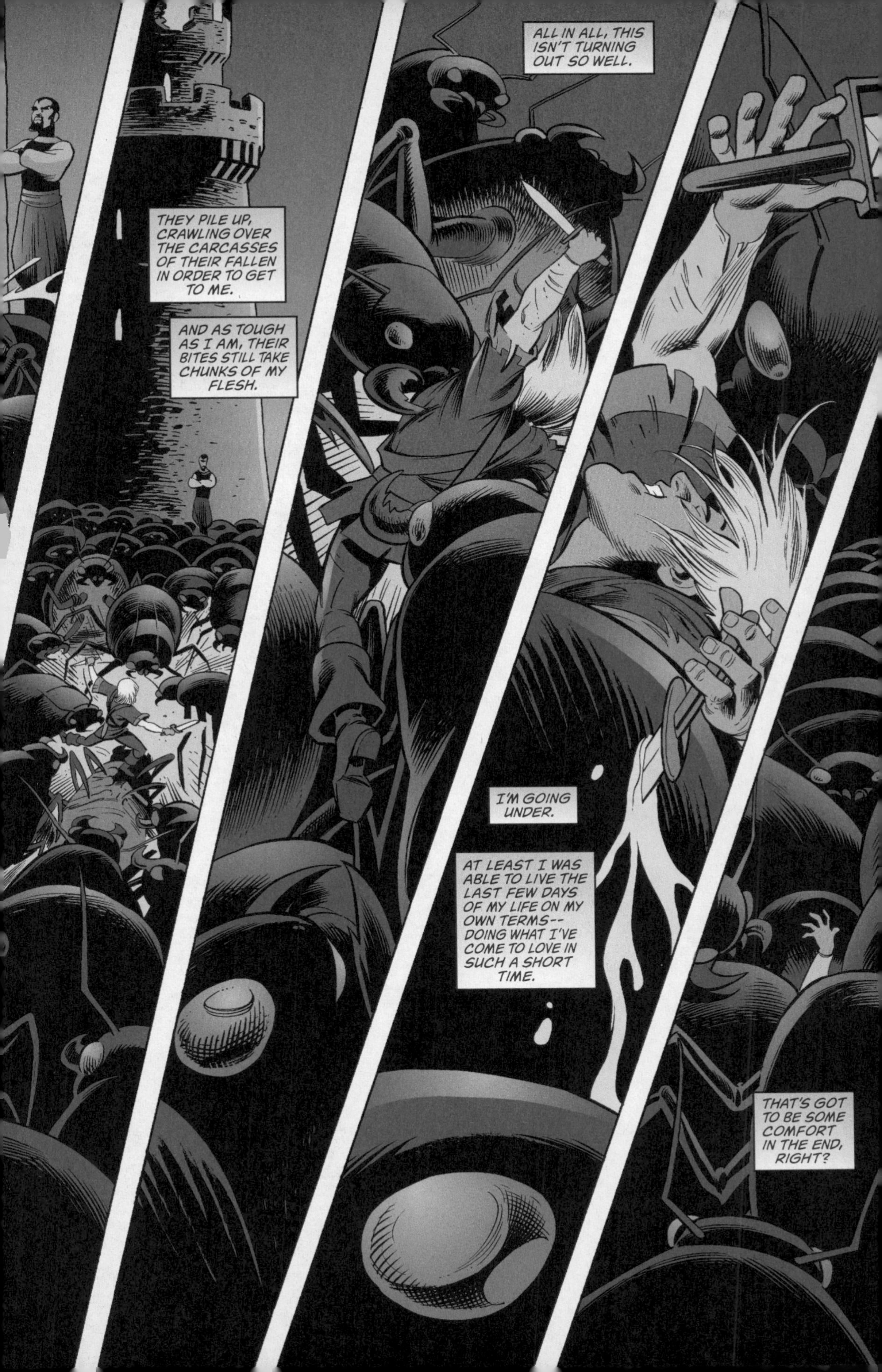
THEY PILE UP, CRAWLING OVER THE CARCASSES OF THEIR FALLEN IN ORDER TO GET TO ME.
AND AS TOUGH AS I AM, THEIR BITES STILL TAKE CHUNKS OF MY FLESH.
ALL IN ALL, THIS ISN'T TURNING OUT SO WELL.
I'M GOING UNDER.
AT LEAST I WAS ABLE TO LIVE THE LAST FEW DAYS OF MY LIFE ON MY OWN TERMS--DOING WHAT I'VE COME TO LOVE IN SUCH A SHORT TIME.
THAT'S GOT TO BE SOME COMFORT IN THE END, RIGHT?

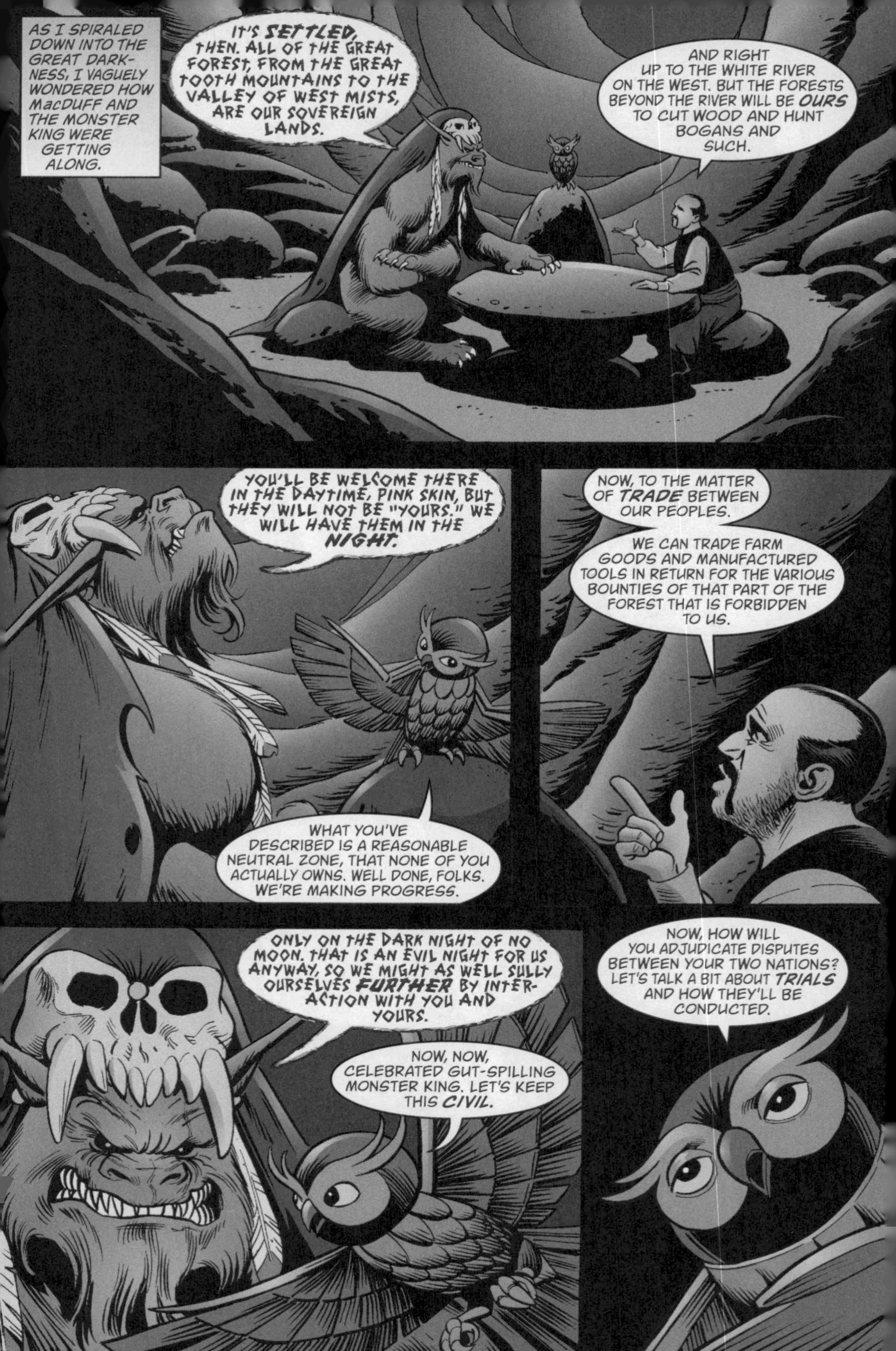
AS I SPIRALED DOWN INTO THE GREAT DARKNESS, I VAGUELY WONDERED HOW MacDUFF AND THE MONSTER KING WERE GETTING ALONG.
IT'S SETTLED, THEN. ALL OF THE GREAT FOREST, FROM THE GREAT TOOTH MOUNTAINS TO THE VALLEY OF WEST MISTS, ARE OUR SOVEREIGN LANDS.
AND RIGHT UP TO THE WHITE RIVER ON THE WEST. BUT THE FORESTS BEYOND THE RIVER WILL BE OURS TO CUT WOOD AND HUNT BOGANS AND SUCH.
YOU'LL BE WELCOME THERE IN THE DAYTIME, PINK SKIN, BUT THEY WILL NOT BE "YOURS." WE WILL HAVE THEM IN THE NIGHT.
WHAT YOU'VE DESCRIBED IS A REASONABLE NEUTRAL ZONE, THAT NONE OF YOU ACTUALLY OWNS. WELL DONE, FOLKS. WE'RE MAKING PROGRESS.
NOW, TO THE MATTER OF TRADE BETWEEN OUR PEOPLES.
WE CAN TRADE FARM GOODS AND MANUFACTURED TOOLS IN RETURN FOR THE VARIOUS BOUNTIES OF THAT PART OF THE FOREST THAT IS FORBIDDEN TO US.
ONLY ON THE DARK NIGHT OF NO MOON. THAT IS AN EVIL NIGHT FOR US ANYWAY, SO WE MIGHT AS WELL SULLY OURSELVES FURTHER BY INTERACTION WITH YOU AND YOURS.
NOW, NOW, CELEBRATED GUT-SPILLING MONSTER KING. LET'S KEEP THIS CIVIL.
NOW, HOW WILL YOU ADJUDICATE DISPUTES BETWEEN YOUR TWO NATIONS? LET'S TALK A BIT ABOUT TRIALS AND HOW THEY'LL BE CONDUCTED.

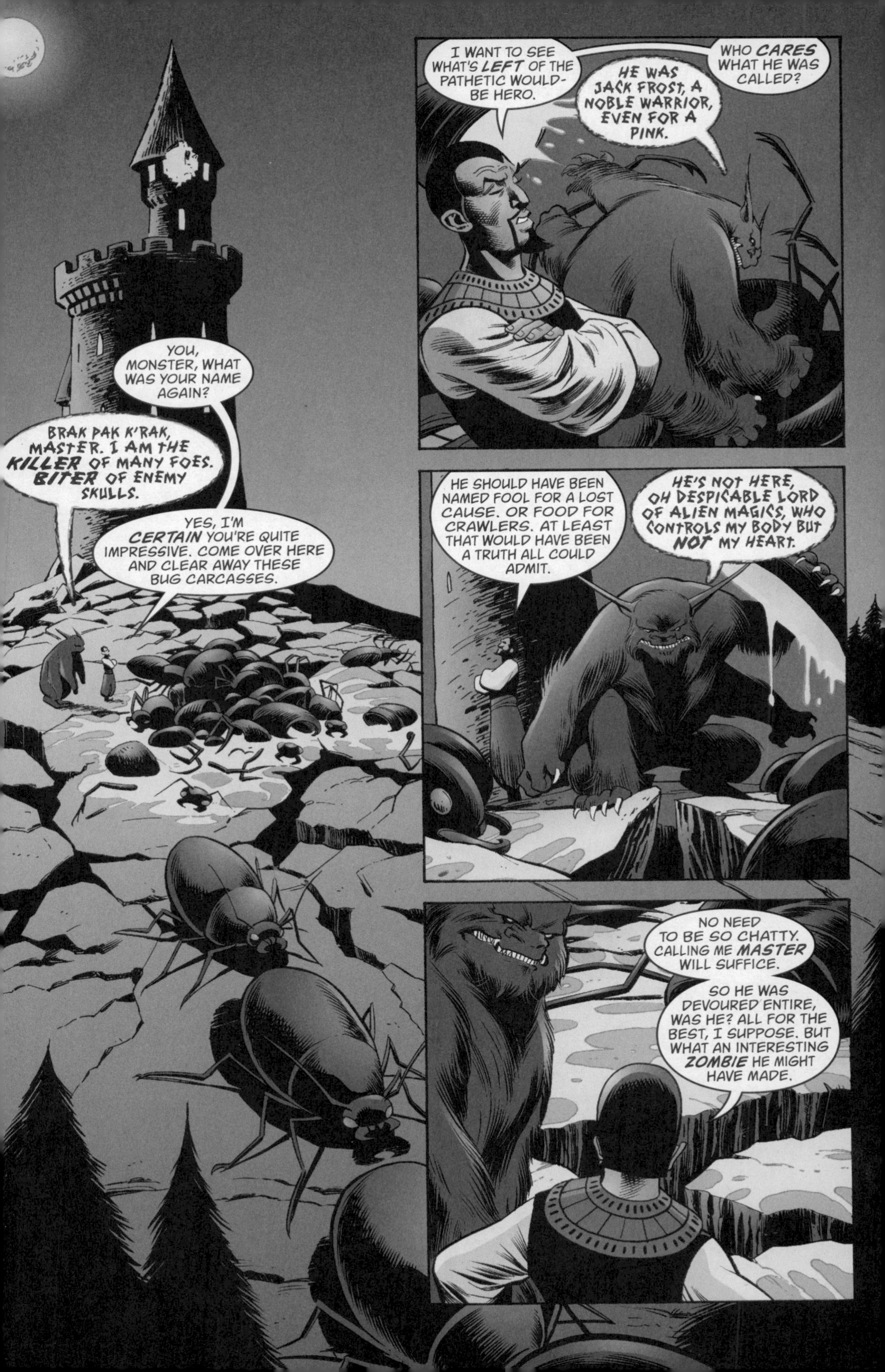
YOU, MONSTER, WHAT WAS YOUR NAME AGAIN?
BRAK PAK K'RAK, MASTER. I AM THE KILLER OF MANY FOES. BITER OF ENEMY SKULLS.
YES, I'M CERTAIN YOU'RE QUITE IMPRESSIVE. COME OVER HERE AND CLEAR AWAY THESE BUG CARCASSES.
I WANT TO SEE WHAT'S LEFT OF THE PATHETIC WOULD-BE HERO.
HE WAS JACK FROST, A NOBLE WARRIOR, EVEN FOR A PINK.
WHO CARES WHAT HE WAS CALLED?
HE SHOULD HAVE BEEN NAMED FOOL FOR A LOST CAUSE. OR FOOD FOR CRAWLERS. AT LEAST THAT WOULD HAVE BEEN A TRUTH ALL COULD ADMIT.
HE'S NOT HERE, OH DESPICABLE LORD OF ALIEN MAGICS, WHO CONTROLS MY BODY BUT NOT MY HEART.
NO NEED TO BE SO CHATTY. CALLING ME MASTER WILL SUFFICE.
SO HE WAS DEVOURED ENTIRE, WAS HE? ALL FOR THE BEST, I SUPPOSE. BUT WHAT AN INTERESTING ZOMBIE HE MIGHT HAVE MADE.

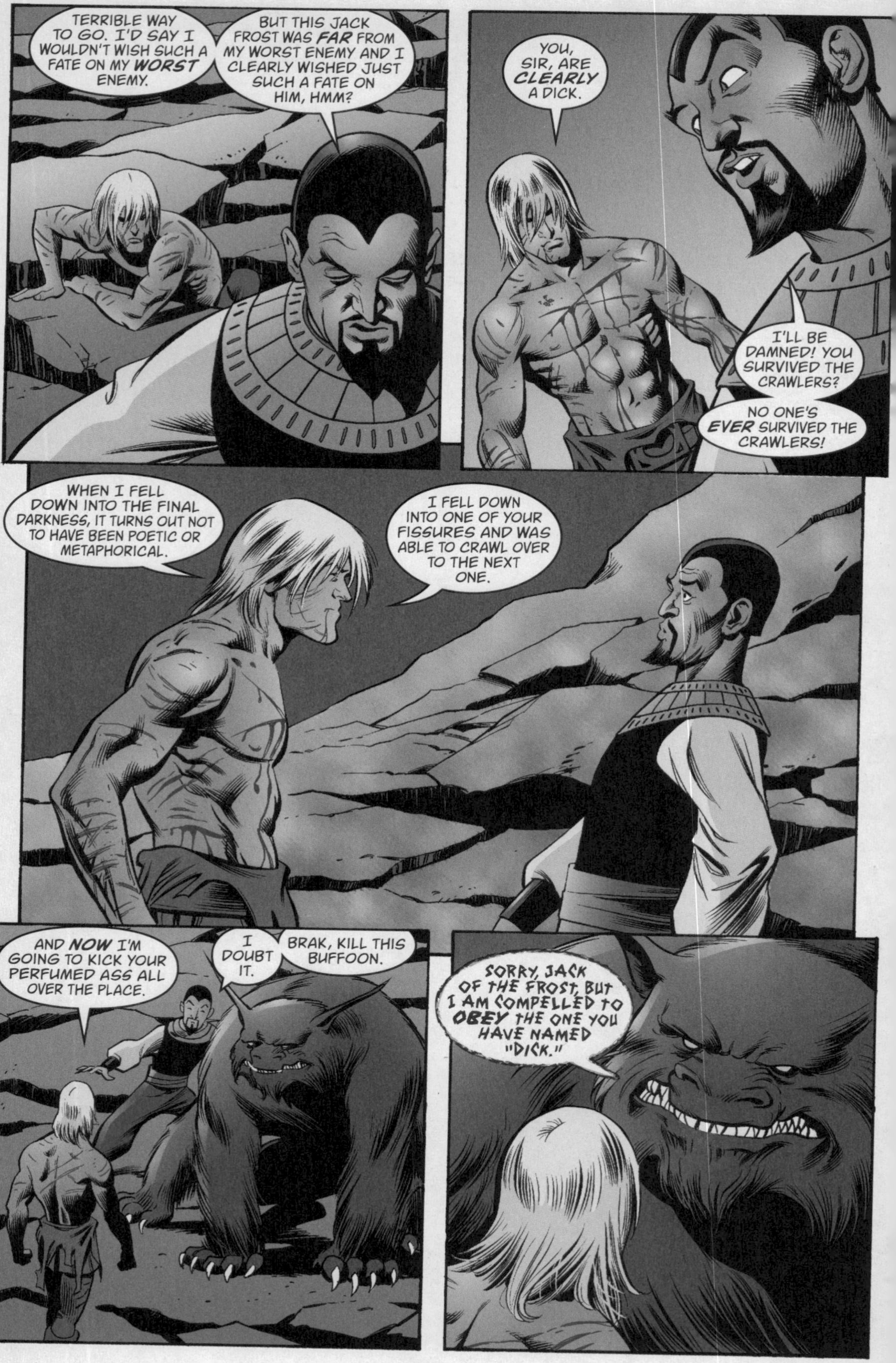
TERRIBLE WAY TO GO. I'D SAY I WOULDN'T WISH SUCH A FATE ON MY WORST ENEMY.
BUT THIS JACK FROST WAS FAR FROM MY WORST ENEMY AND I CLEARLY WISHED JUST SUCH A FATE ON HIM, HMM?
YOU, SIR, ARE CLEARLY A DICK.
I'LL BE DAMNED! YOU SURVIVED THE CRAWLERS?
NO ONE'S EVER SURVIVED THE CRAWLERS!
WHEN I FELL DOWN INTO THE FINAL DARKNESS, IT TURNS OUT NOT TO HAVE BEEN POETIC OR METAPHORICAL.
I FELL DOWN INTO ONE OF YOUR FISSURES AND WAS ABLE TO CRAWL OVER TO THE NEXT ONE.
AND NOW I'M GOING TO KICK YOUR PERFUMED ASS ALL OVER THE PLACE.
I DOUBT IT.
BRAK, KILL THIS BUFFOON.
SORRY, JACK OF THE FROST, BUT I AM COMPELLED TO OBEY THE ONE YOU HAVE NAMED "DICK."

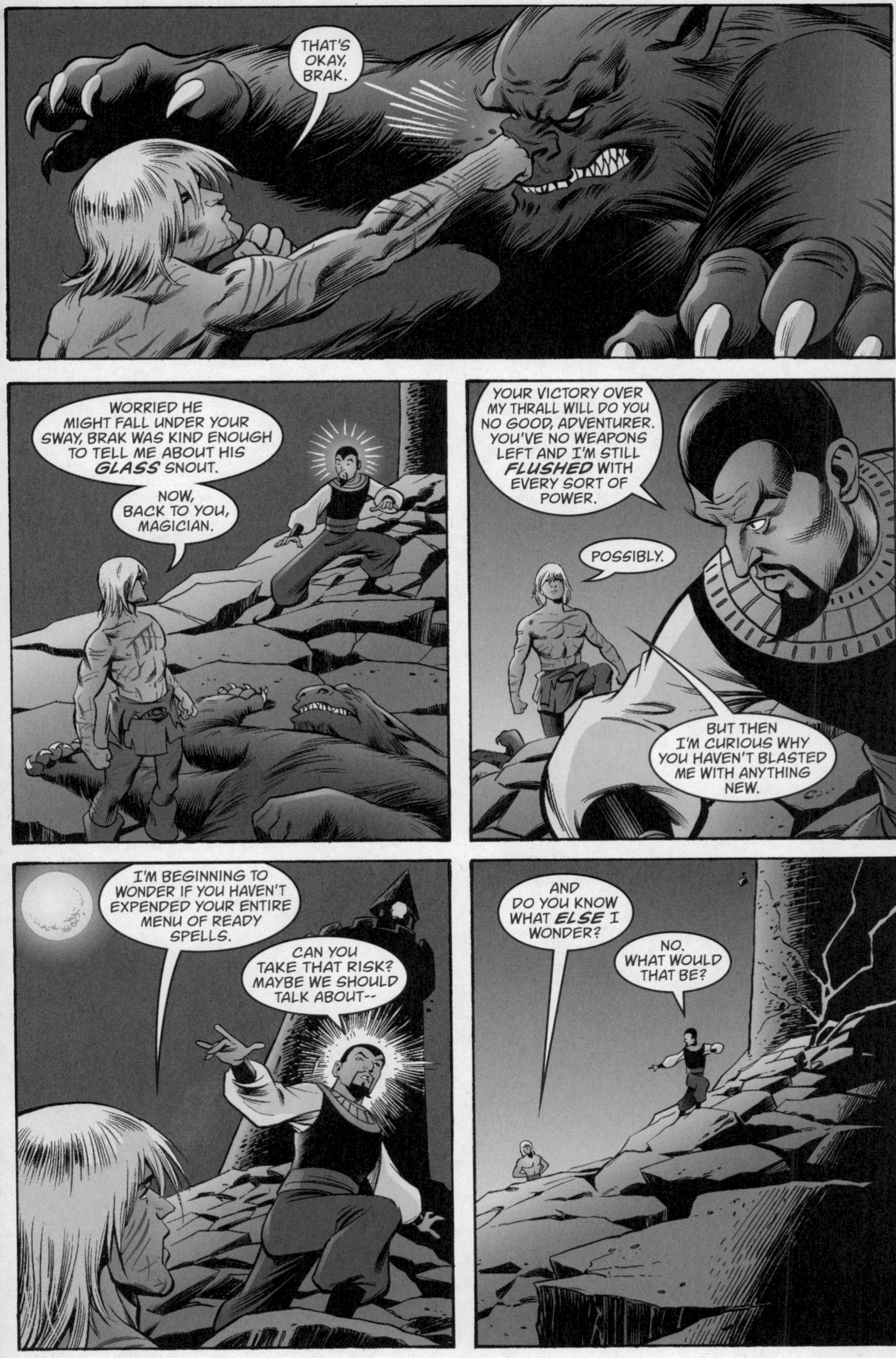

THAT'S OKAY, BRAK.
WORRIED HE MIGHT FALL UNDER YOUR SWAY, BRAK WAS KIND ENOUGH TO TELL ME ABOUT HIS GLASS SNOUT.
NOW, BACK TO YOU, MAGICIAN.
YOUR VICTORY OVER MY THRALL WILL DO YOU NO GOOD, ADVENTURER. YOU'VE NO WEAPONS LEFT AND I'M STILL FLUSHED WITH EVERY SORT OF POWER.
POSSIBLY.
BUT THEN I'M CURIOUS WHY YOU HAVEN'T BLASTED ME WITH ANYTHING NEW.
I'M BEGINNING TO WONDER IF YOU HAVEN'T EXPENDED YOUR ENTIRE MENU OF READY SPELLS.
CAN YOU TAKE THAT RISK? MAYBE WE SHOULD TALK ABOUT--
AND DO YOU KNOW WHAT ELSE I WONDER?
NO. WHAT WOULD THAT BE?

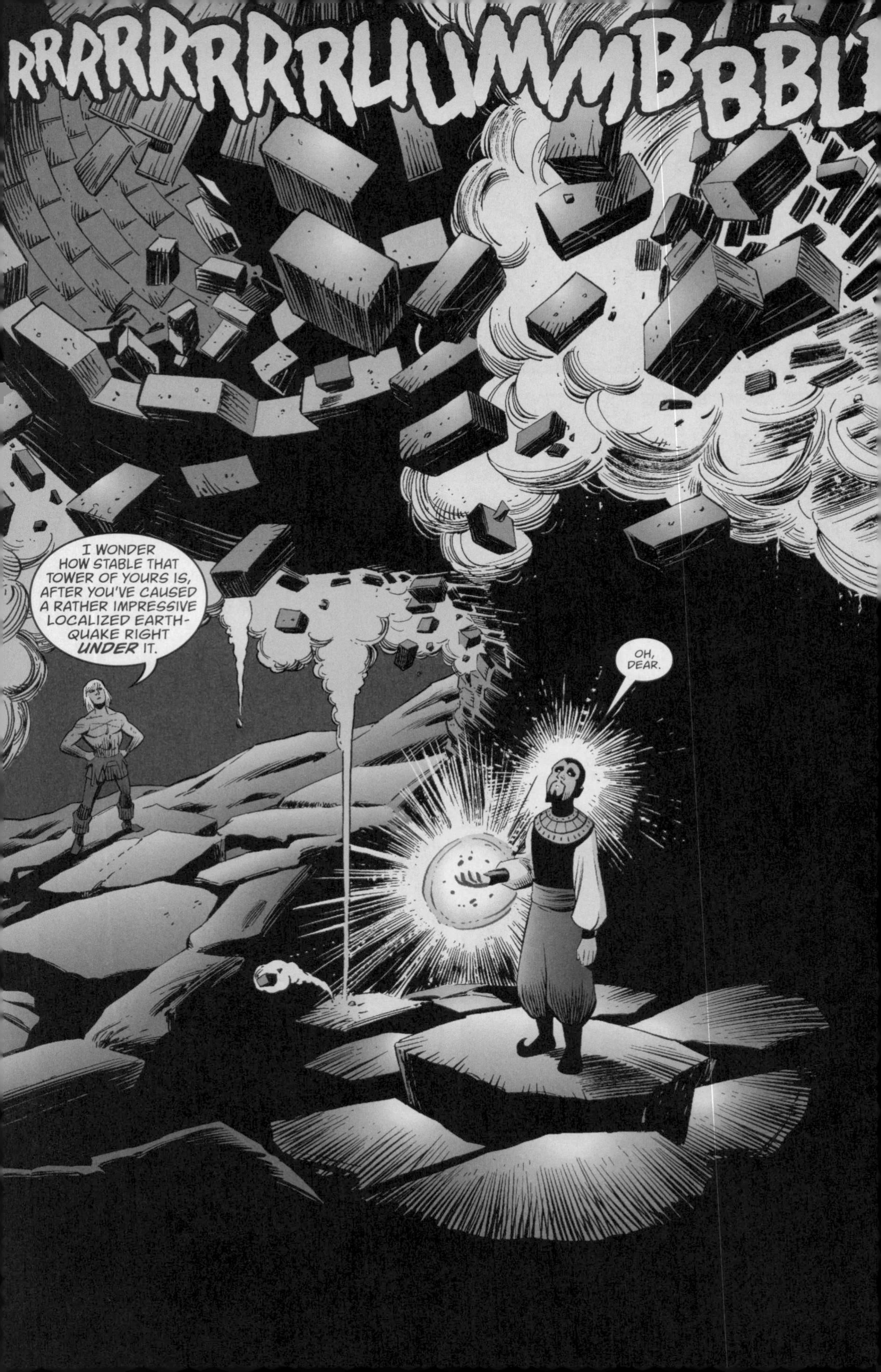
RRRRRRRRLUUMMBBBL
I WONDER HOW STABLE THAT TOWER OF YOURS IS, AFTER YOU'VE CAUSED A RATHER IMPRESSIVE LOCALIZED EARTH-QUAKE RIGHT **UNDER** IT.
OH, DEAR.

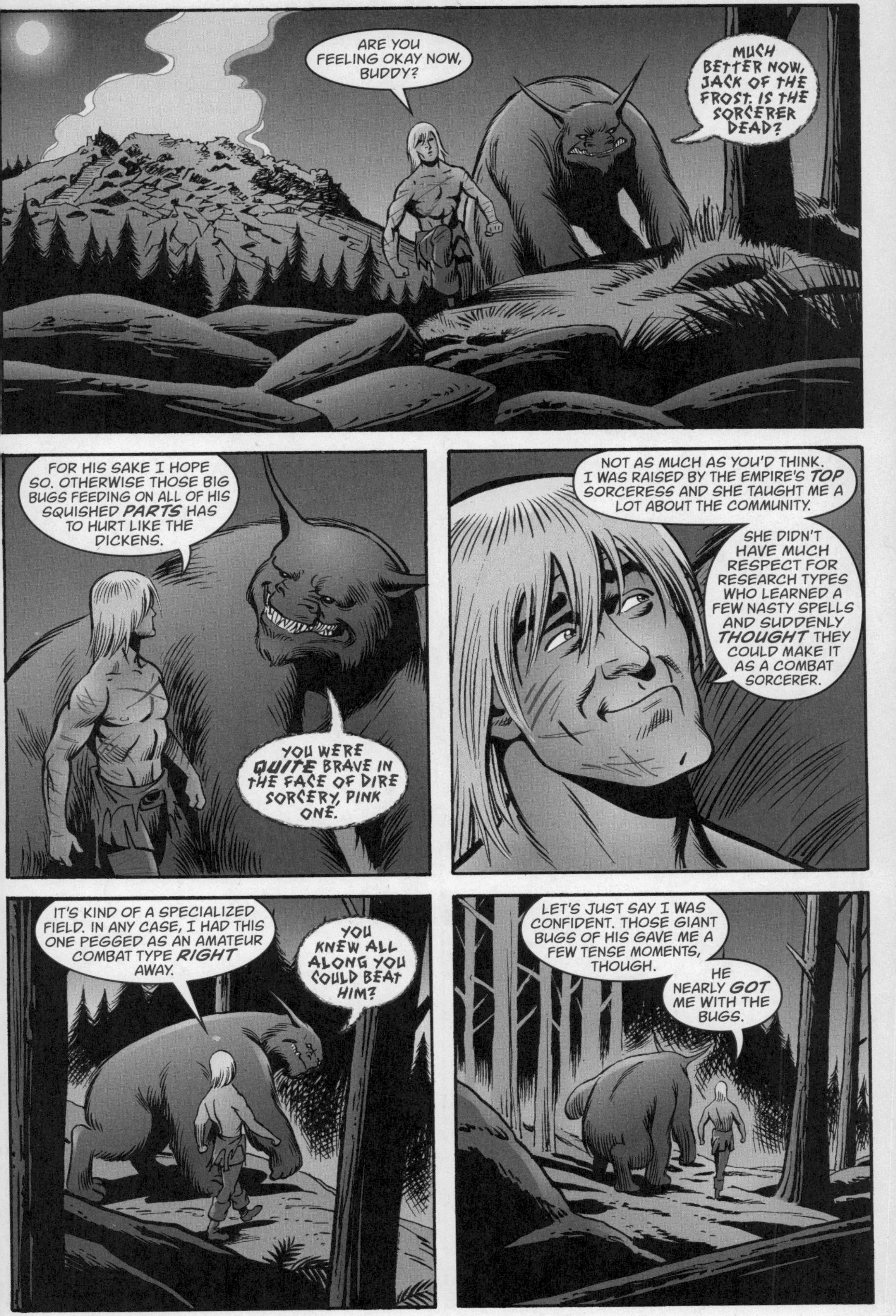
ARE YOU FEELING OKAY NOW, BUDDY?
MUCH BETTER NOW, JACK OF THE FROST. IS THE SORCERER DEAD?
FOR HIS SAKE I HOPE SO. OTHERWISE THOSE BIG BUGS FEEDING ON ALL OF HIS SQUISHED PARTS HAS TO HURT LIKE THE DICKENS.
YOU WERE QUITE BRAVE IN THE FACE OF DIRE SORCERY, PINK ONE.
NOT AS MUCH AS YOU'D THINK. I WAS RAISED BY THE EMPIRE'S TOP SORCERESS AND SHE TAUGHT ME A LOT ABOUT THE COMMUNITY.
SHE DIDN'T HAVE MUCH RESPECT FOR RESEARCH TYPES WHO LEARNED A FEW NASTY SPELLS AND SUDDENLY THOUGHT THEY COULD MAKE IT AS A COMBAT SORCERER.
IT'S KIND OF A SPECIALIZED FIELD. IN ANY CASE, I HAD THIS ONE PEGGED AS AN AMATEUR COMBAT TYPE RIGHT AWAY.
YOU KNEW ALL ALONG YOU COULD BEAT HIM?
LET'S JUST SAY I WAS CONFIDENT. THOSE GIANT BUGS OF HIS GAVE ME A FEW TENSE MOMENTS, THOUGH.
HE NEARLY GOT ME WITH THE BUGS.

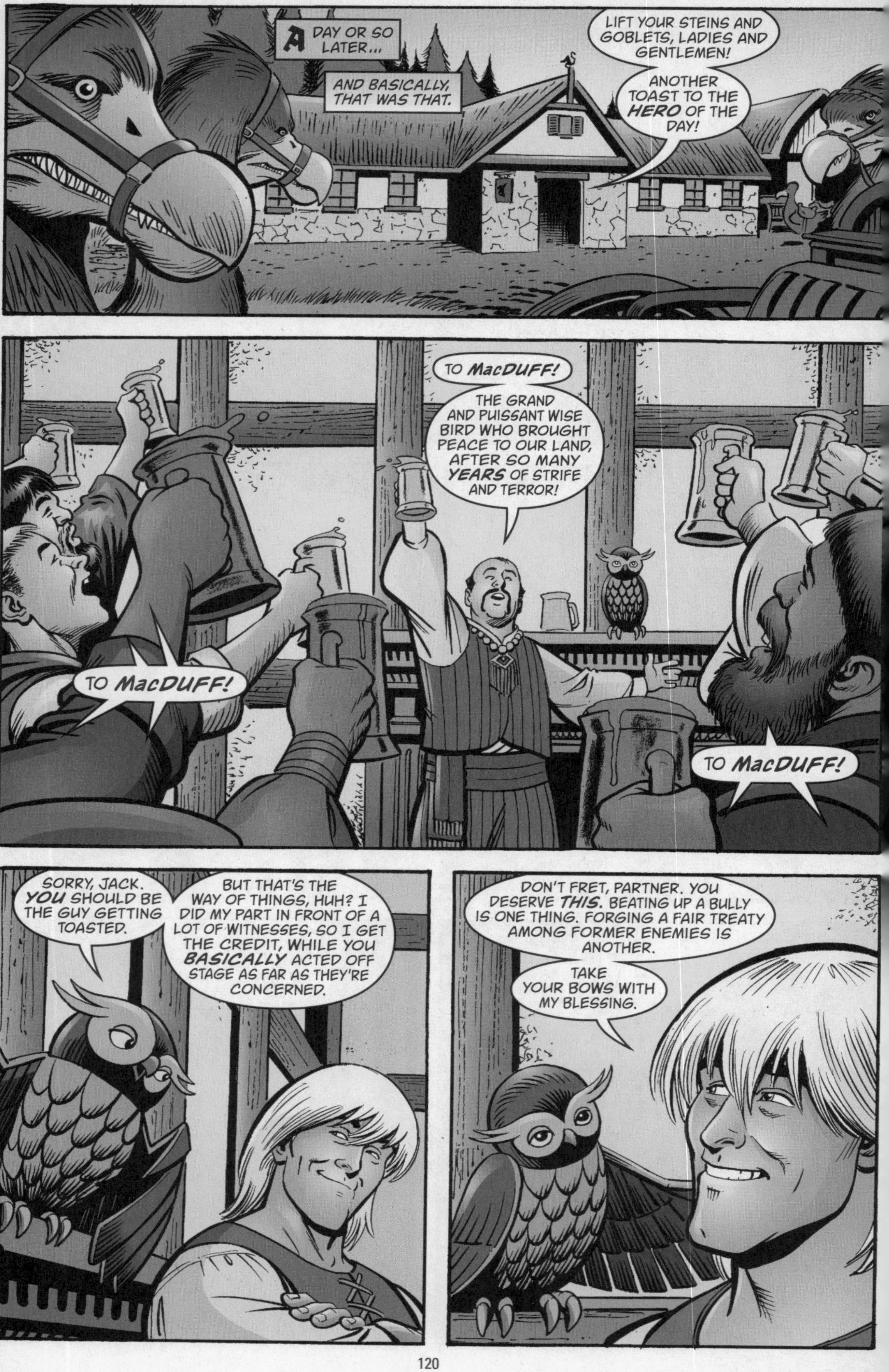
A DAY OR SO LATER...
AND BASICALLY, THAT WAS THAT.
LIFT YOUR STEINS AND GOBLETS, LADIES AND GENTLEMEN!
ANOTHER TOAST TO THE HERO OF THE DAY!
TO MacDUFF!
THE GRAND AND PUISSANT WISE BIRD WHO BROUGHT PEACE TO OUR LAND, AFTER SO MANY YEARS OF STRIFE AND TERROR!
TO MacDUFF!
TO MacDUFF!
SORRY, JACK. YOU SHOULD BE THE GUY GETTING TOASTED.
BUT THAT'S THE WAY OF THINGS, HUH? I DID MY PART IN FRONT OF A LOT OF WITNESSES, SO I GET THE CREDIT, WHILE YOU BASICALLY ACTED OFF STAGE AS FAR AS THEY'RE CONCERNED.
DON'T FRET, PARTNER. YOU DESERVE THIS. BEATING UP A BULLY IS ONE THING. FORGING A FAIR TREATY AMONG FORMER ENEMIES IS ANOTHER.
TAKE YOUR BOWS WITH MY BLESSING.

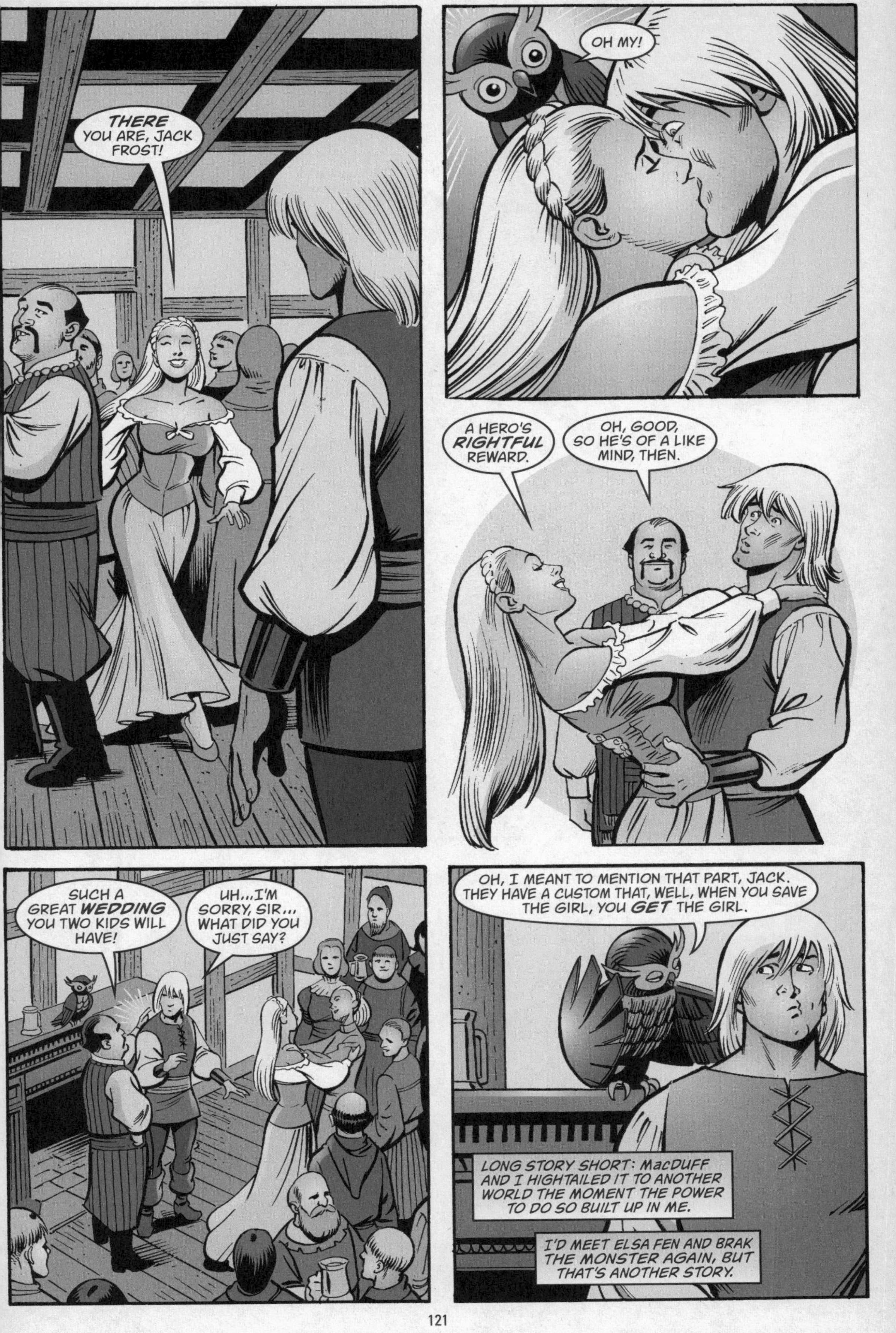
THERE YOU ARE, JACK FROST!
OH MY!
A HERO'S RIGHTFUL REWARD.
OH, GOOD, SO HE'S OF A LIKE MIND, THEN.
SUCH A GREAT WEDDING YOU TWO KIDS WILL HAVE!
UH...I'M SORRY, SIR... WHAT DID YOU JUST SAY?
OH, I MEANT TO MENTION THAT PART, JACK. THEY HAVE A CUSTOM THAT, WELL, WHEN YOU SAVE THE GIRL, YOU GET THE GIRL.
LONG STORY SHORT: MacDUFF AND I HIGHTAILED IT TO ANOTHER WORLD THE MOMENT THE POWER TO DO SO BUILT UP IN ME.
I'D MEET ELSA FEN AND BRAK THE MONSTER AGAIN, BUT THAT'S ANOTHER STORY.

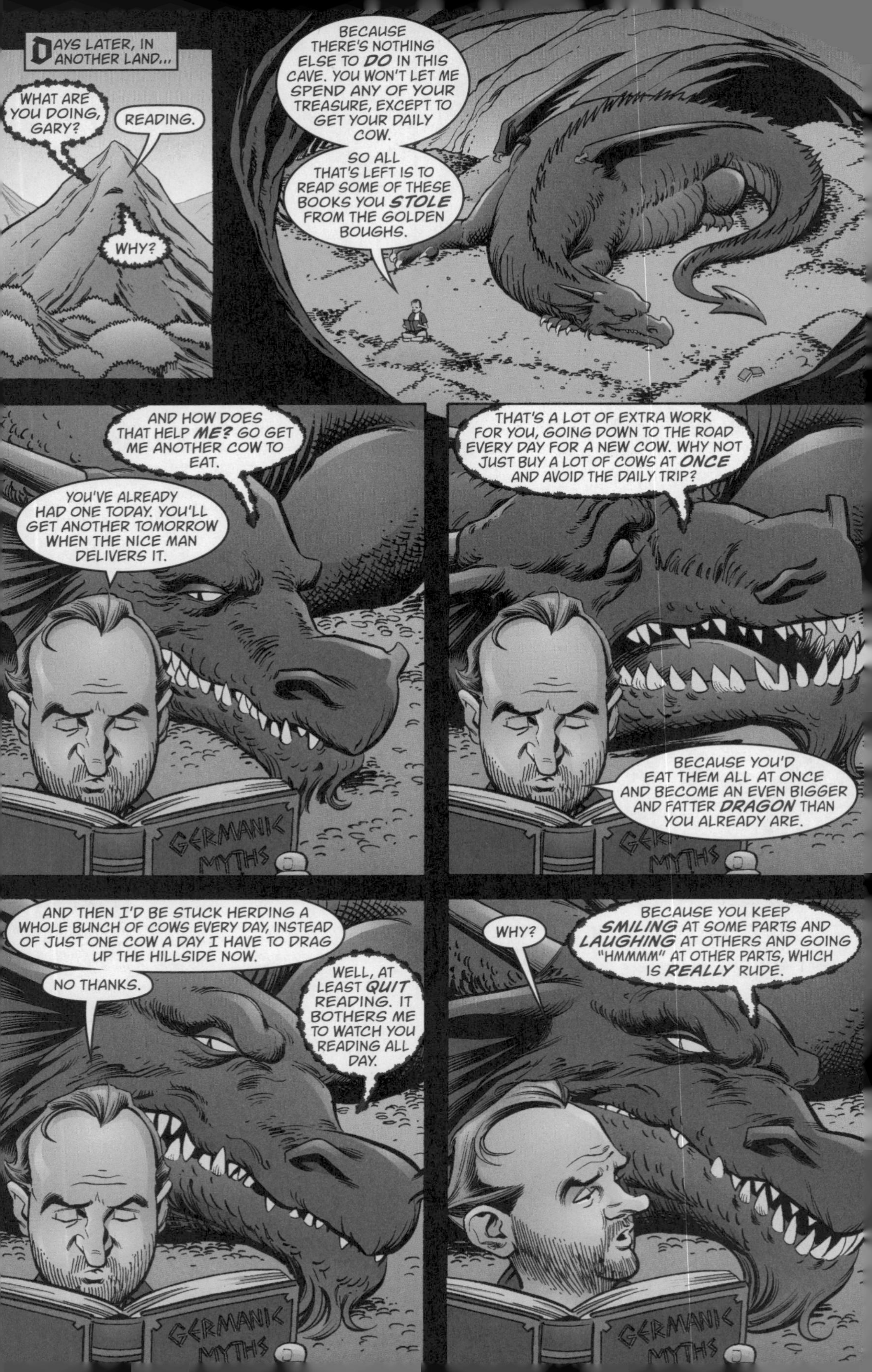
DAYS LATER, IN ANOTHER LAND...
WHAT ARE YOU DOING, GARY?
READING.
WHY?
BECAUSE THERE'S NOTHING ELSE TO DO IN THIS CAVE. YOU WON'T LET ME SPEND ANY OF YOUR TREASURE, EXCEPT TO GET YOUR DAILY COW.
SO ALL THAT'S LEFT IS TO READ SOME OF THESE BOOKS YOU STOLE FROM THE GOLDEN BOUGHS.
AND HOW DOES THAT HELP ME? GO GET ME ANOTHER COW TO EAT.
YOU'VE ALREADY HAD ONE TODAY. YOU'LL GET ANOTHER TOMORROW WHEN THE NICE MAN DELIVERS IT.
GERMANIC MYTHS
THAT'S A LOT OF EXTRA WORK FOR YOU, GOING DOWN TO THE ROAD EVERY DAY FOR A NEW COW. WHY NOT JUST BUY A LOT OF COWS AT ONCE AND AVOID THE DAILY TRIP?
BECAUSE YOU'D EAT THEM ALL AT ONCE AND BECOME AN EVEN BIGGER AND FATTER DRAGON THAN YOU ALREADY ARE.
AND THEN I'D BE STUCK HERDING A WHOLE BUNCH OF COWS EVERY DAY, INSTEAD OF JUST ONE COW A DAY I HAVE TO DRAG UP THE HILLSIDE NOW.
NO THANKS.
WELL, AT LEAST QUIT READING. IT BOTHERS ME TO WATCH YOU READING ALL DAY.
GERMANIC MYTHS
WHY?
BECAUSE YOU KEEP SMILING AT SOME PARTS AND LAUGHING AT OTHERS AND GOING "HMMMM" AT OTHER PARTS, WHICH IS REALLY RUDE.
GERMANIC MYTHS

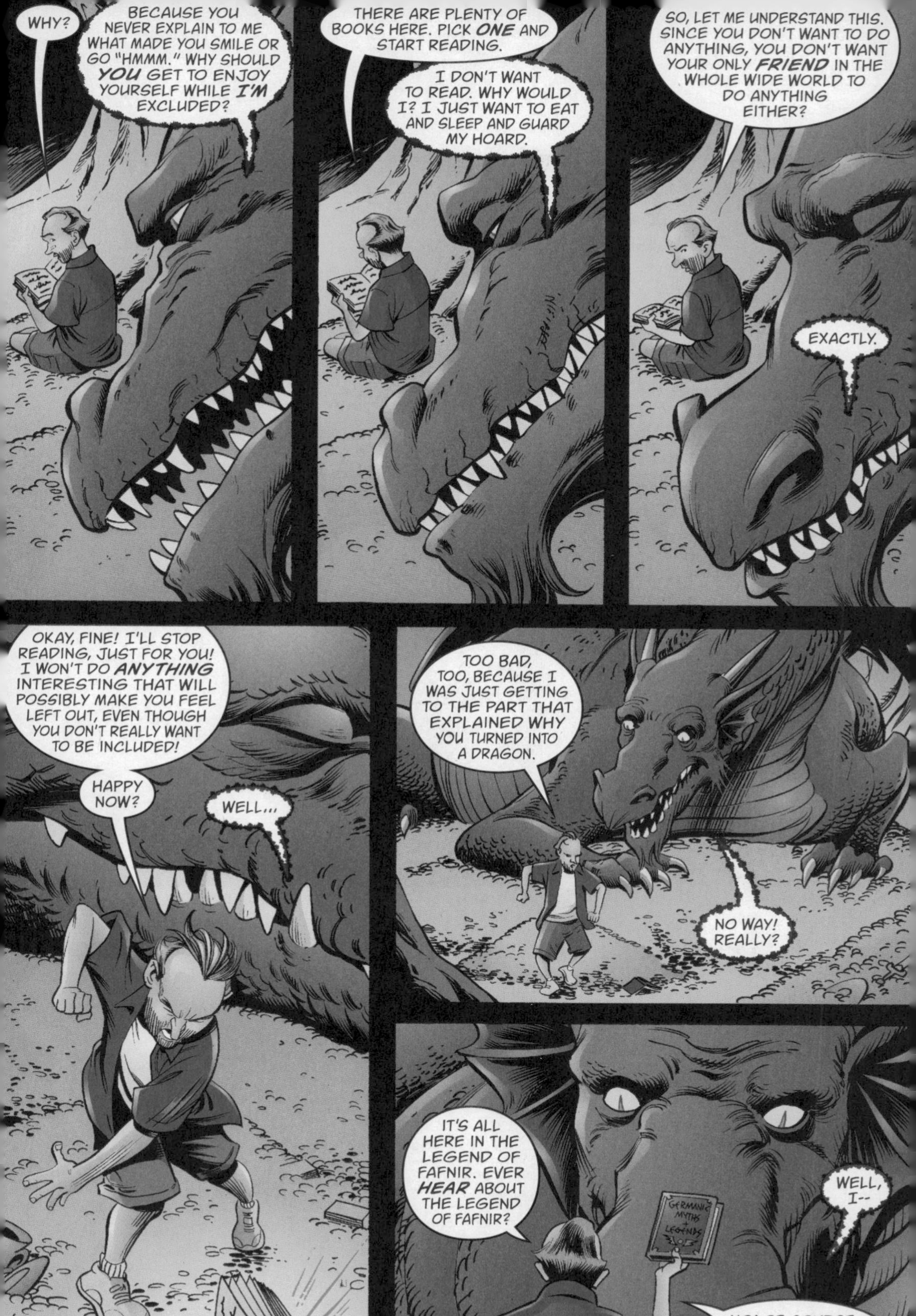
WHY?
BECAUSE YOU NEVER EXPLAIN TO ME WHAT MADE YOU SMILE OR GO "HMMM." WHY SHOULD YOU GET TO ENJOY YOURSELF WHILE I'M EXCLUDED?
THERE ARE PLENTY OF BOOKS HERE. PICK ONE AND START READING.
I DON'T WANT TO READ. WHY WOULD I? I JUST WANT TO EAT AND SLEEP AND GUARD MY HOARD.
SO, LET ME UNDERSTAND THIS. SINCE YOU DON'T WANT TO DO ANYTHING, YOU DON'T WANT YOUR ONLY FRIEND IN THE WHOLE WIDE WORLD TO DO ANYTHING EITHER?
EXACTLY.
OKAY, FINE! I'LL STOP READING, JUST FOR YOU! I WON'T DO ANYTHING INTERESTING THAT WILL POSSIBLY MAKE YOU FEEL LEFT OUT, EVEN THOUGH YOU DON'T REALLY WANT TO BE INCLUDED!
HAPPY NOW?
WELL...
TOO BAD, TOO, BECAUSE I WAS JUST GETTING TO THE PART THAT EXPLAINED WHY YOU TURNED INTO A DRAGON.
NO WAY! REALLY?
IT'S ALL HERE IN THE LEGEND OF FAFNIR. EVER HEAR ABOUT THE LEGEND OF FAFNIR?
GERMANIC MYTHS + LEGENDS
WELL, I--
NO! OF COURSE YOU DIDN'T, BECAUSE YOU'RE ONLY INTERESTED IN YOUR OWN ASININE LEGENDS AND STORIES.

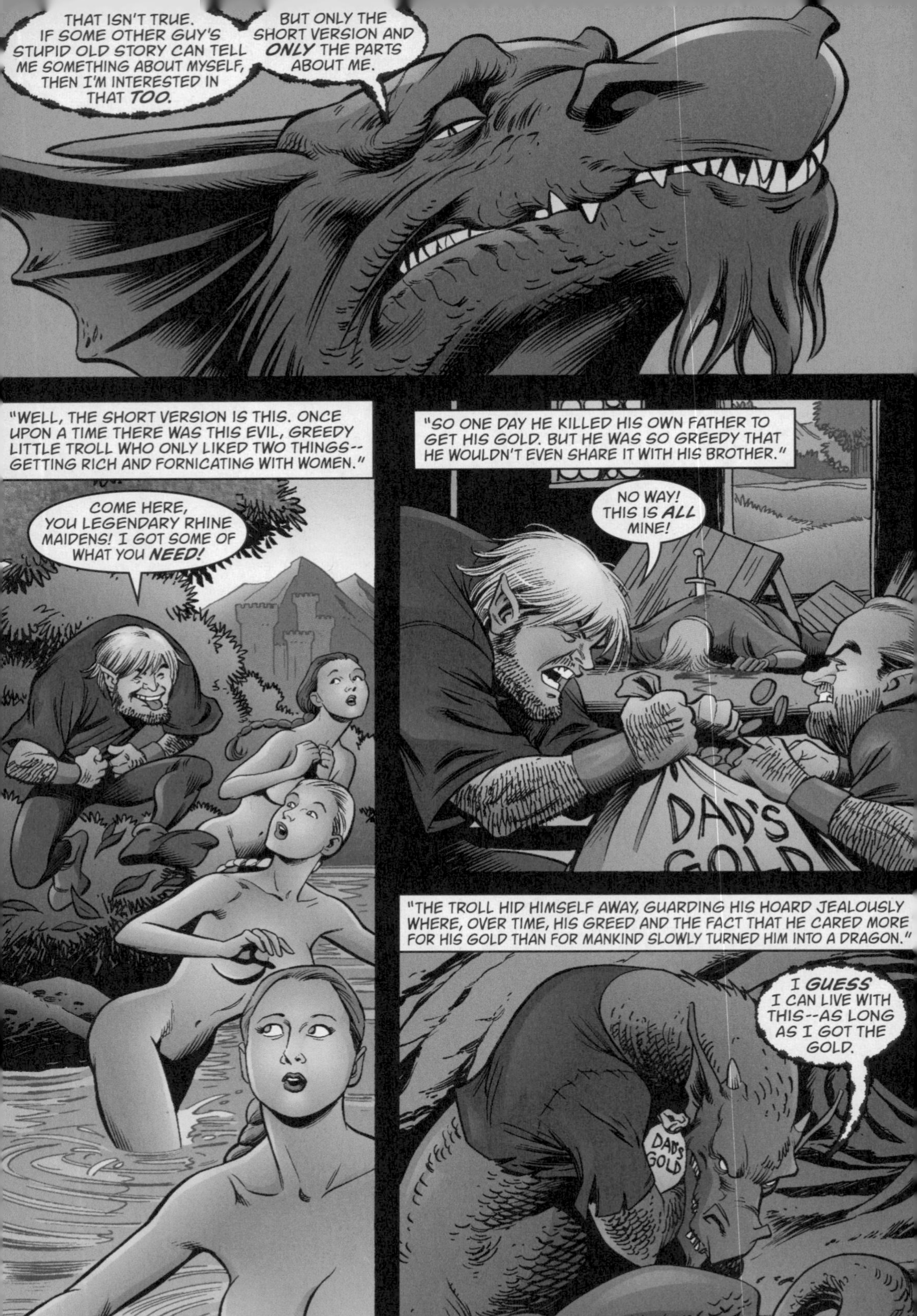
THAT ISN'T TRUE. IF SOME OTHER GUY'S STUPID OLD STORY CAN TELL ME SOMETHING ABOUT MYSELF, THEN I'M INTERESTED IN THAT TOO.
BUT ONLY THE SHORT VERSION AND ONLY THE PARTS ABOUT ME.
"WELL, THE SHORT VERSION IS THIS. ONCE UPON A TIME THERE WAS THIS EVIL, GREEDY LITTLE TROLL WHO ONLY LIKED TWO THINGS-- GETTING RICH AND FORNICATING WITH WOMEN."
COME HERE, YOU LEGENDARY RHINE MAIDENS! I GOT SOME OF WHAT YOU NEED!
"SO ONE DAY HE KILLED HIS OWN FATHER TO GET HIS GOLD. BUT HE WAS SO GREEDY THAT HE WOULDN'T EVEN SHARE IT WITH HIS BROTHER."
NO WAY! THIS IS ALL MINE!
DAD'S GOLD
"THE TROLL HID HIMSELF AWAY, GUARDING HIS HOARD JEALOUSLY WHERE, OVER TIME, HIS GREED AND THE FACT THAT HE CARED MORE FOR HIS GOLD THAN FOR MANKIND SLOWLY TURNED HIM INTO A DRAGON."
I GUESS I CAN LIVE WITH THIS--AS LONG AS I GOT THE GOLD.
DAD'S GOLD

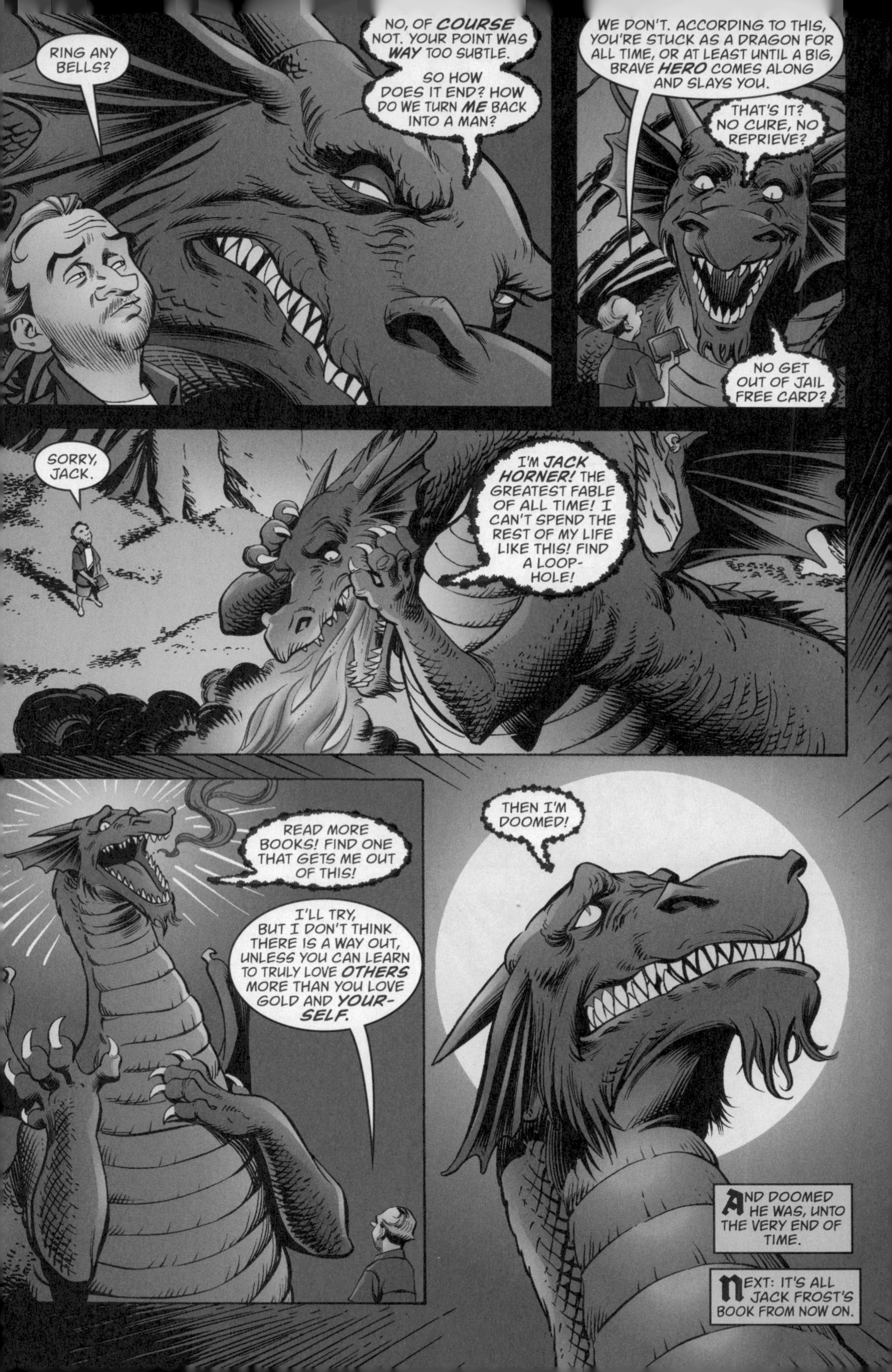
RING ANY BELLS?
NO, OF COURSE NOT. YOUR POINT WAS WAY TOO SUBTLE.
SO HOW DOES IT END? HOW DO WE TURN ME BACK INTO A MAN?
WE DON'T. ACCORDING TO THIS, YOU'RE STUCK AS A DRAGON FOR ALL TIME, OR AT LEAST UNTIL A BIG, BRAVE HERO COMES ALONG AND SLAYS YOU.
THAT'S IT? NO CURE, NO REPRIEVE?
NO GET OUT OF JAIL FREE CARD?
SORRY, JACK.
I'M JACK HORNER! THE GREATEST FABLE OF ALL TIME! I CAN'T SPEND THE REST OF MY LIFE LIKE THIS! FIND A LOOP-HOLE!
READ MORE BOOKS! FIND ONE THAT GETS ME OUT OF THIS!
I'LL TRY, BUT I DON'T THINK THERE IS A WAY OUT, UNLESS YOU CAN LEARN TO TRULY LOVE OTHERS MORE THAN YOU LOVE GOLD AND YOUR-SELF.
THEN I'M DOOMED!
AND DOOMED HE WAS, UNTO THE VERY END OF TIME.
NEXT: IT'S ALL JACK FROST'S BOOK FROM NOW ON.

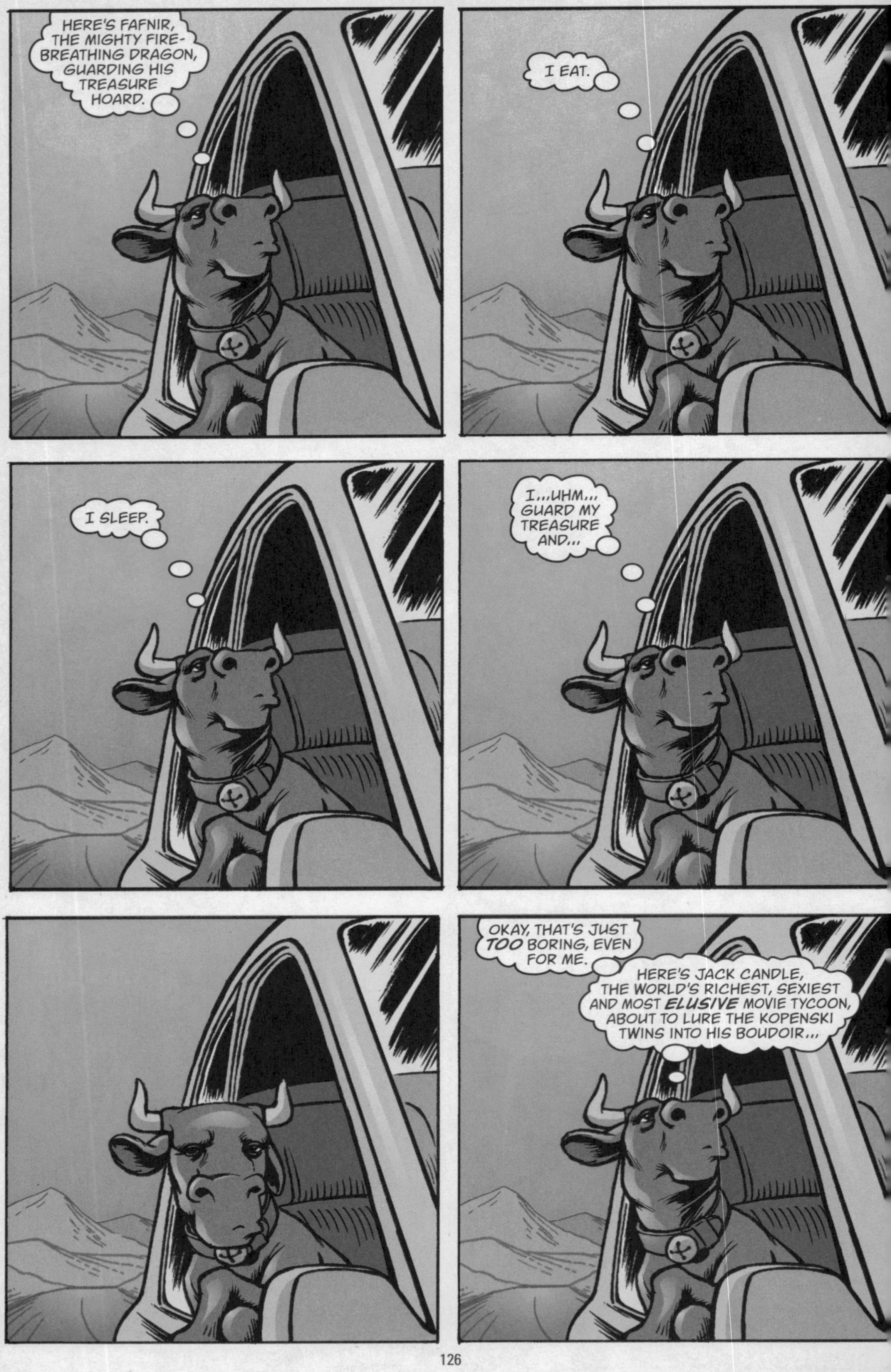
HERE'S FAFNIR, THE MIGHTY FIRE-BREATHING DRAGON, GUARDING HIS TREASURE HOARD.
I EAT.
I SLEEP.
I...UHM... GUARD MY TREASURE AND...
OKAY, THAT'S JUST TOO BORING, EVEN FOR ME.
HERE'S JACK CANDLE, THE WORLD'S RICHEST, SEXIEST AND MOST ELUSIVE MOVIE TYCOON, ABOUT TO LURE THE KOPENSKI TWINS INTO HIS BOUDOIR...